Tony Blair
in his own words

For Alexander James Fabian Richards

Also by Paul Richards
Be Your Own Spin Doctor: a practical guide to using the media
How to Win an Election: the art of political campaigning
The Case for Socialism
Long to Reign Over Us?
Is the Party Over? New Labour and the politics of participation

Tony Blair
in his own words

Edited by

Paul Richards

POLITICO'S

First published in Great Britain 2004 by
Politico's Publishing, an imprint of
Methuen Publishing Limited
215 Vauxhall Bridge Road
London SW1V 1EJ

10 9 8 7 6 5 4 3 2

A CIP catalogue record for this book is available from the British Library.

ISBN 1 84275 089 5

Printed and bound in Great Britain by Mackays of Chatham.

Contents

Editor's Note

I would like to thank the *New Statesman*, the Fabian Society, *Progress* and *Renewal* for their kind permission to reproduce articles from their publications. Graham Dale, Giles Radice and Floris Books were most helpful in allowing me to use Tony Blair's contributions to their books.

Thanks must also go to Mark Fuller, who provided excellent research and support; my wife Sarah Richards; my parents Gordon and Diana Richards; Iain Dale, John Schwartz and Emma Musgrave at Politico's; Steve Blume, and Stephen Lathrope. Thanks of course to Tony Blair – a great Labour Prime Minister.

The texts of speeches and interviews used in this edition are not authorised by Tony Blair or Number 10 Downing Street and any errors are the responsibility of the editor alone.

Some longer speeches, totalling many thousands of words, have been edited to include only the guts of the speech and the memorable or telling phrases. Where passages have been omitted, the symbol * * * appears.

Introduction

Tony Blair has been the dominant figure in British politics for over a decade. Since his election as leader of the Labour Party in 1994, he has proved to be his party's most successful leader. He has led the Labour Party to electoral victory in two landslide elections, in 1997 and 2001, and served continuously as prime minister for longer than any other Labour leader. He has defeated two leaders of the Conservative Party in general elections, and seen off a third before the bell even sounded.

Blair has held together a Labour government as no Labour prime minister has ever managed, despite the ministerial resignations, scandals and rivalries which have time and time again endangered his position. He has been dubbed 'Teflon Tony'. This feat has been accomplished in spite of a war in Iraq which strained Blair's base of support to breaking point, the pursuit of policies which have provoked backbench ire, and the birth in May 2000 of his fourth child, Leo.

The government has delivered a range of reforms, across a broad terrain, from monetary policy, constitutional reforms, changes to public services and institutions, education, taxation and foreign relations. Hardly an area of British life has been untouched by Labour's programme. This has been a reforming, energetic government, brimming with self-belief and the conviction that the state can make things better for the individual. A look at the Prime Minister's weekly diary, with its relentless round of meetings with ministers and MPs, foreign delegations, meetings with officials, parliamentary duties, Labour Party commitments, social engagements and Downing Street receptions, speeches to major conferences, telephone calls from world leaders, his regular fitness regime, and time with his friends, wife and four children shows that Blair is not idle for a second of the day. This is a hyper-active Prime Minister at the head of a hyper-active government.

Tony Blair is the very model of the modern politician. His family life is thoroughly respectable. He goes to church every week. He went to Oxford University, where, despite some sartorial excesses, a summer spent working in a bar in Paris, and a love of rock music, he refrained from drug-taking, flag-burning or student Marxism. He went from Oxford to the Bar, where he became a high-flying young lawyer, and met his future wife, Cherie Booth. Unlike Margaret Thatcher or George Brown, he doesn't drink much. Unlike Harold Wilson, he doesn't smoke cigarettes, or cigars (Wilson's private smoke) or a pipe (his public one). Blair does regular exercise, eats plenty of fruit, and spends his spare time with his wife and children.

Naturally, Tony Blair has had his critics, often fierce and visceral. It is hard to believe today, watching news footage of Britain's Prime Minister returning from a round of overseas diplomacy, an international summit, or a meeting with George W. Bush, with his hair greying and his features showing signs of exhaustion, that once Tony Blair was accused of inexperience by his opponents and given the nickname 'Bambi'. But the Bambi tag was soon replaced by harsher criticism and epithets – the 'control freak', the traitor to socialism, the lapdog of the USA, 'phoney Tony' 'the most dangerous man in Britain', 'Tony Bliar'.

Blair's premiership has been conducted against a backdrop of rapid economic, cultural and political changes. When Blair became leader of the Labour Party, few Britons had used the internet and most did not own a mobile phone or a home computer. A writer in 1994 pitching a script or book synopsis in which Diana, Princess of Wales, is killed after a high-speed car chase in Paris, the British army invades Afghanistan and Iraq, or that terrorists hijack civilian aeroplanes and fly them into the Pentagon and World Trade Center would be dismissed as fantastical. Blair as prime minister has had to deal with these events with a deft political touch.

Blair's greatest skill is as a communicator. Modern politics is about communications: not merely the buzz of the election campaign, but the ongoing dialogue between politicians and voters, mediated predominantly via the newspapers, broadcasters and the internet. His capacity to communicate beyond Labour's traditional heartland is what earned him support to be leader of the Labour Party.

From his early days as an MP, Blair has been a master of the modern political skills of media handling, giving punchy interviews, and churning out resonant sound bites. In 1990 he wrote: 'To criticise politicians for being able to give a good "sound bite" – when, for most of the news media, a bite is all you get – is like criticising a politician for turning up to a press conference in a suit rather than a pair of pyjamas.'

In twenty years of media attention, he has been remarkably gaffe-free. He has raised his own game, and that of the Labour Party, to meet the challenges of the 24-hour media.

The first time I met him was on 14 November 1992, when I chaired a conference for young Labour Party supporters, at the University of London.

Tony Blair was the keynote opening speaker, and the advertisement for the meeting promised 'Blair – seen widely as a rising star in the Labour Party – will kick off the event with a keynote address on Labour's values.' I vividly remember one moment from the speech, which in retrospect is highly telling: in the middle of his speech, Blair paused, nodded to the reporter and crew from Sky News, and embarked on a short passage attacking Saddam Hussein. Once the sound bite had been delivered, which had no relation to the speech, the news crew packed up and left. After another short pause, Blair joked with the audience 'that was a sound bite' and carried on with the speech as scripted.

This small incident proves that Blair's knowledge of the needs of the media was highly developed, even then. No one could have predicted that the subject of his excoriation would have such a profound impact on his career or the history of his country a decade later.

As a Labour Party press officer three years later, I again witnessed Blair's command of the media. He was shadow home secretary and I was his press minder at a Labour Party policy forum in Hammersmith, London. News came in that a prisoner being transferred by the private company Group Four had died in the back of their vehicle. Blair sought me out and gave me a sound bite – 'the farce has turned to tragedy' – for release to the Press Association. Within minutes, Blair's sound bite was appearing on the national news.

I have been in the audience when Tony Blair makes a speech, from a small seminar to an international conference, perhaps fifty times since 1990. Blair is undoubtedly an accomplished public speaker. His conference speeches are consistently of high quality, skilfully crafted and expertly delivered. He has an easily recognisable and easily parodied speaking style. He likes using short sentences, often comprising short verb-less phrases and even single words, for example, 'New Labour. New Britain.'

He often uses humour at the start of a speech. Blair will pick up on some aspect of the introduction he's just received, or his surroundings, or even the weather, and make a light-hearted remark. At a Labour Party meeting in Lewisham, London, in 1995 Blair made light of the retro décor of the Rivoli Ballroom. At the party conference in 2002 he remarked on the sweltering temperature. At a Fabian Society lecture in 2003 at the Old Vic theatre in London he said he had written a proposal for a Fabian pamphlet on why Britain should not sign up to the European convention on human rights. It was rejected.

Even on the grandest of occasions Blair will use this technique. When addressing the US Congress in 2003 he started with an ad-libbed joke about the rapturous applause he received: 'Frankly I don't deserve it, and I'm not used to it!'

I have rarely witnessed Blair rattled on a public platform. He never noticeably loses his place in a speech, or stumbles over a phrase. His greatest disaster came in front of the Women's Institute, when a long, ill-judged speech was booed and slow-handclapped by the stern ladies of the WI. Blair floundered, looked to the chair for help, and eventually abandoned his speech. When confronted by an anti-war protestor at a meeting in a school in Camden in January 2003, he joked about 'Socratic dialogue' and waited patiently for the heckler to be removed.

This has not been an easy book to edit. Because of Blair's prodigious output of speeches and articles over twenty years, much has been left out. This collection does not pretend to be comprehensive, nor is it officially endorsed by Downing Street or anyone else. I have presented the speeches and articles in chronological rather than thematic order. By placing Blair's words in the order they were delivered, I hope to show the development of his thinking, his policies, his convictions and his style. The collection falls into three parts. These three sections are not equal in length of time, but correspond to Blair's political rise.

The first section charts Blair's career as a politician, his decision in the early 1980s to stand as a Labour parliamentary candidate and become a Member of Parliament, his first speech in Parliament, and his rise up the career ladder under the patronage of Neil Kinnock. The latter parts of this section show Blair as shadow home secretary marking out his own clear ideological territory, and breaking with some of his party's own assumptions and traditions. Here the substance of the New Labour narrative can be found.

The second section 'Blair as leader' is the shortest in time – from

1994 to 1997 – but marks the period from Blair's election as leader of the Labour Party to his election as Prime Minister in the Labour landslide of May 1997. This period is filled with excitement, new ideas and language, and the creation of a coherent 'New Labour' message. The mid-nineties witnessed the death of one government, mired in sleaze and desperation, and the birth of the new government, brimming and fizzing with confidence and modernity.

The third section covers Blair as Prime Minister from 1997 to January 2004. It includes major domestic and world events, the 2001 general election and the dominance from September 2001 onwards of world affairs and war. One of the last entries is Tony Blair's address to the United States Congress in July 2003. This section reflects the crises which befell Labour in its second term, the hard slog of governing, and the collapse of international certainties and assumptions after the terrorist attacks on the World Trade Center and the Pentagon.

Because of the wealth of material and the need to be selective, the choice of speeches and articles has been based on three criteria: firstly wherever possible the words are Blair's own, rather than a speech-writer's or ghost-writer's. As party leader and later as Prime Minister, all of Blair's pronouncements owe something to his advisers and civil servants, notably Alastair Campbell, and none can be genuinely accredited solely to Blair. No modern prime minister sits alone crafting major speeches or articles. Major speeches, particularly the annual speech to the Labour Party conference, can be the result of scores of people's efforts. The establishment of the Strategic Communications Unit (SCU) in Downing Street after 1997 allowed former journalists to create an 'article factory' for the Prime Minister, with the results appearing in a broad range of magazines, broadsheets and tabloid newspapers.

I have tried to choose passages in which Blair took a personal hand and which reflect his own views. That means that most of his 'official' speeches and ghost-written articles for newspapers do not appear here.

Secondly, I have selected words which mark a major historical event or key political turning point. What Blair said and wrote at the time of the 1997 general election, or the death of Diana, or the attacks on the 11 September 2001, or during the wars in Iraq and Afghanistan, have historical significance, and are worth recording.

The third criterion is whether the passage chosen illuminates some aspect of Blair's beliefs or values. This is particularly true of the early period, when Blair was finding his political feet, for example, the articles in *Marxism Today*, *Fabian Review* and *Renewal* journal, or his comments on Christian Socialism, the philosopher John Macmurray, or the history of the Labour Party.

During the editing of this book, many people asked me whether a survey of Blair's speeches and articles over twenty years showed his consistency or the contrary. My conclusion is that Blair's own values, as expressed through the written and spoken word, have remained remarkably consistent. Blair may have come to politics relatively late – after university. But once he had established his personal philosophy and belief system, after much deliberation, discussion and soul-searching in his early twenties, he has remained true to it. Here Blair's Christianity is, without question, the dominant influence and the selection reflects this.

On the other hand, much of the rhetoric and many of the buzz-words ('stakeholding', 'young country' 'New Britain') used by Blair sound dated, along with some of the politics which lay behind them. Blair was not above using traditional Labour-speak as a new Member of Parliament, and slipping into the Labour rhetorical comfort zone when he needed to establish his credentials with a Labour audience. His maiden speech in 1983 is pure 'old Labour' rhetoric. Blair's opponents have made much of his support for the Campaign for Nuclear Disarmament (CND) or Britain's withdrawal from the European Union, but these can be explained by his public support for the Party's policies of the day, rather than personal conviction. Blair's views are consistent in some places and a product of time, context and political expediency in others.

It has been an eventful journey for the politician who was once dubbed 'Bambi'. The rise of Tony Blair was extremely fast. An illustration of just how fast is an anecdote I enjoy telling: in October 1993 at the Labour Party conference I helped organise a meeting for the Labour Co-ordinating Committee (LCC) with Tony Blair as the guest speaker. He was addressing the topic of Labour's future. How many of the hundreds of delegates and journalists turned up to hear him? Seven. One of those was a foreign journalist who was in the wrong room and swiftly left. Blair joked about the importance of quality not quantity, and shared some highly thoughtful remarks. Almost exactly ten years later, he was addressing, not six Labour Party activists in a shabby seaside hotel room, but the Congress of the United States of America, and the world.

Paul Richards
London, 2004

Part one:
Blair the politician

Australian lecture
August 1982

At Oxford University, Blair became close friends with two Australian students. One, Peter Thomson, was a 36-year-old theology student and radical minister in the Australian Anglican Church. The other was Geoff Gallop, a Rhodes Scholar studying politics, philosophy and economics, who went on to be an MP in Western Australia and leader of the WA Labor Party. Blair kept in touch with his two friends after their return to Australia, and in August 1982, after being defeated as Labour's candidate in the Beaconsfield by-election, and before being selected for Sedgefield, Blair and Cherie Booth visited Australia. He delivered a lecture at Murdoch University in Perth, Western Australia, where Gallop was then teaching, on 'The British Labour Party Today'.

The lecture is a forensic analysis of the Labour Party's history in the late seventies and early eighties. This period, characterised by infighting, divisive debates and internal elections, and an activist backlash against the Callaghan government, made a mark on the young Blair, newly recruited to the London Labour Party. He sometimes refers to his time in Hackney and Earl's Court Labour Parties with distaste — describing two groups of activists on each side of the room, firing resolutions at one other.

Blair's analysis shows a clear distinction from the Labour Bennite left and its publications, and he is scathing about the recently departed SDP. He refers to the need to broaden the Party's appeal beyond 'the traditional working-class elements of the electorate. To put it crudely, an appeal that reaches only the NUM and the Guardian letter-writers is not going to win Labour a general election'. This obvious truth would remain unproved for another fifteen years. He also welcomes the influence of the women's movement, the election of black councillors,

3

and the move to mandatory reselection of Members of Parliament.

It is a highly technical assessment, based on an analysis of election results and the balance of left–right forces inside the Labour Party and trade unions. There is little of the later Blair here: no mention of values or ethical socialism, and no rhetorical flourishes and sound bites. But this lecture, reproduced here in full for the first time, provides a fascinating insight into the developing political thought of Blair at the start of his political career.

There are three paradoxes in the present British political situation. First, any objective assessment of the Thatcher government must lead to a conclusion that it has failed in the basic tasks it set itself on coming to power in May 1979. The Tories promised to put Britain back to work; their famous advertising slogan was 'Labour isn't working'. Unemployment then was 1.3 million. It is now over three million and still rising. The Tories promised to build up investment in manufacturing industries, by allowing private incentive to prosper. Manufacturing investment has slumped by about 20 per cent since May 1979 and output itself is down 15 per cent. The government's only conceivable claim to success is the reduction of the inflation rate. But that is a reduction only after rampant inflation during 1980 and 1981 and at a cost of greatly, maybe terminally, damaging industry's infrastructure. Even the Falklands conflict (a significant source of government popularity) only arose because of a blunder by the Foreign Office in assessing the sincerity of the Argentines' desire for invasion. Yet, despite all this, the Tory government rides 9–12 points ahead in most opinion polls – an unprecedented situation at this stage of a government's life.

The second paradox concerns the rise of the Social Democratic Party. To read the press, you would think that a major change in British political thought had occurred. 'We are breaking the mould,' say the SDP leaders. They are strange mould-breakers: Roy Jenkins, Shirley Williams, David Owen, Bill Rodgers. If anything they are the failed representatives whose lingering social consciences prevent them from voting Tory; the Tammany Hall working-class Labour politicians; and that ephemeral group of supporters that always clusters round anything new, those that profess to be 'non-political'. Yet it is clear to any but the most evangelical of Labour canvassers that the SDP have touched a powerful feeling amongst a particular section of the electorate: a dissatisfaction not so much with the policies of the main parties, but with their rhetoric and perhaps philosophy.

The third paradox concerns the Labour Party. It is widely seen as intolerant and undemocratic; destructive rather than constructive. Support for the Labour Party should, with unemployment as it is, be dramatic and consistent. Instead it is below that achieved in May 1979. Indeed its supposed intolerance was given as the principal reason for forming the SDP. Yet far from negating democracy, the past few years have seen it flourish within the Party. MPs must now go through a mandatory reselection process prior to renomination as Labour candidates. (This was in a large measure due to difficulties experienced in removing Reg Prentice from the Labour nomination for a safe London seat; once denominated he switched to the Tory Party becoming a minister in the Thatcher government.) The leader of the Party is no longer elected solely by the caucus of MPs. The entire Labour movement participates in the election by means of an electorate college giving 40 per cent of the vote to the unions, and 30 per cent to MPs and constituency parties. The picture is one of power being devolved downwards. It is a picture reprinted in many of the local government manifestos, particularly of the left-wing councils: decentralisation is the theme. But it is the left that is most depicted as being undemocratic.

It is easy to be cynical or careless about these paradoxes; to dismiss them as part of the ebb and flow of political fortunes; or as the expression of the waywardness of electorates. Such an approach would be fundamentally mistaken. Each paradox contains an important lesson for the Labour Party and the Party's task in the immediate future is to resolve them.

The Tory election victory of May 1979 in one sense represented a devastating defeat for Labour. Its Parliamentary strength tumbled from 319 MPs to 268. The Tories increased their share of the vote by 8 per cent. Everywhere the election was hailed as a victory for Thatcherite ideology. Curiously enough this view was most propounded on the left, notably by Tony Benn. It was said that the Labour manifesto of 1974 was radical, promising an 'irreversible shift in the ownership of wealth to working people'; that the mandate given the Labour Party by the October 1974 victory was unfulfilled; that Healey and Callaghan sowed the seeds of Thatcherite monetarism by making pay restraint and cuts in public expenditure the principal foundation of their economic policy; and that the electorate, given no firm socialist lead, decided to have the full-blown self-proclaiming Tories to the closet Tories within the Labour right. Yet a deeper analysis of the 1979 results confounds this view. Although Labour lost 51 seats, it actually polled slightly more votes in 1979 than in October 1974; and its share of the vote declined by only 2 to 3 per cent. Moreover, the traditional left-wing position constantly reiterated by Tony Benn and others – that Labour lost the election by alienating its working-class support – cannot be sustained on an examination of where Labour lost its seats. In Scotland, Wales and the North, the traditional working-class areas, where Labour is much the strongest, Labour retained its seats; in Scotland, perhaps the most economically disadvantaged area of the electorate, Labour's vote increased. The seats were almost exclusively lost in the Midlands and South-East, tradition-ally the prosperous parts of the country. This was especially so in the suburban areas like Basildon and Stevenage, around London.

In *Labour at the Crossroads*, Geoff Hodgson makes the conventional left case. He quotes a survey of electoral opinion which shows Labour support amongst middle and upper working-class people remained constant from October 1974 to May 1979; but semi and unskilled working-class support dropped from 57 per cent to 47 per cent during that period. He cites that as showing working-class rejection of Labour. But, as he admits, the survey also shows that in September 1978 semi-skilled and skilled working-class support for Labour was 58 per cent, 1 per cent up on October 1974. In other words, the drop of support occurred entirely between September 1978 and May 1979, over the period of industrial unrest in 'the winter of discontent'. That is a very different matter from the rejection of the entire government from 1974 onwards. Indeed, on the Benn case, one would expect the most dramatic drop in support to have occurred between 1976 and 1978 when the IMF cuts were imposed and pay restraint under the social contract was being enforced. Certainly, by September 1978, the temper and philosophy of the Labour government was plain. Although the erosion of the Labour vote between September 1978 and May 1979 cannot be ignored, it hardly makes a compelling case for the Benn view.

Moreover, the point about the 1974 manifesto is disingenuous. The electorate cannot seriously have thought that the Labour Party in 1974 headed by Wilson (himself Prime Minister of a very reformist government from 1964 to 1970) and whose leading figures were Callaghan, Jenkins and Healey was going to bring about revolutionary change. Probably the greatest electoral asset Labour had in 1979 from a popular point of view was Callaghan himself, something constantly stressed by the Labour campaign managers.

More challenging statistics than those offered by Hodgson above, are those taken from the Butler and Strokes surveys on the 1964, 1966, 1974 and 1979 elections, and reported in Ivor Crewe's essay

'The Labour Party and the Electorate' published in *The Politics of the Labour Party* (ed. D. Kavanagh).

These figures are more compatible with my own experience, canvassing roughly 8,000 people during the Beaconsfield campaign (all of whom lived in local council estates or the cheaper end of private housing). This experience is that there are growing numbers of young often socially upward-moving people who are simply not prepared to accept our basic ideology just because their forefathers did. There are very few of the younger age group converted to our ideology and we rely to a dangerous degree on the loyalty vote amongst older citizens.

Many, right and left within the Labour Party, suffered similar experiences when confronting the electorate in May 1979. For the right wing, this confirmed to them their suspicion that socialism was dead; Gaitskell had been right when trying to rule out the commitment to public ownership in the Labour Party's constitution. It was this that truly led to the SDP (David Owen's book *Face the Future*, in hardback, used the language of socialism to describe the SDP philosophy; his paperback version, following the hardback, has the word 'socialism' excised).

For the Labour left, precisely the opposite conclusion was drawn. The days of Butskillite consensus politics were over. The failure of Labour ideology was the direct result of the failure of the Wilson and Callaghan governments to campaign for it. No wonder the trade unions were unpopular when they had been attacked by the leader of the Labour Party; of course the public services were not supported when the Labour government was itself cutting them; and naturally nationalisation was a dirty word, when the workers within those nationalised industries had seen the same bosses in charge under public ownership as they had under private ownership.

The powerful appeal of the left to the fundamental socialist instincts of the Party, coupled with the election defeat, easily overwhelmed the tired excuses of pragmatism from the Labour right. As often in politics, it is not how things actually are, but how they are perceived that is important. The May 1979 election defeat was perceived by the Party, and indeed Labour movement as a whole, as a victory for the ideology of Thatcher and a defeat for middle-of-the-road consensus politics.

The left within the Labour Party had been making powerful advances since the early 1970s. Moreover, it now tended to be younger, white-collar and organised. The 1979 election defeat propelled the leftwards movement forward in three ways: first, it lifted the responsibility of power from the shoulders of the Party, and killed off the argument that the left shouldn't, by criticising the Party leader, rock the boat. Secondly, by pointing to the election defeat, the left were able to dispose of the continual refrain of the right wing that moderation was essential to the retaining of power. Thirdly, by asserting that had the more radical policies of the rank and file been followed Labour could have won the election, the left attracted powerful support for the view that the PLP had betrayed the Party and must be made more accountable in future. So in 1980, came mandatory re-election and the electoral college. A further left reform, giving the drafting of the manifesto to the NEC alone rather than the NEC and the shadow cabinet, failed.

But the constitutional reforms in many ways are secondary to the essential change that has taken place in Party membership. It is not really accurate, as Tony Benn would have it, that the rank and file became dismayed with the Party leadership during the 1970s. The rank and file itself altered. The people occupying the positions in general committees of constituencies in the early 1970s are no longer in office. There has been a massive grass-roots change in the Labour Party. Much of this has been beneficial. For example, black councillors are no longer unknown. On the London Council 23 out of its 72 councillors are black.

9

The women's movement has made a colossal input into the Party. So have radical community groups, environmental groups and so on. To a large extent, these groups have been on the left, many of their members being of the 1960s and 1970s student generation. Very often on leaving university, they have gone into the public sector – teaching, local government, social work or research. This change made itself most dramatically felt in the deputy leadership battle last year between Healey and Benn. In the constituency section, Benn took 85 per cent of the vote. MPs, though they had an independent voice in the electoral college, were under strong pressure through the reselection process to vote for Benn.

But the Benn campaign in 1981 may, in retrospect, be seen not only as the highwater mark of his own personal fortunes, but of that of the 'far' left in the Party. Most people on the left supported the constitutional changes and so, crucially, did the left-wing union leaders. There was thus a broad coalition of left forces which proved enormously effective.

Over the battle for the deputy leadership, cracks began to appear. A significant group of left-wing MPs and union leaders slowly began to depart from Benn. This was for two reasons. First, there was undoubtedly a certain element of Benn support that displayed open intolerance of those that did not support him. It was not the shouting down of people at meetings, (this occurred only sporadically), it was the way in which a vote for Benn came increasingly to be put in terms of a socialist imperative. Secondly, as the electoral unpopularity of Labour grew and as the SDP took off, the battle for deputy leadership and indeed Benn himself were seen as running sores doing enormous damage to the Party. Benn's personal unpopularity was plain to any canvasser. It was illustrated when NUPE (the public service union representing the lower paid) voted substantially for Healey, despite the executive of the union being in favour of Benn. The TWGU in its consultation exercise found eight out of eleven regions in favour of Healey. Yet these unions had suffered most during the years of the Healey social contract. Their vote was an anti-Benn vote.

When the deputy leadership votes took place, Neil Kinnock, Joan Lestor and others voted for Silkin (the middle candidate) on the first ballot and then abstained on the second. Still others like Jack Straw, identified with the left, voted for Silkin on the first ballot and only then opted for Benn.

Since October 1981, the split on the left has grown. Kinnock and his supporters were subjected to severe criticism for their 'betrayal' of Benn. Of course, the harsher the criticism, the more isolated they felt from the critics and the more determined to fight back. The position of Lestor and Kinnock was especially vital. They were both members of the NEC of the Party which is charged with the running of the Party and the endorsement of candidates. Michael Foot, from the centre, together with the right on the NEC, possessed insufficient numbers to carry the NEC. The crucial votes were Kinnock's and Lestor's, together with other left union leaders like Alex Kitson of the TWGU.

Over a series of issues they began to support Foot: over the non-endorsement of Peter Tatchell as Labour candidate in Bermondsey (though not Lestor); over the refusal to admit Tariq Ali to membership, and finally over Militant. This last battle has finally been the destruction of the left coalition.

Militant is an avowedly Trotskyist group, whose links go back to the Revolutionary Socialist League in the 1960s. It has 64 full-time workers, including 34 at a regional level. Militant say that they only 'sell the Militant paper'. The centre and right say it is much more than just a group selling a paper; it is, in effect, a Soviet conspiracy, a party within the Party. Following a report by the General Secretary and National Agent into Militant, the NEC voted narrowly to establish a register of all groups in the Party. To qualify, the group has to show it abides by Labour's Constitution. The Constitution in effect outlaws parties within the Party. Thus it is plain, since the report expressly said that Militant was a party within a party, that Militant will not be permitted to register.

That decision by the NEC has now been ratified by the 1982 conference and by a large three or four to one majority. All the major unions (including the normally left-wing NUM), save for NUPE, voted in favour of the register. The vote was seen as a personal triumph for Michael Foot. Thanks to the union vote, the NEC also swung firmly centrewards, if not rightwards. Foot need no longer depend on Neil Kinnock's vote.

There remains one worrying undercurrent to this seemingly omnipotent tide of support for Foot. The unions may have voted overwhelmingly for the register, but the constituency parties did not. In fact, they voted overwhelmingly against it, by a margin of almost 90 per cent to 10 per cent. There is therefore an alarming disparity between the constituency parties and the unions. It may be said that this disparity has always existed. The unions, in particular the union leadership, have usually been more conservative than the 'idealists' in the constituency parties. Nye Bevan's support in the 1950s came, predominantly, from the constituency parties, whilst the right-wing union leaders co-ordinated opposition to him. But the uncertainty of left-wing feeling within the constituencies has never been as it is now. When Hugh Gaitskell lost the 1960 conference vote on unilateralism, some 60 per cent of the constituency parties supported him and were instrumental in achieving the reversal of that decision in 1961. Such constituency support for any 'right-wing' policy would be unthinkable in 1982.

This gap between constituency parties and unions, ties in with the change in Party membership earlier described. It is the manual labour unions – the AOEW, TGWU, EEPTU, GMWU, NUR and the NUM – that dominate the Labour Party conference. NUPE and

ASTMS are the only sizeable white-collar unions, but even NUPE is only partially white-collar. Yet at a constituency level, it is increasingly members of NUT, the teachers, NALGO, the local government officers, ASTMS and the white-collar sections of the manual unions, like ACTSS of the TGWU and TASS of the AUEW, that dominate both debate at a constituency level and party officials. Furthermore, these members tend not to participate as part of their union, in the same way the blue-collar union delegates do or did. They are quintessentially Party members first, and the views they express are their own, not those of their union branch. Many NALGO members active in the Labour Party tend to be on the left. Yet NALGO is not even affiliated as a union to the Labour Party. The membership rejected affiliation by almost nine votes to one a year ago.

So whatever comfort Labour's centre and right can take from the position of the 1982 conference, it is a position that rests entirely on union support, and in the teeth of constituency opposition. The question of the next year is going to be whether the soft left–hard left split within the PLP and the unions becomes mirrored in the constituency parties. If it does not, the Labour Party will begin to develop a schizophrenic personality, with a corresponding confusion engendered in the electorate as to what Labour really stands for.

How can left and right in the Party be reconciled? If a united Labour Party is a prerequisite of electoral support, how does it unite? The Labour Party, left and right, is a prisoner of its own history. It is remarkable how often Labour leaders justify a policy or position on the basis of party tradition. Conference speeches are replete with references to Keir Hardie, Attlee and Bevan. The right recall nostalgically, the days of the 1960s, when the PLP was treated with respect by a largely working-class Party membership and when disagreements could always be patched up over a pint at the local.

The left point to the radical spirit of the Party founders, to the fundamentalist socialism of Cripps and Cole and explode at the description of the left as 'new' when what it is saying is pale in comparison with those early socialist proselytes. Both sides feel a need to represent themselves as the 'true' Labour Party in an historical sense. In doing so, instead of using history to explain the present and point to the future, they chain themselves to the past.

The right of the Party must come to terms with two matters. First, the scale of the problems we face as a people in 1982 are quite unlike those of previous years: 3.25 million unemployed with another one to two million on short-time working or temporary employment schemes; the wholesale devastation of traditional industries such as the steel industry and railways network together with the decline in manufacturing; 10 to 12 million people living at or below the poverty line; so many of our inner cities are just ghettos of the socially deprived. And all this against a background of Reaganomics in the USA and the ever-widening scope of new technology. The mild tinkering with the economy proposed by the Social Democrats alas nowhere near measures up to the problem. A massive reconstruction of industry is needed. However, a reflation of the economy that is unplanned would lead, almost for a certainty, to inflation, and the resources required to reconstruct manufacturing industry call for enormous state guidance and intervention.

If the Labour Party really wishes to reduce unemployment in a secure way by more than short-term schemes of public investment, its difficulty will not be one of increasing central control but of containing that control and marrying it to ideas of industrial democracy. That in turn will bring any Labour government into sharp conflict with the power of capital, particularly multinational capital. The trouble with the right of the party is that it has basked so long in the praise of the leader-writers of the *Financial Times*,

The Times and *Guardian* that it is no longer accustomed to giving them offence. It will find the experience painful, but it is vital.

Secondly, the right must acknowledge to itself that the Party has changed irreversibly. The influence of the new white-collar participants in the Labour Party is open to many criticisms. But it won't go away and there is no doubt that it does represent a genuine, if limited, social movement. The issues they raise are different from the straightforward economics of traditional Party thought. Though on the left, nationalisation is not a great priority, the issues are social issues: nuclear disarmament, ecology, race relations, feminism. Ironically, indeed, they tend to be issues cutting across party boundaries. The 'new' left, so readily accused of being sectarian, often embrace policies that have non-sectarian appeal.

There is a tendency on Labour's traditional right to dismiss these issues as trendy, as part of the student intellectualism of the young left wing, and as irrelevant to what are the bread and butter issues of jobs, housing, health and education. That is an error of enormous proportions. The support of radical campaigns such as CND and environmental protection can be seen across Europe – look at the rise of the green parties in West Germany. And it should never be forgotten that it is working-class people that die through handling asbestos.

These movements around particular issues are real and are finding potent and immediate expression within the Party. There is no point in pretending they don't exist or in attempting to mobilise the union vote to neutralise their effect. Instead, the right should be trying to understand these issues and recognise that they now make up an essential part of 'socialism' and the 'Labour' movement. It should be trying, too, to participate actively in the campaigns, to assist their development by lending them that pragmatism, that hard-headedness of purpose that is the quality of the right, which the left consistently underestimated.

However, the challenge faced by the left within the Labour Party is just as immense. The 1982 conference, on the face of it at least, represents a real slap in the eye. It is quite apparent that the unions mean business. The reversion of the NEC to the right in 1981 and 1982 is a phenomenon unknown for many years. Even the unions thought to be on the left are fed up with the fighting in the Party and, privately at any rate, they blame the left, especially Tony Benn.

There are three courses open to the left: retreat, revenge or reconciliation. The least likely course is retreat, but it is not impossible. It has happened before. The left, demoralised by defeat, loses heart, shrugs its shoulders and goes back to its historic role – the conscience of the Party, but never its hand. It will then fission into countless particles retaining only the common fact of irrelevance. It will be a broad band of dissenters, but without common leadership or goals.

Such a course would be disastrous. Honest people on the right and centre will admit that the left has generated an enormous amount of quite necessary rethinking in the Party. We were in danger of drifting into being 'the natural party of government', but of a society that was unradicalised and unchanged. We had become managers of a conservative country. Fortunately, the left today is probably too large, too tactically astute and too determined for such a course to be taken. Furthermore, the left may have lost the battle, but it keeps intact its power base within the city wall: the constituency parties. A much more pressing danger is that the left now pulls up the drawbridge and casts aside with contempt any form of accommodation.

If it does so, civil war in the Labour Party will break out in deadly earnest. That much underestimated numbers of constituency activists who really don't want to get embroiled in Party fighting at all, will be increasingly driven off neutral ground and forced to take 'positions'.

Above all the unions, reluctant though they are to have a fight, will not duck it if it is pushed on them. The 1982 conference was the foreseeable consequence of 1981.

The last course open to the left is reconciliation. That will require painstaking self-criticism and a willingness to learn. If the left simply dismisses what the unions are saying to the constituency parties as no more than the manifestation of the power of the union leaders, it will commit a political act of huge folly. The left should learn four things.

First, the Party appeal must encompass more than the traditional working-class elements of the electorate. To put it crudely, an appeal that reaches only the NUM and the *Guardian* letter-writers is not going to win Labour a General Election. This is straightforward, obvious, psychological sense. But it is remarkable how often it is ignored. The left is fond of pointing to the radicalism of early socialists as justification for their own views. If that means the left should draw on the spirit of Party founders, that is positive; if it means a blind obedience to traditional doctrine, that is misguided atavism.

The left may well be right as a matter of history. *The Labour Party in Government* is a collection of essays, published in 1933 by Cripps, Cole, Attlee and others. It should be compulsory reading for right-wingers who talk paranoically about the 'new' left. The essays represent politics way to the left of Benn and not far from the revolutionary left.

But since 1933 there has been an enormous sociological shift in the class composition of Britain. Almost 50 per cent of British people now live in owner-occupied houses. The average wage is almost £7,500 p.a. Over 65 per cent of people own their own car. Almost 50 per cent of people now work in service industries or the public sector. Crosland was right in 1956 when he identified, in *The Future of Socialism*, major alterations in British society; in particular, the rise in living standards of sections of the working class and the emergency of a new white-collar class.

Where he was wrong was in assuming continuing economic growth at the rate of the 1950s and therefore that these changes would continue and intensify. Instead, the 1970s plunged Britain and the Western world into a recession from which they have not yet emerged. This recession, unusually, has been accompanied by inflation. There is, thus, a large group of unemployed; and an even larger group of low paid, about 7 million. In total perhaps 10 to 11 million of the workforce fit into these two categories. That is 40 to 45 per cent of the entire country's workforce. They are the reason the Social Democrats haven't a hope of winning a general election; they are forced by sheer self-interest, even if nothing else, to vote Labour. Moreover, they are concentrated in particular areas the inner cities, the North, Scotland, Wales, etc. Electorally, these are Labour areas. Certainly under the present electoral system, they will provide Labour with a solid 200-seat base.

But whereas the Social Democrats refuse to face up to the irrelevance of their politics to this group of workers, the left is at risk of confusing them with the mass of the British people or the Labour electorate. There may be 40 to 45 per cent of the workforce unemployed or lowly paid, but that leaves 50 to 55 per cent who are not; who, even with the cuts in living standard of the past few years, still maintain a lifestyle incomparably better than their ancestors. Disraeli saw Britain as two nations: the rich and the poor. The modern truth is more complex: Britain is becoming two societies: those in work in traditionally high-paid jobs or in industries where there are unions with muscle; and those out of work or in jobs where unions are non-existent or powerless. An electoral appeal exclusively to one section will disinterest or alienate the other.

The most vivid demonstration of this is the often quoted regional divide: north and south. The disparities in wealth are matched by the disparities in voting. The South-East region (i.e. leaving aside London) of the Labour Party now has only one MP – Joan Lestor in Slough. In the South as a whole there are only eleven MPs. On the boundary changes Labour's base will narrow still further. Yet there is still a myopic tendency to dismiss the South; to treat the 'real' Labour Party as that or of the archetypal mining/industrial town in the North. Frequently (indeed in the right as well as the left), people describe Crosland as out of date, failing to take account of the structural decline of capitalism, etc. That is as foolish a view as the view that class distinctions are a thing of the past. The reality is complex and relative, not absolute.

The second lesson for the left leads on from the first; or perhaps should precede it. The left is keen on democracy, and rightly so. But 'democracy should not be seen as something abstract, something the Party has within itself. The Party must have a democratic relationship with the electorate. The key word is relationship. It would be absurd if the Party descended into oblique populism, merely parroting the views of 'the electorate', however those views could be gauged. Equally absurd, though, is the view that there is anything to be gained from capturing control of the Labour Party machine whilst leaving the voters behind. The left's position is often inconsistent on democracy. It will advocate Party democracy, yet refuse one member one vote in the constituency section of the electoral college. It will talk of decentralisation yet find itself at a bizarre and remote distance from most of the opinions of those to whom 'power' is supposed to be given.

Part of the problem stems from the failure of Party activists to mix sufficiently with the electorate. It is a social difficulty. Party members will attend five or six or more meetings a week. The trouble is that they can end up with little or no time for meeting those with whom they disagree.

A dialogue with the electorate is impossible if you only ever meet them on a canvass. A local party should grow out of a local community – the Party members having roots in that community. That is not only for reasons of political efficiency; it is because the Party will then be more sensitive to the needs and wishes of the electorate. I will give two deliberately controversial examples of the difficulties Labour is experiencing in its relationship with the electors.

Labour would disallow the sale of council houses. That is for perfectly sound reasons of political principle. Yet there is something mildly distasteful about owner-occupier Party members preaching the virtues of public housing to council tenants. Secondly, London *Labour Briefing* (a left-wing Labour Party organisation which publishes a monthly paper) is perhaps the most powerful grouping in the London Labour Party, with a hegemony as complete as that which used to be enjoyed by Labour's right wing. But I venture to suggest that most Labour voters in London would regard *Briefing*, if they were to read it, as incomprehensible at best and at worst as scary.

The left have got to come to terms with the quality of relationship they have with the people they wish to represent. Moreover, it is no use blaming the press for this poor relationship. Blaming the press won't alter its influence and, in any event, press paranoia can become (as it has for Tony Benn) an immunity from self-criticism.

This leads on to the third lesson. It is impossible to define, in terms of a strategy, what the left must do to correct the impression of the voters that it is indifferent, if not hostile, to their feelings. There is no detailed blueprint that can be examined and followed to the letter. There is no logical master plan. It requires the exercise of political judgement and an amount of political maturity. To many on the left, those are dirty phrases. They suggest pragmatism; which spells sell-out. So they must be resisted, no matter what the cost. Sometimes not even if the cost is failure in a general election.

Political judgement, however, does not mean cowardice. It means knowing when to fight and when to accept defeat. It acknowledges that not every compromise is a sell-out. Above all, it means an appreciation that there must be some system of priorities. For example, the proposal that Labour nationalises state assets sold off by the Tories without compensation has a gut appeal to many activists. But, quite apart from questions of parliamentary democracy, such a policy would cause much more trouble for Labour – in terms of Labour being portrayed as an extremist authoritarian party both at home and abroad – than it could possibly be worth. Ultimately, it would be a demonstration of political virility, not a rational policy taking account of practical reality. As Lenin wrote (significantly after the Bolsheviks had taken power): 'to reject compromises "on principle", to reject the possibility of compromises in general, no matter of what kind, is childishness, which it is difficult ever to consider seriously.' (*Left-Wing Communism – An Infantile Disorder*).

Lastly, the left must look for its political philosophy to something more sensitive, more visionary, in a word, more modern, than Marxism, whether in the crude vanguardist form preached by Militant or in its broader libertarian form practised by groups like *Labour Briefing, Chartist,* Clause IV and so on. There is a strange irony in left-wing socialist thought. The group of intellectuals who left university in the late sixties or early seventies derives its fundamental political philosophy almost exclusively from Marx. Marxism is the foundation, whatever vague philosophical additions have been superimposed on top of it. Not just the analysis, but the style of most of the periodicals and journals influential on the young Labour left is that of Marx, Lenin and Trotsky: savage in the denunciation of opponents, especially within the Party; constantly assessing and reassessing tactics; studied in the avoidance of any analysis which has gained favour in the mass media; and most particularly, with a political language that requires the readers to be *cognoscenti*.

The irony lies in the homage paid to Marx at a time when most casual political observers and certainly most voters hold him and the regimes founded on his political philosophy in fear and distrust. The major political change since the 1930s, for Europeans, is the existence of the Eastern bloc of Europe. It is impossible to underestimate the influence which this has had on the thinking of the post-war generation. It has destroyed faith in Marxism as a liberating force and is a remorseless deterrent to experimenting with such a philosophy here. It is quite vain for Marxists to effect explanations for repression in Marxist states, no matter how plausible they are. People will not risk it.

Doubly damaging to the cause of Marxist socialism is the fact that it isn't even efficient – working people in Eastern Europe are, if anything, worse off. No doubt Marxism will always have an influence within Labour Party thinking. But countenancing its domination is political suicide. The early socialists had plenty of vision; their socialism was young, and fundamentalist. But it was untrammelled by experience. What might inspire hope then would inspire fear today.

I return to the paradoxes with which I began. The reasons the Tories are popular are twofold. First, they have a plain political philosophy: individualism. It has a simple gut appeal. Its essence in a troubled world is survival – look after yourself, root out 'inefficiency', those that can't cope, those that don't fit. Retaining the 'misfits' or 'unfits' is a liberal luxury the Tories say, which in this time of austerity we cannot afford.

A country in deep recession becomes scared and fear makes the people selfish. It's no real surprise, therefore, that a regime of each for himself is popular or that alternatives based on ideas of the common weal and social justice find it hard to be accepted. That is especially so when the conventional wisdom in the pubs and parlours of the nation for so long has been that we are unproductive and lazy as a workforce and that the current economic difficulties are in a real sense our own fault. If Mrs Thatcher has furthered any collective feeling, it is a collective sense of masochism.

But it is not just the simplicity of the Tories' message. It is also the conjunction of that simple message with the fractured nature of the opposition. The combined anti-Tory vote is still much higher than the Tory vote. However, the opposition is fractured not merely into different parties but within the parties.

The Labour Party sits uneasily, squashed between traditional Clause IV, Part 4 socialism and an acceptance of the mixed economy. Its rhetoric may be more consistent with the former but its policies are consistent with the latter and do not appear likely to undergo very severe change in the near future. Indeed the more 'consensual' its economic policies, the more Labour speakers find it necessary to extirpate consensus from their language in order to appease those who regard 'consensus' as betrayal. The result is that people find Labour's philosophy incomprehensible and confusing.

The policies seem favoured by popular opinion, but they are sold in the language of the Party faithful. It should be the other way round: policies should be formed by the Party faithful (or at least by them in conjunction with the broad Labour movement) but sold in a popular way to the people at large. If you asked a member of the present Tory Party to define Tory philosophy, the task would not be difficult. A member of the present Labour Party would find it extremely difficult to define Labour's philosophy. He or she might find it easy enough to place their own position or conception of the Labour Party but not that of the Party as a whole.

Moreover, no credible opposition at all is presented by the SDP or Liberals. They show a humane, bland, unobjectionable face that says very little that is not 'moderate', and nothing that is efficacious.

They lack any distinctive image save for one of niceness. Having cut themselves off from the trade unions by their disastrous embracing of the Tebbit Bill, which curbed trade union rights, they have isolated themselves from organised Labour, a fatal mistake for any radical party.

Yet their, still high, level of support is not surprising. To the lower middle to middle income people of the post-war generation, they offer at least some compromise between the overt callousness of Mrs Thatcher and the old-fashioned collectivism of Labour. The greatest political error Labour could make is, in defeating the SDP at the next election, to misinterpret the reasons for the support the SDP has and has had. The SDP does express a real sociological challenge to Labour. If Labour ignores that challenge, it will find the opposition vote split between it and the SDP/Liberals and the prospects of wresting power from the Tories remote. Labour will be the major opposition party because the grouping giving rise to the SDP is too small to break the traditional Labour or Tory constituency, certainly under the present electoral system. But Labour needs those middle-ground voters to be sure of defeating the Tories. If this is so now, then it will be so to an ever greater degree when the boundary changes take effect in 1983.

The crucial point that I would make is that Labour can achieve this support without altering its policies at all. Its policies, indeed already recognise, if sometimes unconsciously, the changes that have taken place in our social and economic attitudes. In fact in so far as policy issues – unilateral disarmament, withdrawal from the EEC and incomes policy – divide Party members, they are really much less fundamental to a concept of socialism than is often supposed. But the Labour Party must cease being a victim of its own past. It must recognise that its goals of social equality and justice cannot be realised in the abstract, but must be realised in a relative and often shifting world.

There exists within the present Labour Party the necessary strands of radical thought: traditional trade union militancy; a new and vital commitment to democracy and accountability within the institutions that govern us; an appreciation of the ever-growing danger posed by the nuclear arms race; a recognition of the multi-cultural society in which we now live; and a traditional belief in social equality and justice through public ownership and the welfare state. These strands exist but are often disparate in their recognition in the Party. Members agree with them, if asked, but don't see them as part of a whole. The task now must be to weave them into a coherent philosophy for the future, understood by the Party and communicated to the people.

Sedgefield parliamentary selection CV
May 1983

In May 1983, less than one month before the general election, the thirty-year-old Tony Blair sought selection to be the parliamentary candidate for the safe Labour seat of Sedgefield, in the North-East of England. Blair, staying with friends in Durham, hastily produced a curriculum vitae to win support from the delegates to the Sedgefield Labour Party general management committee. The document is both a product of the pre-computer age, without spellcheckers and delete keys, and of the speed with which it was written: it contains a number of howlers and typos, including Bluir's own name. The references to left-wing causes including the Campaign for Nuclear Disarmament (CND) and employment rights are calculated to appeal to Labour members choosing their candidate. He fails to mention his membership of the Fabian Society, which he joined in 1976, seen as 'right-wing' by many Labour members. There is no record of an article in the Guardian by Blair at this time – nor any such body as the 'Society of Labour Congress' to which he gave the annual lecture. He meant the Society of Labour Lawyers. This is the CV of a young man in a hurry.

NAME: TONY BLAIR

AGE: 30 YEARS

TRADE UNION: Transport and General Workers Union

PREVIOUS PARLIAMENARY EXPERIENCE
I stood, during the Falklands war, in the Beaconsfield by-election, a Tory seat with a majority of 23,000. I lost (unsurprisingly) but

gained valuable experience. Michael Foot speaking on BBC Newsnight on 26 May 1982 said,

"In my view Tony Glair will make a major contribution to British Politics in the months and years ahead".

BACKGROUND

I lived in County Durham from i958 to i975, first in Durham City and then from i963 to i975 on a new housing estate at High Shincliffe. From i972–75 I attended Oxford University (St John's College) where Iread Law. I graduated in 1975 with a B.A. (Hons) in Law.

I975/6 I was a student at the Inns of Court School in London, passing my professional exams in the summer of 1976.

I976/7 I was pupip to Alexander Irvine Q.C. At the end of my pupillage, at the age of 24 years, I was awarded a full place in Chambers as a practicing barrister. Since 1977 I have worked as a practising barrister in those Chambers.

NATURE OF WORK

I specialise in trade union and industrial law, which, in effect, has meant living and working in London . I also work for several major County Councils and in the area of Civil Liberties. In addition I have represented the Labour Party. The unions I have worked for include: T.GW.U; I.S.T.C; N.U.R; G.M.B.A.T.U; T.S.S.A; A.U.E.U; N.A.L.G.O. Amongst the major cases in which I have been involved over the past few years are;

- Defending the Labour Party in court action against Reg Prentice and his supporters
- Defending the Labour Party in the court action against it by Militant

- Defending ILEA in its decision to peg school meal prices at 35p
- Several cases arising aout of redundancies by the British Steel Corporation, inclusing winning the unfair dismissal claim of the 30 Birmingham steelworkers
- I have, in particular, worked in cases where trade unionists have been selected for redundancy, especially in the TGWU and ISTC
- Most recently I acted for the Port Talbot steelworkers in their case against the BSC.

PUBLICATIONS AND LECTURES

Amongst the papers I have written for are – The Guardian, New Statesman, Spectator, Labour Weekly. These articles habe concerned trade union law, civil liberties, and race relations. I have lectured regularly in Trade Union law over the years, giving the i982 Society of Labour Congress lecture on the Tebbit Act.

In addition I as a discussion leader at the TGWU weekend in Durham City in June 1982, speaking on the Labour Party, and I was invited and gave a lecture on the Labour party and its future in Perth, western Australia to Murdoch and W.A universities, later published in Australia.

PARTY OFFICES

I have held offices in three London constituencies, and have been a member of each G.C. I am at present a TGWU delegate on Hackney South GC (a Labour seat with a sitting SDP defector).

I am a member of the Executive of the Society of Labour Lawyers concentrating particularly on trade union and logal government law.

MEMBERSHIP OF OTHER ORGANISATIONS

C.N.D; N.C.C.L.; L.C.C

FAMILY
I am married to Cherie Booth, who was born and bred in Liverpool. Cherie is now a barrister (having come top in her professional exams in 1976 in the whole country). She specialises in child care and adoption work. Cherie's father is the actor Anthony Booth of 'Till Death Do Us Part' fame. Anthony and Pat Pheonix, from 'Coronation Street' both came and canvassed for me when I previously stood for Parliament and would be happy to do so again.

Cherie and I, as yet, have no children.

SHORT STATEMENT OF VIEWS AND INTENT
I have always wanted to come back to the North East to represent the community here. I would, of course, live in the constituency if selected, and would be a full-time M.P. Cherie's work, unlike mine, could transfer to the North.

I believe an MP has two tasks: to know and work with the community he or she represents; and to put the best possible case for that community in Westminster.

I believe in a united Labour Party offering radical solutions within a framework that people understand and that touches their everyday lives. I support party policy as determined by Party conference. When arguments do take place, they should take place within the party, not on the media; and in a spirit of democracy. That means not only the right to express your views, but the right to have them listened to.

Maiden speech

House of Commons, 6 July 1983

A newly elected Member of Parliament has to make his first 'maiden' speech in the chamber of the House of Commons. Traditionally, the speech contains tributes to the former MPs for the seat, and some pleasantries about the MP's constituency and constituents. The tradition is that the maiden speech is non-controversial. Blair decided to follow the convention in the early part of his maiden speech, but in the section published here he launches an attack on the Thatcher government's Finance Bill, which cut taxes for the wealthy. (Twenty days later, Blair won the right to hold an adjournment debate, in which he addressed the issue of the closure of the Fishburn Coke Works.) He closes his maiden speech with some fiery socialist rhetoric, and language ('common weal', 'fellowship') which plays to an older Labour tradition.

I thank you, Mr Speaker, for allowing me this opportunity to make my maiden speech, especially on such an important Bill, as the new Member of Parliament for Sedgefield. I only hope that I can acquit myself as well as the Hon. Members who have preceded me in this difficult task.

* * *

In the area of the Wingate employment exchange, which covers a very large part of the constituency, unemployment now stands at over 40 per cent. A large proportion of the unemployed are under 25 years of age. It is said with bitter irony that the only growth area in the constituency is the unemployment office. Those young people are not merely faced with a temporary inability to find work. For many, the dole queue is their first experience of adult life. For some, it will be their most significant experience. Without work, they do not merely suffer the indignity of enforced idleness – they wonder how they can afford to get married, to start a family, and to have access to all the benefits of society that they should be able to take for granted. Leisure is not something they enjoy, but something that imprisons them.

The Bill offers no comfort at all either to those people or to the vast majority of those of my constituents who are fortunate enough to be in work. Indeed it adds the insult of inequality to the injury of poverty. It gives a further clutch of tax concessions to those who are already well-off. Some 200,000 people are taken out of the higher rate bands, whereas only 10,000 come out of the poverty trap. This is a good illustration of the sense of priority shown in the Bill.

* * *

You may wonder, Mr Speaker, why, contrary to tradition, some maiden speeches have been controversial. Perhaps it is pertinent to ask in what sense they can be controversial, since the deprivation and unhappiness that afflict our constituencies seem beyond argument. What impels us to speak our minds is the sense of urgency. As I said, in the Wingate area, unemployment is over 40 per cent. A government who are complacent or uncaring about a level of unemployment of over 40 per cent are a government who have abdicated their responsibility to govern. A government who refuse to govern are unworthy of the name of government.

* * *

What Sedgefield and the north-east desperately need is a government committed to marrying together the resources of the area – a government committed to the north. Over the last few years the level of investment in manufacturing industry in the north has dropped not merely in absolute terms but relative to other parts of the country. That situation must be reversed. In practical terms, the government must pledge themselves to a massive investment in the region and must plan that investment.

I and others will continue to press for a northern development agency to perform for the north the task that the Scottish Development Agency performs for Scotland. That is not a request for fresh bureaucracy but a realistic assessment of need. Experience of the present government may teach caution in hoping for such a commitment, but a refusal does not make the case for such a body any less strong. The aim would be to harness the considerable resources of the constituency and the region and to let them work to create a better standard of living for the people. After all, that is the essence of socialism.

I am a socialist not through reading a textbook that has caught my intellectual fancy, nor through unthinking tradition, but because I believe that, at its best, socialism corresponds most closely to an existence that is both rational and moral. It stands for co-operation, not confrontation, for fellowship, not fear. It stands for equality, not because it wants people to be the same, but because only through equality in our economic circumstances can our individuality develop properly. British democracy rests ultimately on the shared perception by all the people that they participate in the benefits of the common weal. This Bill, with its celebration of inequality, is destructive of that perception. It is because of a fear that the government seem indifferent to such considerations that I and my colleagues oppose the Bill and will continue to oppose it.

'The Constitution after Westland'

New Statesman, 7 November 1986

The Westland affair rocked the Thatcher government, and precipitated the dramatic resignation of Michael Heseltine from the Cabinet. It concerned the awarding of government contracts to build helicopters, but soon became an issue about government secrecy and Thatcher's own role as prime minister. Blair, an MP for only three years, wrote a savage piece for the New Statesman *upholding parliamentary democracy and ministerial accountability.*

Some of the language Blair uses – 'the attacks on the BBC ... the increasing reluctance on the part of ministers to answer questions (frequently mentioned by older parliamentarians), the politicisation of the civil service' – would be echoed twenty years later against his own government following the death of Dr David Kelly.

The government is trying desperately to bury Westland. It may succeed: public interest has waned. Yet last week's debate marked the unceremonious junking of a crucial centuries-old convention of our constitution: ministerial responsibility.

On 6 January 1986, the Solicitor-General wrote a letter to the then Defence Secretary, Michael Heseltine, drawing his attention to 'material inaccuracies' in a letter from the latter to the Westland company. It is clear, as the All-Party Select Committee on Defence found, that the PM instigated the letter and did so with a view to its being published. It was ultimately leaked, by the Department of Trade and Industry. It has been admitted under pressure by the PM that No. 10 knew of the leak and, as Sir Robert Armstrong the Cabinet Secretary said, 'accepted' it.

The point missed is that this is a fundamental admission with direct consequences for the PM. To protect her, the government continuously stressed that the leak was by the Department of Trade and Industry, not No. 10 and that No. 10 never 'approved' the leak. But this assertion, in any event highly questionable, is a diversion. The DTI was simply the means of distribution for the leak. It was a subordinate ministry to the PM's office. That is why it sought the sanction of No. 10. The duty of the PM's officials, in these circumstances, was not simply to be indifferent to the leak, still less to 'accept' it, but actively to oppose it, to say no.

If this were the duty of the PM's office, then it is quite impossible to see how the PM herself is not liable for the acts of her officials in accordance with the doctrine of ministerial responsibility. The doctrine lacks firm definition. But where a minister instructs officials to secure an objective and a senior official does so, but in a way that is improper, it is difficult to see how the doctrine does not apply.

The doctrine is essential because it ensures that civil servants are protected from being made liable for carrying out their orders; and to ensure that the ministers are accountable to Parliament for the acts of their departments. The consequence, of course, of a minister not being responsible is that the civil servant is.

Yet, perhaps the most extraordinary element in the whole Westland affair is the absence of punishment or disciplinary proceedings against anyone, civil servants or ministers. Leon Brittan resigned, not because he or his officials had behaved improperly in leaking the Solicitor-General's letter, but because he had 'lost the confidence of his colleagues'.

Is it paranoid to see this as part of a pattern? Westland, the *Belgrano*, the attacks on the BBC, the fiddles on the unemployment register, the increasing reluctance on the part of ministers to answer questions (frequently mentioned by older parliamentarians), the politicisation of the civil service. What really distinguishes the modern Tories from the old, or Thatcher from Heath, is that they want, above all, to win. It is an obsession. For her and for those like her, scruples simply clutter up the path to victory.

Interview in *Marxism Today*
July 1990

Part of the left-wing magazine Marxism Today's *attempt to make theoretical politics accessible (and even interesting) was their use of questionnaire-style interviews with politicians. Here, Blair gives his answers, which reveal him to be a family man who changes nappies, anchored in his north-east constituency, fond of holidays in the west of Scotland. He mentions his main influences as being his Oxford contemporary and mentor Peter Thomson, and is unafraid to mention his schooling at the public school Fettes. His favourite advert — for Hamlet cigars — would be banned ten years later by his government along with all other tobacco advertising.*

What newspapers/magazines do you take?
Daily Mirror, the *Financial Times,* the *Guardian,* the *Independent, Marxism Today* and *The Economist.*

What foreign languages do you speak?
French.

When do you listen to music?
In the car.

When was the last time you prayed?
Yesterday.

What was your first thought this morning?
Kathryn's nappy needs changing.

What is the most common colour in your wardrobe?
Dark blue.

What is your favourite meeting place?
The Fox and Hounds, Trimdon village, for its atmosphere.

What is your favourite piece of architecture
Durham Cathedral and Holly Street Estate, Hackney, London.

Who do you reveal your secrets to?
Depends on the secret, but usually to Cherie.

What makes you feel secure?
Love.

What do you blame your parents for?
Thinking that sending me to public school would be a good career move!

When did you last visit your parents?
Last month.

How do you envy your children's lifestyle?
Getting up early in the morning and apparently enjoying it.

You're driving through a hot, desolate expanse. What's playing on the stereo?
Tom Petty; *Runnin' Down A Dream.*

What is your city of the 90s?
Any capital of Eastern Europe, I hope.

Where do you wish you were living?
County Durham.

Where is your favourite holiday destination?
The west coast of Scotland.

How has your diet changed in the past 10 years?
Less fat, more balance.

What physical exercise do you do?
Tennis and walking.

Tony Blair in his own words

Under what circumstances would you use private medicine?

If my kids were ever at risk and it was the only way I could help them.

At what age do you want to stop working?

When I die.

Do you really need your car?

No.

Do you own shares?

No.

What is your favourite advertisement?

Hamlet cigars.

What are you doing for the environment?

The usual things, lead-free car, etc. But more importantly, making it connect with my politics.

What part of your life would you take with you into another life?

Childhood.

Who is your hero?

I don't have a hero, but the person who most influenced me was Peter Thomson, the principal of St Mark's College, Adelaide.

What do you no longer believe in?

Certainty.

What would you die for?

That's not something you can answer until the choice is real.

What campaign do you most support?

Campaigns for the Third World.

What do you now own that you had never dreamed of owning?

A British car with a Japanese engine.

What is the greatest amount of money you've spent on an item of clothing?

Two hundred pounds on a suit.

What hi-tech device scares you?

Any.

How much time do you spend each day on the phone?

Too much.

What were doing when Mandela was freed?

Watching it on TV.

In one word, how has the Rushdie affair left you thinking?

Depressed.

Complete this sentence: if I was dictator for a day...

I'd make sure my political monument was more than a gesture.

How do you personally hope to change by the end of the millennium?

To have a sense of achievement.

'Forging a new agenda'

Marxism Today, October 1991

In this long think-piece for Marxism Today, *Blair set out a coherent political position in the face of the recent collapse of the Soviet Union and the right's political ascendancy. Like many on the left, Blair saw the disappearance of Communism as an actual system as the opportunity to restate the ethical socialist position. Blair's conviction that 'citizenship without community, and without the willingness to act as a society, is empty rhetoric' is both a nod backwards to Christian Socialism and R. H. Tawney, and a taste of the predominant themes of new Labour to come.*

The right wing in the West would love to see the collapse of Communism in the East crush all forms of socialism beneath it. It is certainly true that all fixed points on the landscape have changed. There are no safe havens of political doctrine. Everything and anything can be thought or rethought. We start again. Yet there is an irony. Even as events in the East unfold, the potential for advance by socialist and social democratic parties has not been greater for many decades. The 1980s saw a frontal attack on the public sector by governments claiming to act on behalf of the individual. In the 1990s the agenda for 'public action' is back. It is the same whether in Europe or the USA.

But, here is the rub. The limitations of individualism are plain. But there is no appetite to return to old-fashioned collectivism either, whether of the full-blooded sort now dying in Eastern Europe or the milder corporatism of the 1960s practised in the West. The error of conservative ideology is to believe all problems can be solved by the market without the need for public action; the challenge for socialists is to re-establish the agenda for public action without the old failings of collectivism.

To do this, we must take the fundamental principle of socialism – the need of society to act together to achieve what the individual cannot do alone – but apply it entirely afresh to the world today. Modern socialism has much to learn from twentieth-century history, but it still has much to teach. We should accept the lessons of our history and build on them, not be intimidated or shackled by them. We must fashion a modern view of society or public action, which recognises the vested interest of both market and state and articulates a new over-arching concept of the public interest standing up for the individual against those vested interests. At the core of this modern view of society lies a new settlement between the individual and society which determines both their rights and obligations; so that public action is effective in achieving its objectives for the individual, and individuals can be protected against the possibility of abuse by the very action supposed to assist them.

This is a much stronger notion than citizenship, whether of the sort advocated by John Major or Paddy Ashdown. The more the word 'citizen' is used, the less satisfying it becomes – unless the idea of citizenship is allied to economic and social rights, as well as rights as consumers of public and private services, and unless it implies obligations as well as rights. In other words citizenship must be distinguished from individualism by an insistence that a citizen is part of a wider community. Citizenship without community, and without the willingness to act as a society, is empty rhetoric.

The consequences of a new approach – neither old-style collectivism nor new-style individualism – is to alter the terms of the policy debate. It ceases to be dominated by a battle between state and market. Instead, it is about how we make both state and market subject to the public interest, creating a modern, active society with a modern notion of active government to go with it.

The historical problem of socialism is not hard to define, though it is essential to define it correctly. Socialism, as its name implies, was founded on a belief: that individuals cannot be separated from the society of which they are a part. As a political force, it advocates the use of society to protect and advance the individual. It therefore requires the notion of a clearly identified community, embodying the public interest or public good, standing up on behalf of individuals, against the vested interests that hold them back. Note that socialism in origin was based around the individual, not the other way round.

In the latter part of the nineteenth century, and the early part of this century, it was clear what those vested interests were. They were those of wealth and capital. Labourers produced the wealth but had it taken from them by the capitalist. So the objective was to wrest control of wealth and capital on behalf of the broad mass of people excluded from the fruits of their labours. The instrument of control was the state. The policy was ownership of the means of production, distribution and exchange. Owned by all, they would be used for all.

The public interest became synonymous with public ownership. In addition, Marxism, in offering a scientific explanation of why such development was inevitable, gave intellectual coherence to the popular movement. Critically, in its Leninist form in particular, it also started to place society above the individual, as an abstract ideal to which the individual should conform.

Of course it would be absurd to say the British Labour Party was ever Marxist or that it failed to take individual liberty seriously – as Tawney illustrated so clearly. But firstly, socialism, in its democratic form, was inevitably tainted with by its caricature in undemocratic form – the Soviet Union.

Secondly, democratic socialists equated the public interest with public ownership. So that, though their motivation and values were, and remain correct, and though they correctly analysed the shortcomings of the early capitalist system, they had no developed analysis of the limitations of public ownership through the state as a means of helping the individual. To be sure, they recognised the capacity of the state to do wrong. Even elements of the Trotskyist left condemned the Soviet Union as state capitalism. But early socialists always assumed these problems were remediable within a fixed political framework. They never perceived either that the problems were fundamental and required a fundamental reappraisal of the role of the state; or that capitalism itself had drastically altered with the advent of a modern sophisticated market. Socialists spent the next 50 or 60 years trying to escape from the consequences of these developments.

The state, of course, succeeded at first. It provided basic essentials – housing, education, health, social security, public services. But two things happened. First, the state became large and powerful, a vested interest in itself, every bit as capable of oppressing individuals as wealth and capital. The majority of people became taxpayers funding the activities of the state and therefore anxious as to how their money was used. Secondly, as economies developed and individual wealth grew and was spread more widely, people came to regard themselves as consumers as well as producers. They wanted choice. They needed the market to exercise choice. The institutions of the collective – whether government, state industry or trade unions – became unpopular. Those who advocated less government and 'free' markets took the initiative. Hence Thatcherism. Socialists, in attempting to defend the state against this attack, appeared, however unfairly, to be merely defenders of the status quo against new radicals from the right.

But it is critical to note: Thatcherism enjoyed far greater popularity as an attack on the vested interests of the collective than it ever did as a positive political philosophy in its own right. The essential values of the country, actually socialist values, remain. They believe in the right to own property and create wealth, but also in social justice, the removal of poverty and the reduction of inequality. They accept the need for a market economy, but also for market intervention in the interests of the community.

They want public services to be accessible and of high quality, but they do not want them privatised or run for profit. They want trade unions to be accountable but not neutered.

There is no desire to substitute the market for all collective provision, though the boundaries between the two may alter significantly. But both should be subject to the governing principle of the public interest. Whether that public interest is advanced through state or market, public or private sector, is still of vital importance. For example, it is clearly right for there to be a market in consumer goods; and for the Health Service to be publicly owned. But no power should exist without accountability and no vested interest, whether of wealth or state, should interfere with, or transgress, the fundamental rights and freedoms of the individual.

Let us be clear: we do not say that concentrations of wealth and capital have ceased to have the potential to exploit. On the contrary, plainly, private wealth and capital can and do have the potential to exploit the individual. Failure to recognise this properly is surely the fundamental error of the Liberal Democrats and the abiding inadequacy of the Tories. The vested interests of the market have not disappeared. It is merely that our notion of society must recognise the similar potential in collective institutions and transcend traditional views of the state. The real task, then, is to give effect to this modern idea of society embodying the public interest – as opposed to the vested interests of the public or private sector. In turn, this requires a new political settlement between individual and society, a bargain between the two which determines rights and obligations on both sides.

Of course this means difficult choices. Taxation restricts the individuals' ability to spend their own money, but it is self-evidently necessary to fund public services, defence, social security and so on. The right of the individual to free speech can conflict with the needs of the community for racial harmony.

No amount of careful thought about the nature of this bargain between the individual and society can exclude the role of subjective judgement when the rights of the one clash with the requirements of the other. But the debate is now centred on the right issue. The framework within which the choices are made can be properly defined. By modernising our view of society, by acknowledging the need for society as integral to individual freedom, yet defining its role as triumphing over vested interests, a new policy agenda can be forged.

This is not the place to do more than sketch out the headings of such an agenda. But they will be fundamentally different from the issues that dominated debate in the past.

A modern society requires a modern constitution. Democracy requires content as well as form; openness and plurality as well as merely the right to vote. Action by the community does not mean action by central government. At present our whole political system is a conspiracy against reason: outdated, unfair, and with the minimum of checks and balances. There is a clear case for a written constitution, including the guarantee of certain inalienable civil liberties. Decision-making should be devolved as far as is practical from the centre and as close to the impact of the decision as is sensible. There should be fundamental reform of the system of government to make it representative and accountable, with the process of government open to proper scrutiny and information freely available. Constitutional reform can no longer be treated as peripheral. If it is right that we need a modern view of society and its relationship with the individual, then the constitutional question becomes central.

In economic policy, the battle over theoretical forms of economic organisation is dead, or at least relegated to means, not ends. We need to develop instead a new economics of the public interest, which recognises that a thriving competitive market is essential for individual choice; not a threat to ordinary people, but without seeing it as an ideology in itself, which we must obey, even if it conflicts with the objectives we, as a community, have identified as part of the public interest. It acknowledges the market's worth and its limitations.

The public interest demands action by government to ensure a fully competitive market to prevent monopoly to encourage choice. It also demands that companies operating within the market do so with social responsibility both to the customer and the wider community. For example, a public interest view of the market and the environment would go much further than saying companies should not pollute, or should pay for the pollution they cause. The government should be prepared to intervene actively in order to promote environmentally beneficial products and methods of working. But in return the company and the consumer would have to accept some restrictions in freedom and cost.

A public interest view of the market also recognises its obvious limitations. For example, whether a major infrastructure project like the Channel Tunnel is worth doing is a judgement we should make as a society. If it is, then we should act to ensure it happens. Whether this is achieved by private or public sector, or by a mixture of the two, can be determined pragmatically on the basis of which satisfies the public interest. But to leave the judgement about whether it is done at all to the 'market' is fatuous.

With the new framework of public interest, we can make sense of the need both for the existence of the market, and also for co-operation in the overall management of the economy. Debate about the 'social market' in the hands of Major or Ashdown becomes a mix of Tory or even Thatcherite economics with Labour welfare policy, as if the 'social' and 'market' operated in the same spheres. The true meaning is surely that the market's importance is recognised but is itself still subject to the needs of society. To say, as the Tories do, that the government has no role in industrial policy is nonsensical. The government should play a full and active part assisting industry to grow and modernise. The difference is that instead of government's relationship with industry being part of an ideological fight for territory between public and private sector, it becomes a partnership for the achievement of certain specific objectives in the public interest. The real debate should be about the nature of these objectives and the manner of securing them. This is not to say that difficult decisions do not arise as to when interference in the market is justified or not, but we should not be forced to choose between two outdated views, which hold the market to be either good or evil.

Similarly, with other policy areas the agenda becomes changed. For example, it would be absurd to say that the individual no longer needs protection at the workplace from potential abuse by vested interests. But the task of social or collective action today is not to abolish capital as part of some war for supremacy between labour and management, but rather to enhance the power of the individual employees, not just to protect their position from abuse, but also to grant them the capability to use or exploit capital.

This is the real case for investment in training, not just for economic success, but to allow each individual the opportunity to develop his or her talents to the full and thus have much greater power over their future. With it would go the right to fair treatment for employees – the message of the Social Charter – and rights to information, consultation and the right to participate in the decisions affecting them. The public interest view of modern industrial relations starts with people – their vast, untapped potential and the need to liberate it. If the 60s was about technology replacing people, then the 90s should surely be about the application of ever more sophisticated technology by ever better educated workers.

The debate about public services becomes not about how we provide the basic minimum, but about how society guarantees to each citizen, as of right, equal access to the best, not basic, services; about services based on quality and choice; about how public services are paid for and how they are made accountable.

The crusade against poverty is not simply one of compassion for the poor, or of Tory notions of charity or even of some loose notion of a safety net for the most disadvantaged. It becomes the infinitely more powerful idea of a society having a duty to prevent the individual being held back by poverty, of each individual having the right to decent living standards as the price society must pay for the obligation of citizenship to be fulfilled. The existence of an underclass of deprived and poor, with vast disparities of wealth existing between rich and poor, is seen not just as morally wrong but as an obstacle to the creation of the social cohesion necessary to function effectively.

There is one final point of importance. A new settlement between individual and society must recognise, more than ever before, that it is a settlement not just within our own nation, but with Europe and the broader world. Labour's internationalism was, in origin, one of its greatest attractions. It is now urgently required in modern form.

Of course this goes much wider than Europe, but in Europe at least we should be leading events not following them from a distance, stopping every so often to ask ourselves whether we want to be on the road at all. That we fail to do so now is in part a reflection of our failure to forge a new national identity. We know the days of the Empire are over but we can't relinquish the memory sufficiently to grasp the new opportunity.

If Britain was confident in itself, in its modern identity as a European nation, it would be supporting the movement towards a single currency and closer European integration, but focusing the debate on where it should be – on the measures that must accompany monetary union to make it work, and updating radically the institutions of the European Community to insist that, as power increases, so must its democratic accountability. Instead, under the present government, we languish at the back, hesitating to join in and terrified to leave.

The notion of a modern view of socialism as the driving force behind the freedom of the individual is in truth the important governing philosophy of today's Labour Party. It will benefit us greatly both internally and with the public if we spell it out with confidence and show how it means not just a different set of policies, but a different view of Britain as a nation.

'Pride without prejudice'

Fabian Review, May 1992

Labour's election defeat in April 1992, the fourth in a row, was a major shock to the party. John Major's narrow victory meant that Labour had not won an election since 1974. It led to the replacement of Neil Kinnock with John Smith as leader, and a soul-searching debate about why Labour lost and how it might win. In 1992, there were serious commentators who argued that the Labour Party could never win an election again without a pact with other parties.

Inside the Party, some argued that what was needed was 'one more heave' to dislodge the Tories; others wanted far-reaching reforms of both Party and policy, for fear of losing a fifth time. Blair's article in Fabian Review *in May 1992 was written just days after the election defeat, and during Labour's leadership contest between John Smith and Bryan Gould, when the direction of the party was being decided. Blair's rallying cry to 'continue and intensify the process of change' placed him firmly in the modernisers' camp. Here, he even uses the expression 'New Labour' for the first time.*

There was much of which Labour could be proud on 10 April. Over forty seats have been taken from the Tories. In many more we are a mere handful of votes behind. There has been a tremendous infusion of new blood and talent into the Parliamentary Labour Party. There is now no way the new Tory government can carry on oblivious to public opinion or reason. Politics has changed. This sense of achievement must be weighed against the bitter disappointment of defeat.

This is important because otherwise defeat turns to despair and becomes defeatism. That would be wrong. The opportunity is with us to reflect and then rebuild. This should continue far beyond the leadership election. The identity and attributes of the new leader are, of course, vital. But more so are the nature and character of the Party he leads.

We became contenders for government at the election because of the changes made under Neil Kinnock. There can be no serious doubt about that. They made the Labour Party electable. Labour's resulting rise in public standing caused the dissatisfaction in the Tory Party that led to the downfall of Mrs Thatcher. The poll tax had to be abandoned. Even now, the appointment of Michael Heseltine to the DTI and the clear attempts to change at least the image at other departments are indications that the Tories are under pressure. But in the end, as the election results showed, the public was insufficiently sure of the new Labour Party to put it into government.

The lesson in my view is clear: neither to stand still and simply change leader; nor, certainly, to go lurching back to the early 1980s; but to continue and intensify the process of change. This must happen at the level of both ideas and organisation. This is more profound than policy. Of course, policies are crucial and those for the next election will be formed in quite a different context from the last. But the struggle to establish a clear identity for the radical left of centre politics in the latter part of the twentieth century goes much deeper than individual policy issues.

The choices facing the British Labour Party are not unique. All social democratic or democratic socialist parties have been confronted by them in not dissimilar ways. Where, as with the socialists in France or the Labor Party in Australia, we gained power in the early 80s we have, by and large, kept it, though not without huge internal tensions. Where we failed to win, our spell in opposition has been long and painful, as with the SPD in Germany, the Democrats in the USA or the British Labour Party. There are great movements of history at work here and the beginning of understanding lies in recognising this simple truth.

The essential task is to retain the values and principles underlying social democracy or democratic socialism but apply them entirely afresh to the modern world. This modern world has a number of altered characteristics: the collapse of Communism and the acceptance of a market economy; the growth of the public sector, funded by taxpayers, who are now in the majority and who want value for money; a global economy where international cooperation is replacing the possibility of any country 'going it alone'; huge changes in industrial production and technology; a more educated and prosperous electorate that wants a more varied and individual set of life choices.

At the same time the world still has vast interests in the private sector that often go unchallenged; the need for good public services is probably more important than ever; and there exists still cruel poverty for many millions amidst great wealth. Moreover, many of the changes – for example, a more international perspective and the urgent need for a better trained workforce to cope with new technology – are changes which Labour values are better equipped to tackle than Tory ones. Labour's values are therefore not in any sense historically redundant. That is both our hope and our opportunity.

Labour must, once again, be the Party that stands up for the individual against the vested interests that hold him or her back, wherever they are, using the power of the community to achieve what people are unable to achieve on their own. This is its historic mission, as necessary today as it was 100 years ago. But the means of fulfilling it will be very different. There should be no preconceptions whatever, no areas of intellectual abstinence, and we should go out of our way to build common cause with other parties around the world in searching out the way forward.

We should also ensure our Party organisation is reformed fundamentally to mirror these changes in approach. By the time of the next election, Labour must be ready, in ideas and organisation, to govern. If we fail it will be our own responsibility.

'Why crime is a socialist issue'

New Statesman, 29 January 1993

With his appointment as shadow home secretary in 1992, Blair had the opportunity to do three things: to establish his credentials as a top flight politician with his party and the public; to match his 'rights and responsibilities' rhetoric with practical policy development; and to position the Labour Party as modern, in touch and capable of tackling the Conservative government on its own traditional issues.

The slogan Blair adopted to demonstrate his approach – 'tough on crime, tough on the causes of crime' – is more than a mere sound bite. It reveals Blair's political strategy: to appeal to the traditional, liberal left with the will to deal with the perceived causes of crime – unemployment, poor education, family breakdown, drugs – and simultaneously to appeal to the middle England desire, and that of working people on housing estates, for harsher sentences and more police. In two years as shadow home secretary, Blair destroyed the Tories' credibility as guardians of law and order, as his friend and rival, Gordon Brown, destroyed their credibility as custodians of the public purse.

This short period, more than any other, enabled Blair to be widely seen as the obvious candidate for leader of the party when the opportunity tragically and unexpectedly arose in May 1994.

The Tories have given up on crime. Not just their policies but their philosophy has failed. For crime is quintessentially a problem that the individual cannot tackle alone. Crime demands that communities work as communities to fight it. Labour's commitment is to match popular concern with a constructive and broad-based programme of action.

Stop any random group of people and ask them what are the key issues, not so much for the country, but for them as individuals, and the chances are that crime will be at the top, or almost at the top. Fifteen million offences were committed last year. Most house-holders or car owners have been victims at some time in their lives. In 1993, there are expected to be close to one million assaults, muggings, rapes and murders.

But it is not just the daily lurid headlines that are a cause for concern; it is the constant round of abuse, vandalism and petty disorder. Of the 14,000 fire service call-outs in Tyne and Wear during the first five months of last year, more than 8,000 were either arson or hoaxes. The perpetrators are often young teenagers. Frequently cars are stolen and set alight – for no reason, with no financial gain.

Many of our old people live in a state of fear and do not dare go out at night. When two sixteen-year-olds were mugged in a Glasgow shopping centre one Saturday morning, the police told their parents they shouldn't really have been in the centre unaccompanied. They weren't blaming the parents, just stating a fact of contemporary life. A survey on a north London housing estate found that more than half the residents of any age would not use public transport at night for fear of being attacked.

Crime profoundly affects the quality of our lives. It is ultimately linked with the strength and cohesion of the community. It is a cliché, but true nonetheless, that it is people who live on inner-city estates or use public transport – many of them Labour voters – who suffer most. Many of these people feel disenfranchised after fouteen years of Tory neglect of inner-city crime. It therefore intensely interests our core voters, who look to Labour to reflect their anxiety and anger, not to respond with patronising sympathy or indifference.

However, it is an issue that stretches way beyond our traditional boundaries to the electorate we need to win. Rural England and

Tory suburbs are now scarred by almost routine violence, affrays, assaults on the police on Friday and Saturday nights, which local people feel powerless to prevent.

Finally, it is an issue on which the Tories have patently and comprehensively failed. Crime has risen by 50 per cent in the past three years. Even the Tory press has begun to turn on its government.

There is a growing and open determination both inside and outside the Parliamentary Labour Party to make crime a genuine 'people's' issue, the subject of a national campaign for better and safer communities. To do that, we are setting out the principles of our approach clearly, so that old perceptions and misrepresentations are dispelled.

First, we are moving the debate beyond the choice between personal and social responsibility, the notion that there are only two sides to the 'law and order' debate – those who want to punish the criminal and those who point to the poor social conditions in which crime breeds. The obvious common sense of the matter – which would be recognised instantly by any member of the public – is that the choice is false and misleading.

People have a right to go about their business without being attacked or abused or having their property stolen. They have a right, and society has a duty, to bring those who commit these crimes to justice, and to a punishment that properly reflects the seriousness of the crime. To act otherwise would be to betray the interests of those we serve.

Equally, the purpose of any system of justice should not just be to punish and deter, but also to rehabilitate, for the good of society as well as the criminal. Which is why there are practical reasons, as well as those connected with civil liberties, for reforming our monstrous prison regime.

Above all, any sensible society acting in its own interests as well as those of its citizens will understand and recognise that poor education and housing, inadequate or cruel family backgrounds, low employment prospects and drug abuse will affect the likelihood of young people turning to crime. If they are placed outside mainstream culture, offered no hope or opportunity, shown no respect by others and are unable to develop respect for themselves, there is a greater chance of their going wrong. This cannot be challenged other than through active community intervention. To see this requires not a PhD in sociology, but a small experience of life. Yet the Tories are destroying hope for young people, slashing training programmes, closing youth clubs. They are inert in the face of rising youth unemployment.

We should be tough on crime and on tough on the underlying causes of crimes. We should be prepared and eager to give people opportunity. But we are then entitled to ask that they take advantage of it, to grant rights and demand responsibilities. The public – contrary to conventional wisdom – does not ignore the social context of crime. But, rightly, they only listen to people who show understanding of their own plight as potential victims.

Second, we should support clearly and help the actual victims of crime. At present they are poorly treated and, on occasions, end up feeling they have become victims twice over. In particular, charges can be dropped or reduced without any input from the victim at all. This should not happen until the victim has been consulted. The police and the Crown Prosecution Service should be obliged to keep the victim fully involved at every point of the case.

Third, we should champion the cause of putting policing back in local communities. This does not just mean more policemen and women on the beat – though we should not underestimate the importance of this to ordinary people; but it means involving local people in the policing of their local communities, with the police acting in partnership with them, not as remote unaccountable experts. There is no reason why policing priorities should be the exclusive preserve of the police. The worries of local people about those priorities – for example, the drift towards ignoring certain types of offence – should be addressed.

There should be a comprehensive crime prevention strategy, led nationally but implemented locally, that is concerned not just with personal security, but identifies the nature and type of crime locally – that searches out and eliminates drug peddling, the lawlessness of gangs of youths and networks of criminal activity, and establishes a real basis of trust between police and people. This needs more local input, not less. It would be disastrous if, as rumoured, the government abolishes police authorities and replaces them with boards of appointees.

Fourth, we should bring the courts and criminal justice system up to date, getting rid of antiquated procedures and ensuring that the possibility of miscarriages of justice, all too frequent in the past, is significantly diminished.

Finally, we should not be hesitant about applauding the government if it does things that are right. The Sheehy inquiry into police terms and conditions of employment may or may not come out with sensible reforms. But if it does, it would be absurd of Labour to defend police vested interests. Rather, we should state positively that reform is necessary, support reforms that are sensible, judge whether they improve standards of service and assist in bringing police closer to the community. But we should resist what will undoubtedly be the Tory desire – to use the reforms as part of an exercise to shift blame for rising crime from government to the police.

We face the future with only two options. We could end up like parts of the US, where there are more murders in a year in New York and Chicago combined than in Northern Ireland since 1969; where those who can afford it buy ever more expensive security systems and those who can't suffer increasing despair. Or we can start anew.

Tony Blair in his own words

Labour is the only party seriously confronting all the issues connected to with crime. Our approach is rooted in our belief that society needs to act to advance the interests of individuals. For crime, ultimately, is a problem that arises from our disintegration as a community, with standards of conduct necessary to sustain a community. It can only be resolved by acting as a community, based on a new bargain between individual and society. Rights and responsibilities must be set out for each in a way relevant for a modern world. The longer we leave it, the harder the task will become.

'Why modernisation matters'

Renewal, October 1993

Renewal *is a small-circulation journal of Labour policies and ideas launched in early 1993, following Labour's election defeat the previous April. It was created by leading members of the Labour Co-ordinating Committee (LCC), a modernising pressure group inside the Labour Party, to which both Tony and Cherie Blair belonged since the early 1980s.* Renewal *included Tony Blair, Robin Cook, Clare Short, Patricia Hewitt, Margaret Hodge, Fiona MacTaggart, and Tony Wright on its editorial board.*

This article appeared in October 1993 when Blair was Labour's shadow home secretary, and John Smith was leader of the Labour Party. Whilst Blair's contribution contains no overt criticism of Smith's leadership, it appeared at a time of growing disquiet amongst Labour modernisers at the slow pace of Party reform and policy renewal, characterised by one moderniser's warning that Labour was 'sleepwalking into oblivion'.

It is almost as if we have been conducting an election campaign for three years – ever since Mrs Thatcher departed. The election itself came and went without any appreciable difference in the pace and frenzy of the battle. The spectators hover somewhere between bewilderment and boredom. Meanwhile, the political soul aches for something more satisfying than the daily round of press release and counter press release about who is winning the war.

Now is the time to stand back and think and reflect. In part, the harshness of the struggle derives from an understandable feeling of revulsion and frustration about a government that has tipped itself and the country into disarray. But, more profoundly, it belies a sense that politics has a vacuum at its centre, that its future is unclear. The country feels an increasing and acute loss of purpose, of direction. The old certainties have gone, but new ones have not yet appeared. There is an urgency about the fight and, underneath the clamour, there is a search for the ideological initiative.

The thesis set out here is that politics this century have alternated between the ideologies of fairly crude individualism and collectivism and that what is required today is to define a new relationship between citizen and community for the modern world; and that the task for the Labour Party and the left-of-centre is to make itself a credible expression of that relationship.

I don't link the left to this task just because I am a member of the Labour Party. The phase of politics we are in now – which recognises the limitations of crude individualism – is one naturally suited to the left. The country now wants and needs a confident, revitalised left-of-centre. Perhaps the most frustrating part of being in opposition is the instinctive belief that the left could, if only it wanted to, shape the politics of the next generation. But that can only be achieved if the failures of the past are properly faced and a clear modern identity is established in which people can believe. This article will therefore deal with both aspects of this task: the new principles by which our society should be governed; and how the Labour Party can embody them.

The first fifty years of this century saw huge and necessary social change. It began with no welfare state, no universal suffrage, trade unions which were barely able to function legally and a class structure in which the upper, middle and lower ranks were sharply delineated. The majority were without their own homes, without suitable or well-paid employment and had little or no education. They saw their only hope in collective action: what they could not achieve alone they could do together. The economic forces of mass production were pushing them closer together anyway.

But without public intervention or co-operative action, change could not come. So trade unions sprang up and soon trade unionists wanted their own political representation to protect and advance their interests. The state grew as the instrument of intervention to bring increased opportunity, to guarantee the basic amenities of life and, through better housing, employment, health and education, to allow people to prosper. The state became powerful, as indeed it was intended to be. It employed a lot of people. It raised taxes to carry on its work of intervention. In time living standards increased and the fruits of growth were much more widely shared.

There is a myth that at some point, the nature of the people themselves then changed: they *were* collectively minded and *became* selfish. In fact, if you speak even to miners in County Durham, never mind people in the south of England, about voting Labour in 1945, they weren't voting for everyone else or for some abstract notion of the public good, they were voting for a collectivist government because that government was going to do good by them.

People didn't change. Society changed. Alongside the vested interests of capital and wealth sat the vested interests of the state and the public sector, not always faithfully delivering what they were supposed to. What's more, an increasingly prosperous electorate was paying more taxes to fund the state. They became consumers anxious to participate in the luxuries of life which the better-offs had always taken for granted. A conflict was born between the desire of the individual to consume and the necessity for us all to invest. Moreover, the old industrial base of the economy was breaking up and, with it, so were notions of 'class', based on a static view of the process of production.

In retrospect, it is easier to see that these changes were actually taking root in the 1950s, but their political focus was blurred. By the

1970s, that focus had become sharper. There was an antagonism towards the institutions of the collective, a perception, rightly or wrongly, that rather than making people free they were holding people back. Thatcherism caught this mood. It pitted individual enterprise against collective action, and set about dismantling collective power in the name of individual freedom.

Today, however, we are now in a new phase of development. The supposed changes of the Thatcherite revolution have turned out to be less enduring and more questionable than its supporters wished. In particular, the fragility of our economic position has become painfully transparent. There is no desire in the country to go back; but no wish to stand still either. People do not regret that collectivism in its old form was challenged, but they do not have much faith in the crude individualism that replaced it.

It is not that people now want to see the end of a market economy, any more than, even during the heyday of Thatcherism, they wanted an end to the welfare state. But they recognise that the problems we face cannot be solved by the market alone. Economically, we are not competitive because we lack sufficient capacity and skilled labour. We have failed to invest in building and modernising our industry over a long period of time and are poorer as a result. Our public services are bad and in urgent need of improvement. At work, many people remain badly treated and underpaid, in need of proper union representation. Socially, we are severely divided, with the growth of an underclass that may be a minority but is frighteningly large. The notion that the less the government does, the better for the country, just seems outdated. There is an inchoate but perceptible belief that we have lost our way – that we need, but have not got, a more clearly shared sense of community.

It is worth inserting here that this dilemma, about the fracturing of social cohesion in a more individually assertive culture, is fairly precisely replicated around the world. The Democrats won in the USA only because they seemed, in opposition, to overcome it, though whether they will in government remains an open question. In France, Spain, Italy and Germany, a very similar debate is now taking place on the left, albeit in different ways.

The need to construct new principles to govern the relationship between individual and society is underlined by the distortion of policy debate by this concentration on an outdated ideological battle about public versus private sector. It leads to wholly meaningless political rows that obstruct real issues. By not accepting that the ideological battle between state and market for total supremacy of one over the other is actually over, this battle still defines the positions of left and right. So as reality and public opinion drive each to make common sense concessions to the other on the territory fought over, many commentators and even some politicians end up saying that 'the parties are both the same' and nothing substantial separates them because the line of separation is drawn by reference to past ideology.

What then should this new relationship consist of? First, it involves a new concept of citizenship in which rights and responsibilities go together and where we cease to posit an entirely false choice between social and personal responsibility. As is so clear the more you examine the rise in crime and social disorder in Britain, the problem has been that the left has tended to undervalue individual responsibility and the right has ignored the influence of social conditions. Indeed, to the right, talk of the link between social conditions and crime is to excuse crime. So the obvious common sense – namely that children brought up with no chance of a job, with poor education, with family breakdown, and in bad housing, are more likely to drift into crime than those that aren't – is denied.

A modern notion of citizenship gives rights but demands obligations, shows respect but wants it back, grants opportunities but insists on responsibility. So the purpose of economic and social policy should be to extend opportunity, remove the underlying causes of social alienation, but it should also take tough measures to ensure that the chances that are given are taken up.

It means too, that constitutional reform becomes integral not peripheral. The fundamental rights of the citizen should be guaranteed with the ability to challenge the state or government. Local government – heading for dereliction – should be reborn so that decisions are taken closer to where people live. The process and machinery of government should be opened up and made accountable.

Second, this new relationship between society and individual needs new principles of public intervention and action. Economically it requires the creation of a genuine partnership between public and private sector, the purpose of which is to intervene to enhance individual economic opportunity, and rebuild the economic base. That is the key to both individual prosperity and economic success.

In public services, the emphasis should be not on *who* provides, but on *what* is provided and the efficiency and standard of service. We should open up the issue of how public services are funded, how we raise money and how we spend it; and how we link tax and spending more clearly to the objectives the public want. In fighting poverty, the aim is not to maintain dependency on the state, but to create the conditions for people to escape it.

We need new instruments of public intervention. In this, the voluntary sector has a central role to play. The left has for too long misunderstood its role as if it were simply nineteenth-century philanthropic charity, while the right uses it as a convenient way to relieve government of its own responsibilities. In fact, the voluntary sector can often provide services more effectively and more creatively than either public or private sector.

Above I mentioned local government in the context of enhancing democracy, but it is utterly central also to a regeneration of the principles of government intervention. The destruction of local government is one of the most foolish, almost wicked, dogmas of the Thatcher years. The stupidity of one or two councils has been used as a cover for the wholesale dismantling of a large part of our machinery of government. Yet properly harnessed to clear public policy objectives, we should be seeking to do more, not less at a local level.

That is particularly so as power shifts to Europe, where again there is need for fundamental change. I have no doubt at all that Britain's future lies in Europe. All the more reason for those of us that are pro-European to tackle the problem of democratic accountability in Europe that will, if unresolved, kill the dream of greater European integration.

So we come to the second part of the argument: the Labour Party as the credible expression of this new relationship between society and individual. It is here that the economic and social change in the country meets the need for political change in Labour. As change in the former has happened, support for the latter has declined, from a peak of over 50 per cent in 1951 to just under 27 per cent in 1983.

Yet it is Labour, because of its historical commitment to social action, that is best placed to take up the challenge the country now faces. It is from this belief and the idea of using the power of community or social action to advance individual liberty that all notions of democratic socialism or social democracy stem. Social justice, compassion, equality, the provision of opportunity – these motivating values all arise from one single belief about human beings and the way they live. The last election should have been won and was lost by seven and a half points, a larger margin of defeat than in 1979. That is why, despite the government's problems and its lurch into almost unprecedented political disasters since the election, we cannot ever minimise the need to build our support.

The great danger is here is not actually complacency as such, it is delusion. Most political parties have an almost infinite capacity for self-delusion because self-criticism is painful and easily confused with uncertainty about basic beliefs. The Tory right is a case in point as their increasingly vociferous and extreme youth section indicates. When they lose an election, the Tories will split thunderously.

There are two delusions Labour must guard against. Curiously, one is the delusion of defeatism. This theory holds that by some hidden and mysterious process it has been decreed that whereas the Tories can win elections, Labour can't. Accordingly, it should acknowledge this and concentrate its efforts on either making alliances with other parties or – worse – abandoning hope of winning and becoming a kind of permanent, institutionalised opposition.

This is a depressingly determinist view of politics. The truth is that elections are won and lost for reasons. No serious political party, when defeated, gives up. It asks why it lost and remedies the reason. If it doesn't, then no short cut to success can be found through electoral partnership. If Labour is unelectable, then any alliance it forms elsewhere will likewise be unelectable. This is particularly so since Labour would necessarily be the leading party in such an alliance. Even if it were desirable, the precondition for the feasibility of any such arrangement would be the electability of Labour. Otherwise it would be seen as merely a deal struck between politicians to win power, not an agreement of principle based on ideas. If the public decided they did not want a Labour government, they wouldn't vote in by the back door what they had excluded from the front.

The second dilemma is more difficult because there is an element of truth in it, which is then transformed into delusion by a sleight of hand. This is the delusion of betrayal. The theory holds that Labour lost because it was not sufficiently 'bold' or 'radical' standing up for its principles against the Tories. Indeed this is a frequent charge against Labour now, echoes of which can be found even in serious commentators sympathetic to Labour's case.

The element of truth is that because Labour embarked on a review of its policies prior to the last election and because this was inevitably a response to the defeats of the 1979–87 period, then there probably was some confusion in the public mind as to what Labour stood for. In this context, policy change could appear opportunistic rather than, as it was, genuine. It is also right to say that Labour has no future other than as a bold and radical party.

The sleight of hand, however, is then to jump to the conclusion that removing the confusion about what Labour stands for means going back to where Labour was. The brutal truth is that where we were, before Neil Kinnock began the process of change, was on the brink of political extinction.

Between 1983 and 1987 Labour kept its head above water. But people should recall again that at the beginning of 1987 campaign Labour lost the Greenwich by-election and went into the election neck and neck with the Alliance. Thanks to a brilliant campaign, with Neil Kinnock showing real strength as a campaigner and with an excellently argued presentation of Labour's case, Labour did well enough to hold on to second place.

It was *only* after the policy review began in 1988–89 that the Party truly revived and began to look a serious contender for government. And, as every single piece of independent analysis shows, the worry of the electorate in 1992 was not that Labour had changed, but the concern that the change was superficial.

There are two subtexts to this delusion. One is that the Labour Party is too much concerned with 'image' and 'sound bites'. This is just daft. No one believes that image is a substitute for policy, but image and good presentation are important and necessary complements to policy. To criticise politicians for being able to give a good 'sound bite' – when, for most of the news media, a bite is all you get

– is like criticising a politician for turning up to a press conference in a suit rather than a pair of pyjamas. Getting the image right is part of the job; no more, no less.

The other subtext expresses the tendency of those peddling the delusion of betrayal to believe that what is 'radical' is what any pressure group, operating in a particular area, says is 'radical'. Pressure groups are a vital part of our democracy, but they are not the same as political parties who aspire to govern. And they are never satisfied. If we attempt to build a platform for power around the agenda of pressure groups, then we will go down a political cul-de-sac, where we will end our journey by being obliged to turn round and retreat, offending deeply on the way back all those we earlier sought to placate. The issue is not whether to be radical or not; but what being radical means in today's world. In this lies the key.

The reason Labour lost in 1992, as for the previous four elections, is not complex, it is simple: society had changed and we did not change sufficiently with it. Policy prescriptions for one generation became confused with basic principles that are timeless. The rather paternalist, centralised view of collective power wielded *for* people rather than *by* them became, for the very reason given earlier, discredited. Precisely because socialists worked to change society, people became more educated, prosperous, prepared to question and demand. This was and is a natural part of social evolution. But it has a natural political consequence.

The changes in social composition – the break-up of the old class structure – mean that to form a new electoral majority, the left has to reach out beyond its traditional base. This has to be based on an appeal about the values and nature of our society, not on a snapshot of its economy.

Most important of all, such a reaching-out – creating a basis of support that is value-based, not simply class-based, in the traditional economic sense – is not a jettisoning of principle. The principles of the Party surely *are* its values. It is the means of their implementation that will and should change with each generation. To tie ourselves to the policy perspective of one era is to chain ourselves to history rather than learn from it. Neither does such a change involve letting down Labour's traditional support from the poor and unemployed because this strategy of change is precisely what is required to win power and it is the absence of power and the impotence of opposition that is the real let-down for them.

Labour does need a clear identity based on principle, not a series of adjustments with each successive electoral defeat. But the identity should be one for the modern world, not a throwback to a romanticised view of the past. The process of what is called 'modernisation' is in reality, therefore, the application of enduring, lasting principles for a new generation, not just by creating a modern party organisation, but by inspiring a programme for a modern society, economy and constitution. This is not to destroy the left's essential ideology; on the contrary it is retrieving it from an intellectual and political muddle.

Once freed from the constraints of confusion between policy and principle, the left is then able to address the political dilemma which the country as a whole faces – how to construct a new relationship between society and individual which turns out, on analysis, to be precisely the same task as the left faces. Rebuilding Britain as a strong community, with a modern notion of citizenship at its heart, is the political objective for the new age. Labour must transform itself into a credible vehicle for achieving it. The project of renewal for Labour mirrors that for Britain. What the country wants is what Labour needs. In this way, we can reshape coherent, up-to-date principles of government. The task has never been more urgent. Otherwise the drift to disillusionment with our political process will continue.

Foreword to *Reclaiming the Ground: Christianity and Socialism*

ed. Chris Bryant (Hodder & Stoughton), 1993

If there is a defining characteristic of Tony Blair's personal and political beliefs it is his Christianity. This consists of deeply held convictions developed at university in late night discussions over coffee and cigarettes, personal commitment to personal prayer and collective worship, and a desire to put Christian teaching into action. Blair asked to be confirmed into the Church of England as a student. If you want to trace the provenance of Blair's politics, you should start with Christianity. In this, Blair fits into the lineage of Christian Socialists within the Labour tradition, from Keir Hardie, to R. H. Tawney, to John Smith.

With Smith as leader of the Labour Party after 1992 willing to talk publicly about his faith, the Christian Socialist Movement (CSM), which is affiliated to the Labour Party, enjoyed a renaissance of membership and interest in its values. In this short contribution to the CSM's 1993 book Reclaiming the Ground, *Blair, a member of CSM, makes his first published and most overt statement of Christian belief.*

It is an uncompromising passage, filled with moral certainty. Blair writes: 'Christianity is a very tough religion. It may not always be practised as such. But it is. It places a duty, an imperative on us to reach our better self and to care about creating a better community to live in ... It is judgemental. There is right and wrong. There is good and bad. We all know this, of course, but it has become fashionable to be uncomfortable about such language.'

A decade later, when Blair wanted to end his television broadcast to the British public at the eve of the war in Iraq with the words 'God bless you' Alastair Campbell said, 'We don't do God.' But reading

Blair's own words on Christianity and social action, it is clear that he definitely does 'do God'.

This book is not about using religion to advance a political party, or staking out a claim that one set of religious beliefs is superior to another. Neither is it an attempt to solve political problems by simplistic theological solutions. It is a book written by Christians who want to reunite the ethical code of Christianity with the basic values of democratic socialism.

Like any great cause, Christianity has been used for dubious and sometimes cruel purposes wholly at odds with the essential message. But at best, it has inspired generations of people throughout almost 2,000 years to believe in and work for a better, more humane and more just world.

To radicals it has always had an especial validity. Radicals want change, and change, both personal and social, lies at the heart of the Christian religion. But it is change of a particular sort, based on a fundamentally optimistic view of human nature. It accepts the existence of our faults and weaknesses; it is not in any sense utopian. But it believes that there is a potential in human beings to do good that can be brought out and developed and made real.

Central to Christianity is the belief in equality; not that we are uniform in character or position, but on the contrary that despite our differences we are entitled to be treated equally, without regard to our wealth, race, gender or standing in society. It is about justice. Everybody should get the opportunity to make the most of themselves. The waste of human talent in our country and in the world today is an affront. It is shameful that millions of our fellow citizens are out of work, that many of our young people are left without hope and opportunity. And it is a brutal outrage that countless millions starve to death in a world that has abundance and plenty.

It is about compassion, the recognition that we will have to and should pay a price to help those less fortunate than ourselves, not as an act of charity to help them in dependence upon our bounty, but as a means of allowing them to achieve a better life for themselves.

It is about liberty, personal and social, freedom from unnatural restraint and freedom to enjoy and develop character and personality.

But above all, it is about the union between individual and community, the belief that we are not stranded in helpless isolation, but owe a duty both to others and to ourselves and are, in a profound sense, dependent on each other to succeed. This philosophy is sometimes used in such a way as to distinguish it from selfishness or even individualism. In one sense it is distinct from the notion of life about more than personal acquisition or consumption. But this can give rise to a false choice between self and others. In reality the Christian message is that self is best realised through communion with others. The act of Holy Communion is symbolic of this message. It acknowledges that we do not grow up in total independence, but interdependently, and that we benefit from that understanding. In political terms, this belief in community expresses itself through acting collectively to provide the services we need, the infrastructure of society and government without which modern life would be intolerable.

Therefore the values of democratic socialism are founded on a belief in the importance of society with others, and are closely intertwined with those of Christianity – hardly surprising in a view of the Christian beliefs of many of the Labour Party's historical and present-day members. By rethinking and re-examining our values, and placing them alongside those of the Christian faith, we are able, politically, to rediscover the essence of our beliefs which lies not in policies or prescriptions made for one period of time, but in principles of living that are timeless. By doing so, we can better distinguish between values themselves and their application, the one constant and unchanged, the other changing constantly. To a Labour Party now undertaking a thorough and necessary analysis of our future, this is helpful.

However, it is also a powerful compass for the direction of changes in our country. The new agenda in politics will reach out past old debates between economic ideologies of state control and *laissez-faire* and embrace different issues: the development of new economic opportunities for the individual; the environment, the third world, the international economy, the creation of modern, efficient public services. These issues must derive from some political values and we are as well to be sure of what they are.

A return to what we are really about, what we believe in would be a healthy journey for our country as well as the Labour Party.

It would also help us comprehend more fully the importance of personal responsibility in our lives and its relationship to society as a whole. Christianity is a very tough religion. It may not always be practised as such. But it is. It places a duty, an imperative on us to reach our better self and to care about creating a better community to live in. It is not utilitarian – though socialism can be explained in those terms. It is judgemental. There is right and wrong. There is good and bad. We all know this, of course, but it has become fashionable to be uncomfortable about such language. But when we look at our world today and how much needs to be done, we should not hesitate to make such judgements. And then follow them with determined action. That would be Christian socialism.

Part two:
Blair the leader

Principle, Purpose, Power

Election leaflet for party leadership contest, May 1994

On 12 May 1994 the leader of the Labour Party, John Smith, died from two heart attacks at his home in London's Barbican. Although Smith had suffered and survived a heart attack in 1988, he had lost weight and seemed in good health. On the eve of his death, John Smith had spoken at a Labour Party fundraising dinner in central London, at which he famously asked the British public for 'a chance to serve'.

The leader's death shocked his party, and resonated deeper with the broader public and there was a genuine sense of loss and grief amongst the British public.

Much has been written about the manner in which Tony Blair emerged as the modernisers' candidate for the leadership over his rival Gordon Brown. By the time the following leaflet was issued to party members across the UK from the Blair campaign HQ in Westminster, Brown had put his ambitions on hold, and Blair was the clear favourite to become leader of the Labour Party.

The leaflet has a clear Blairite ethos, and predates many of the later themes of the Labour government. In style, it marks out Blair's fondness for simple, direct language and short, even single word, sentences.

We must change the tide of ideas, state a new vision of our country, a vision of hope, justice and renewal.

The Labour Party will soon have an historic opportunity. To rebuild Britain. To create jobs. To ensure our schools are centres of excellence. To make the NHS once more the envy of the world. To wage a crusade against crime. To give hope back to the people whose trust we seek.

We seek that trust at a time of widespread cynicism about politics and politicians. The reaction to John Smith's tragic death showed the public's clamour for decency, honesty and integrity in British politics. Labour will continue to provide that. Our democratic socialist values are shared by the vast majority of the British people. Fairness. Justice. Community. Equality of opportunity. Responsibility. Self-respect and respect for others. A recognition that using the power of society is the key to delivering prosperity and opportunity to the individual.

Above all, the scar of mass unemployment must be removed, not just because it is a moral evil but because of the waste of the talents and skills of those without jobs and the cost of keeping them idle.

We must devolve power to the regions and nations of Britain and dismantle the Tories' unaccountable quango state. That means rebuilding local government and granting everyone the constitutional and workplace rights and freedoms commonplace in the rest of Europe.

We must strive to end the poverty and misery of those who starve in a world of plenty, roll back the proliferation of nuclear weapons and rebuild the United Nations to construct a peaceful international order.

These are ambitious goals. But they are the absolute minimum required for the renewal of Britain ruled by a short-termist government which has served a narrow section of society at the expense of the majority.

To meet those goals will require tough leadership of a strong and talented team. It will require discipline, unity of purpose, fresh ideas and energy.

A whole generation has grown up knowing nothing but Conservativism and the disillusionment that has flowed from it. The child born in 1979 comes of age in 1997.

We must give that child born of the Thatcher-Major age powerful reasons to vote for a party that they have never seen in government. Even more, we need to attract them into the party by showing them that it is a mass membership party with roots in every community, and in which the vote and the views of every individual count, whether as members of the party or their trade union. I joined the Labour Party straight after college. After serving as a local branch and constituency officer I fought the Beaconsfield by-election. The next year I was elected for the Sedgefield constituency and held Treasury, Energy and Employment portfolios before becoming shadow home secretary after the last election.

I am seeking the leadership of our party because I believe I possess the vigour, the devotion, the beliefs and the principles to lead it in its tasks of devising policies and communicating them to the whole electorate.

Let us work together for a Labour government radical in intent, underpinned by conviction, confident in its beliefs and strong enough to defeat this decaying Tory philosophy, not just for a term but for a generation.

* * *

Dear Friend,

This is an election no one wanted. John Smith was more than a good man; he was a fine leader of our party, and would have been a great prime minister of our country.

We must stand up for what John Smith believed in, above all his passion for social justice and his vision of economic prosperity. We must transform Labour from a party of protest to a party of government.

I believe Labour must stand where it has always stood – for the values of democratic socialism, for the people who rely on hard work and fair pay to keep them away from hardship, and who aspire to a better life for themselves and their families.

The Conservatives have failed; and that is our opportunity. But we cannot wait for them to lose the election. We must win the battle of ideas. Only then will we secure not just election victory, but a radical government. Above all we must show how our enduring values have modern relevance, by responding to the new challenges of the 1990s and beyond, and answering the British people's hunger for a national renewal.

I entered politics to achieve change in our country. With your help, I believe we can do it.

Yours sincerely,

Tony Blair

Socialism
Fabian Society pamphlet, 1994

In June 1994, as the new leader-in-waiting of the Labour Party, Tony Blair found an increased interest in his personal philosophy and credo. In a serious intellectual contribution, Blair wrote a Fabian Society pamphlet which sought to position his political thought within the context of British socialism. By rejecting Marx and a socialism based on economic prescriptions, Blair developed the idea of an ethical socialism, based on values. He coined the phrase 'social-ism' with the all-important hyphen denoting a renewed emphasis on society, the community, and the balance of rights with responsibilities. Socialism was an attempt to redefine British socialism in a modern age based on an older ethical tradition; it was also part of Blair's bid for the Labour Party leadership, which was decided in his favour the following month.

Ethics, Marxism and true socialism

For almost two decades, the left has felt itself on the defensive. Having fashioned the post-war consensus of 1945, its intellectual confidence became sapped by its own inner doubts, the problems of government in the 1960s and 1970s and the onslaught of the right through Thatcherism. It had a choice in 1979: to accept defeat; to wait unchanged in the hope of the world turning back to it; or to change and rediscover its purpose. Essentially it split in all directions, in the process splitting the Labour Party, the main party of the left. The great achievement first of Neil Kinnock and then of John Smith was to take the Labour Party back on a course towards renewal.

There have been three phases of political development this century. In the first, capitalism and the market were regarded as

81

having failed. The majority lived in poverty and ignorance. So the great institutions of collective power were created and developed to give the majority access to opportunities previously denied – proper housing and sanitation, universal education; insurance against unemployment; a national health service free at the point of need; public ownership of essential industries and services; and a trade union movement with the legal freedom to advance the interests of its membership at work. Government and state became repositories of great power and public expenditure.

In the second phase the majority became more prosperous, and began paying taxes and there was a reaction, not against the institutions themselves but against the manner in which their power was exercised, which came under attack in the name of the individual.

Reaction

Now we are entering a third phase. The limitations of Thatcherism are clear. The claims of an economic miracle have evaporated. Society is divided. The people are insecure. The public is once again ready to listen to notions associated with the left – social justice, cohesion, equality of opportunity and community. They do not want to go back; they want to move on.

The left can lead this new popular mood but only if it understands its nature and presents a clear vision of the country's future that is both radical and modern. In turn, this cannot be achieved unless it continues to regain the intellectual high ground, stating with clarity its true identity and historic mission. In doing so, it must show how this is not a break with its past or its traditions but, on the contrary, a rediscovery of their true meaning.

Different strands

There are two strands of socialist thought that have dominated the left this century. One is based on the belief that socialism is a set of values or beliefs – sometimes called ethical socialism and closely allied to European Social Democracy. It does not deny the existence of class divisions but its definition of them is not time bound. The other is a quasi-scientific view of socialism that is based on a notion of economic determinism and a particular view of class. This is usually associated with Marxism and other parts of the left grouped around a narrow view of class interests. The Labour Party has never been Marxist but it has been influenced by the second strand of thought. In particular, many student radicals and union activists of the 1960s and 1970s were reared in the belief that the ethical strand of socialism was weak and inadequate and that the economic determinist version based around class interests was harder edged and more radical.

This second strand became entangled with various other elements of left thought – syndicalism in the trade unions and the new movements around issues such as the environment and nuclear weapons (though in the latter their influence was always limited). It also believed strongly in 'activism' – the idea that the politically conscious few have to drag the politically unconscious many in the direction of the true faith.

Ethics

The main consequence which flowed from the influence of the second strand was that, when defeat came in 1979, one part of the left then believed that the reason for defeat was that 'true' socialism had never been tried; and therefore instead of altering the path of the left, it decided instead to plunge down the same path much more vigorously.

But the first strand of thought was still there. Since 1983, it has come back into its own. Indeed, since the collapse of Communism, it has been the only serious view of the left's future that can remain. What is necessary now is to give it some clarity and content.

The socialism of Marx, of centralised state control of industry and production is dead. It misunderstood the nature and development of a modern market economy; it failed to recognise that the state and public sector can become a vested interest capable of oppression as much as the vested interests of wealth and capital; and it was based on a false view of class that became too rigid to explain or illuminate the nature of class today.

Reasserting social-ism

By contrast, socialism as defined by certain key values and beliefs is not merely alive, it has a historic opportunity now to give leadership. The basis of such socialism lies in the view that individuals are socially interdependent human beings – that individuals cannot be divorced from the society to which they belong. It is, if you will, social-ism.

It contains an ethical and subjective judgement that individuals owe a duty to one another and to a broader society – the left view of citizenship. And it believes, objectively, that it is only through recognising that interdependence – and by society as a whole acting upon it – that the individuals interest can be advanced. It does not set apart individual interests and the interests of society as the Tories do. It takes an enlightened view of self-interest and regards it, broadly, as inextricably linked to the interest of society.

It is from this combination of analysis of the world as it is and prescriptions of the means of changing it that values of democratic socialism – social justice, the equal worth of each citizen, equality of opportunity, community – came.

Time limited

Once socialism is defined in this way as a set of principles and beliefs, based around the notion of a strong and active society as necessary to advance the individual, rather than a set of narrow time-bound class or sectional interests or particular economic prescriptions, then it can liberate itself, learning from its history rather than being chained to it. It then no longer confuses means such as wholesale nationalisation with ends: a fairer society and more productive economy. It can move beyond the battle between private and public sector and see the two working in partnership. It can open itself up to greater pluralism of ideas and thought.

The problem with an ideology based on a particular economic prescription or time-limited view of class is that it may be valid for one time, but quickly becomes historically redundant. Society or the economic changes and the disciples of the ideology are left trying to fit the world to the ideology, not the ideology to the world.

For example, there are at least three obvious changes in the post-war world. First, the economy is global and the trading future of our economy is completely interlocked with those of our main trading partners. Economic isolation is neither desirable nor feasible.

Second, there has been an explosion in service industries coupled with the development of a consumer culture, where people regard themselves as economic consumers as well as producers.

Third, the world of work has been revolutionised. Almost half the workforce is women. Many choose to work part time. The pattern of working hours has changed. People will change jobs several times in their lives.

Above all, as a modern economy develops, the premium on knowledge and education becomes ever greater. It is now virtually a platitude to say that the success of a modern economy is built on the skill and talent of its workforce but it is true nonetheless. It is the amount of value they can add to what they produce that is the key to overcoming competition from low wage or low skill competitors.

Reclaiming the ground

Yet we have failed to answer the scale of this challenge. Large numbers of people are still unskilled or under-educated. There are still frightening proportions of young adults who are both illiterate and innumerate. We have a higher education system that the majority fail to reach. We are in danger of dividing into two groups in the working population: those with careers and those with jobs. The former have some definable notion of progression; the latter are increasingly demoralised and demotivated, undervalued and often very poorly treated by a management style that is neither right nor, in the end, efficient.

The old extreme left has no real answer to those problems, believing that addressing them is a form of collusion with an irredeemably exploitative market system. The right either ignores them or, in the case of bad management practice, endorses it.

This is the chance for the Labour Party and the left to capture the ground and language of opportunity for itself by policies that are entirely consistent with its traditional principles – namely intervening to equip the individuals ability to prosper within this new economy – but applying them in a different way for the modern world. How it does so should be where the new thinking and ideas are developed, released from false ideological constraints.

The result is not a policy vacuum or a retreat into philosophy rather than political action. It is, rather, the development of a new policy agenda and in many ways a broader one at that.

The broad agenda

In economic terms, we need a new industrial policy that addresses the structural weaknesses of British industry; a new social partnership at work; absolute priority to education and skills as the means of both enhancing opportunity and creating an efficient economy; direct measures to reduce unemployment; rebuilding our infrastructure; and international co-operation at macroeconomic level to co-ordinate measures for stable and sustainable growth. In all these respects, society, through government but in many other ways, is acting to promote the public good. In other words, we are not trying to run a Tory economy with a bit of social compassion but acting to ensure the economic public interest is upheld.

In social terms, we act to modernise our welfare state and eliminate poverty, to reduce levels of crime and to improve our environment and quality of life.

And we renew the way we govern ourselves, our outdated and decrepit constitution that now contains the worst features of the centralising tendency of government with unaccountable quangos and cartels taking over local services. A new settlement between citizen and society requires radical reform of our constitution and such reform should be pursued by a Labour government with urgency. It is not an issue of insignificance, relevant only to the chattering classes; it goes to the heart of the nature of power and the way it is abused in Britain today.

Most of all, by re-establishing its core identity, the Labour Party and the left can regain the intellectual self-confidence to take on and win the battle of ideas.

Vision

For too long, the left has thought it has had a choice: to be radical or to be cautious and electable.

Whilst being 'radical' is defined as the old-style collectivism of several decades ago this may be true. But that is not really being radical at all; it is just neo-conservatism of the left. Once being 'radical' is redefined as having a central vision based around principle but liberated from particular policy prescriptions that became confused with principle, then in fact being radical is the route to electability.

Once this destination – a strong, united society which gives each citizen the chance to develop their potential to the full – is properly mapped out and the ideological compass reconstructed on true lines, the journey can be undertaken with vigour and confidence. We can then go out as a Party to build a new coalition of support, based on a broad national appeal that transcends traditional electoral divisions.

The future will be decided not on the basis of pacts or deals or horse trading between politicians or parties but through the power and energy of our ideas and our vision for the country. If that vision for Britain is strong, if it can create a popular movement in this country for change and national renewal and show how this can be achieved, then we will win; if we cannot, then no deal or pact can save us and neither does it deserve to.

The Thatcherite project of the 1980s is over. The present government has no project, except political survival. As a result, the country drifts without serious purpose or coherence of direction. The prospects for a regenerated left-of-centre have never been better, nor is duty to grasp them greater. It is now time to rediscover our central mission of social advancement and individual achievement. This is a time in which we will make our own history; not power at the expense of principle, but power through principle and for the common good.

'No favours'

New Statesman, 18 November 1994

This article appeared in the New Statesman *at the time of the Trades Union Congress annual conference. It was designed as a warning shot across the bows of the trades unions, which, whilst affiliated to the Labour Party, had been instrumental in defeating Labour governments in 1970 and 1979. Blair stakes out his formula for dealing with his party's paymasters: fairness, not favours. The article was part of the strategy to reassure middle England voters that Labour would not buckle under union pressure once in government.*

With more part-time, flexible patterns and the challenge of a global economy, trade unions are needed more than ever before. But their role is changing, and will continue to change.

The revolutions in work and family patterns have created an insecure society. With no job for life, people need to know there will be opportunities to move from one job to another. With women making up half the workforce, we need to find new ways of ensuring that work and family life can be balanced. Unions have a vital role in making sure that working families prosper in a changed world.

A Labour government would provide the basic framework of the rights for fairness at work: the Social Chapter, a minimum wage, proper treatment for part-time workers and, where employees want it, the ability to have their union recognised. Unions will also be vital partners in the partnership economy we hope to build, working with management to make sure British industry is competitive and has a highly skilled workforce.

The unions must adapt to this changed world. They will have to supply decent services to their members, of course – but their role goes much wider. Work is still central to most people's lives. People want a collective voice in the workplace. People want services tailored to their individual needs.

There is a bond of belief between Labour and the unions that goes beyond a few lines of the rule book. At their best, unions represent in the workplace the values that Labour shares with the British people: social solidarity, community rights and responsibilities, fair reward for hard work. Unions, working intelligently and flexibly, can back up the efforts of individuals in the workplace.

Unions can be at the forefront of the debate on training, reskilling and full employment. This year the TUC ran a successful conference on full employment with a broad range of voices, including that of the CBI, taking part to address a most vital issue for our country.

Unions are once again showing that they are in touch with the needs of employees. They are beginning to adapt to their new needs. Unions are becoming the voice of working people and not of narrow sectional interests. Influence should not be based on favours from government.

Many unions are making these changes. Just as Labour is now looking again at the culture, the organisation and the constitution of the party, so are many unions who see that the present structures and objectives are out of date.

I have been heartened by the response to the review of our constitution, which I announced at our party conference. I welcome the fact that all sections of the party are contributing to the debate, among them unions, CLPs, MPs, and indeed the *New Statesman*.

The sort of things that unions should be doing and in some cases are already doing include:

- job searching advice including advice phone-lines;
- a support service for career mobility;
- advice with taxation, pensions;
- help with individual pay negotiations as well as collective bargaining.

The GMB, for example, is doing much good work on pensions; and the TGWU have just set up a 24-hour legal advice helpline.

It is clear that if unions do not revolutionise their services and tailor them to the changing needs of employees, then someone else will provide these services. The private sector will come in and cherry-pick the profitable services, leaving many without the vital help they need. Already the Citizens Advice Bureau has noted an increase in employment law enquiries – enquiries that unions ought to be gearing themselves up to answer.

Unions are also rethinking their campaigning role: how they use their collective voice intelligently so that public opinion is carried with them.

The UCW's part in the successful campaign to stop post office privatisation has shown how effective unions can be, however much the Tories have put them on the defensive for the past few years. The UCW used intelligence and subtlety to win support. They lobbied Tory MPs as well as the other parties. They did not try to persuade them through threatening strikes. They refused simply to defend the status quo, and instead proposed public ownership but with commercial freedom. Every public statement was based on how the service to the customer would suffer and not just the impact, important though it is, on the UCW workers. The result was that public opinion was won over and, in turn, enough Tory back-benchers sided with Labour in opposing privatisation.

The UCW has shown the way forward for unions. Unions will be listened to if they are seen not as an adjunct of party politics but representing working people. If they put forward constructive proposals on the major employment and economic issues, they will once again be an essential part of the debate on the key issues.

As the new general secretary of the TUC has recognised, it is in the unions' best interests not to be associated merely with one political party. The influence of the trade unions will come from being a broad voice of working people, not a direct party political voice or one that is concerned for the narrow interests of individual unions.

Labour has changed over the past fifteen years because we lost touch with the voter. A similar rethink is happening in the unions and this has been given new momentum by the impressive work of John Monks. All institutions need to change to adapt to new realities. Unions realise this. They have a legitimate and important part to play in the economy and workplace. They do not want, nor will they get, favours from a Labour government. They will get fairness. Unions should be able to thrive with any change of government or no change in government, because they speak for the broad interests of working families.

The growing insecurity of millions of families will create an opportunity for unions which they can grasp if they rethink their role and respond to the new wishes of employees. There is no reason why declining union membership should not be reversed as people realise that more than ever before they need a voice in the workplace that backs up their own hard work and effort. But, like any organisation, unions must make sure they get their vital services delivered to the frontline where their members can see they are getting the best deal possible for their money.

We must return to the situation where unions are in the news because they are acting for their members by defending individual rights, providing innovative services for people and contributing to important debates on industry and the economy.

Labour Party conference speech
Blackpool, 4 October 1994

This first speech by Blair as party leader was pure drama. I watched it from the back of the Winter Gardens in Blackpool, where the backdrop was a bizarre pistachio colour.

Towards the end of the speech, a member of the Blair team whispered in my ear, 'He's going to abolish Clause IV', and indeed he was, although at the time, the exact meaning of the latter sections of the speech were not immediately clear to the audience. Even the journalists' copies of the speech, handed out in advance, had this section missing.

Michael White of the Guardian *wrote the following morning: 'Tony Blair seemed likely last night to pull off the most sensational political coup for a generation as the Labour conference embraced his unexpected call for an overhaul of the Party's time-honoured aims and objectives – including the controversial Clause Four commitment to nationalisation.'*

Across the nation, across class, across political boundaries, the Labour Party is once again able to represent all the British people. We are the mainstream voice in politics today.

To parents wanting their children to be taught in classrooms that are not crumbling, to students with qualifications but no university place, let us say: the Tories have failed you. We are on your side. Your ambitions are our ambitions.

To men and women who get up in the morning and find the kitchen door smashed in again, the video gone again; to the pensioners who fear to go out of their homes, let us say: the Tories have abused your trust. We are on your side. Your concerns are our concerns.

To the small businesses, pushed to the wall by greedy banks, to employers burdened by government failure, to employees living in fear of the P45, to the thousands of others insecure in their jobs in every part of the country, let us say: the Tories have forgotten you, again. Labour is on your side. Your aspirations are our aspirations. We are back as the party of the majority in British politics, back to speak up for Britain, back as the people's party.

Look at Britain fifteen years after Mrs Thatcher first stood on the steps of Downing Street. Where there was discord, is there harmony? Where there was error, is there truth? Where there was doubt, is there faith? Where there was despair, is there hope?

Harmony? When crime has more than doubled?

Truth? When they won an election on lies about us and what we would do?

Faith? When politics is debased by their betrayal?

Hope? When three million people are jobless, almost six million are on income support, and one in three children grow up in poverty?

They have brought us injustice and division, but these have not been the price of economic efficiency. Because tax is also up – £800 a year extra for the average family. Spending is up, and growth over the last fifteen years is down.

Look at what they wasted on the way. Billions of pounds gifted by nature – the God-given blessing of North Sea oil. Billions we could have invested in our future. Billions they squandered. One hundred and eighteen billion pounds – £5,000 for every family in this country – gone, wasted, vanished.

And to hide the truth of the nation's problems they have sold our nation's capital assets, built up over many years, and have used the proceeds not to invest but to cover current spending. Seventy billion pounds gone for ever.

It's time to take these Tories apart for what they have done to our country. Not because they lack compassion – though they do – but because they are the most feckless, irresponsible group of incompetents ever let loose on the government of Britain.

And why are they incompetent? Not just because of the individuals. It is not this or that minister that is to blame: it is an entire set of political values that is wrong. The Tories fail because they fail to understand that a nation, like a community, must work together in order for individuals within it to succeed. It is such a simple failing, and yet it is fundamental.

Go and look at a company that is succeeding. It will treat its workforce not as servants but as partners. They will be motivated and trained and given a common purpose. Of course sweatshop conditions in the short term can make do. But in the end they fail. The quality and commitment aren't there.

It's the same with a country. It can be run on privilege and greed for a time; but in the end it fails.

This is not theory. We have living proof of it. At the end of fifteen years, we are taxing and spending more – not to invest in future success but to pay for past failure.

I don't mind paying taxes for education and health and the police. What I mind is paying them for unemployment, crime and social squalor.

After fifteen years we spend more of our national income on unemployment and poverty and less on education. If the share of national wealth invested in housing was the same as in 1979, we would spend £11 billion more; next year we will spend £11 billion on housing benefit.

Now they want to cut the benefit. Instead of cutting benefit, why not cut the homeless queue, cut unemployment, and build houses? And if it needs an initial capital investment, release the money tied up in local-authority bank accounts and put it to work to start the house-building programme.

The Tories' economics is based on a view of the market that is crude, out of date and inefficient. And their view of society is one of indifference – to shrug their shoulders and walk away. They think we choose between self-interest and the interests of society or the country as a whole. In reality self-interest demands that we work together to achieve what we cannot do on our own.

* * *

It is time we had a clear, up-to-date statement of the objects and objectives of our party. John Prescott and I will propose such a statement to the NEC. Let it then be open to debate. I want the whole Party involved. I know the whole Party will welcome that debate. And if it is accepted, then let it become the objects of our Party at the next election and take its place in our constitution for the next century.

This is a modern party living in an age of change. It requires a modern constitution that says what we are in terms the public cannot misunderstand and the Tories cannot misrepresent. We are proud of our beliefs, so let's state them – and in terms that people will identify with in every workplace, every home, every family, every community in the country. And let this Party's determination to change be the symbol of the trust they can place in us to change the country.

Let Us Face the Future:
the 1945 anniversary lecture

Fabian Society pamphlet, 1995

One year after becoming leader of the Labour Party, Blair occupied a strong position. He had unleashed a programme of party policy and organisational reform, and his poll ratings remained high. By contrast, his Conservative opponents were in the middle of allegations of corruption and sleaze.

Blair made the fiftieth anniversary of Labour's 1945 election landslide to deliver a lecture on his predecessors, and what lessons could be learnt. The lecture was published by the Fabian Society in July 1995. It contains some significant content about Blair's belief that his party needed to win voters across the social and political spectrum to form a government.

Blair says: 'I am not interested in governing for a term, coming to power on a wave of euphoria, a magnificent edifice of expectations, which dazzles for a while before collapse' – a laudable, if tough, ambition.

He also makes the case for the 'progressive century' – a coalition of support for progressive measures drawn from beyond Labour's traditional political boundaries. In a prescient aside, Blair even warned Tory MP Michael Portillo that if Labour repeated the success of 1945, it would win the Enfield constituency from the Conservatives.

At the time, the audience laughed.

In 1945, as now, we faced enormous changes in the global economy and in society. Then, as now, Labour spoke for the national interest

97

and offered hope for the future; the Tories spoke for sectional interests and represented the past. Then, as now, Britain needed rebuilding and the voters turned to Labour to take on that task; because, then as now, the people knew that market dogma and crude individualism could not solve the nation's problems. That is why I honour the 1945 generation: to learn the lessons of their victory and their achievements, and to set out how the enduring values of 1945 can be applied to the very different world of 1995.

It is also appropriate to do this under the auspices of the Fabian Society, which also holds a special place in Labour history. It was founded before the Party itself. Before the Second World War, the society's summer schools had an enviable reputation – for parties as much as or more for than for politics. In 1945, the Society boasted Guild socialist GDH Cole as its Chair. On its executive were Michael Young (now Lord Young of Dartington), the author of the 1945 manifesto and much else. Also on the Committee was Evan Durbin MP, author of the important book *The Politics of Democratic Socialism*. Today, the Society is again a source of political education and new ideas. The Fabians have undergone a real revival in the past few years – for example, the pamphlets in the *Southern Discomfort* series have been important in turning the attention of the Party towards lost voters in the south.

Labour past, present and future

As we celebrate the 50th anniversary of a quite momentous date in the history of the Labour Party and of our country, I have no hesitation whatsoever in describing the 1945 Labour government as the greatest peacetime government this century. It was led by statesmen of enduring stature: Attlee, Morrison, Bevin, Bevan. Its achievements were immense: demobilisation and full employment, the welfare state, the NHS, as well as significant contributions to international relations. And it was so secure of the British people that it lost no by-elections, gained votes on its re-election in 1950, and gained votes again in 1951 when it won more votes but fewer seats than the Tories.

The record of that government makes me proud to call myself a democratic socialist. Its confidence, exuberance and commitment to the jobs that needed to be done are an inspiration to all in the Labour movement. 26 July 1945: 393 seats, 209 gains, overall majority 146.

This speech has two constant themes. First, I wish to highlight both the achievements of the 1945 government, and the lessons we can learn from it. Second, I want to put today's modernisation of the Labour Party in its historical context.

With the grain

In respect of the 1945 government itself, I shall argue that its achievements were enormous, its impact enduring. But it is important to understand where its strength came from, what it really represented as well as what it didn't. The reality, I shall try to show, is that the Labour government's agenda grew out of the coalition government of the war; that it cut decisively with, not against, the grain of political thinking; and that its prospectus at the election was strongest in the direction it offered, not in the minutiae of policy detail.

The real radical strength of the 1945 government was the utter clarity and determination with which its purposes were defined and carried through. Its objectives – jobs for all, housing, proper health and education services – were magnificent. It was a government massively driven by a sense of national purpose and renewal, extraordinary unified in its aims, and entirely unashamed of building a broad consensus to achieve them.

It was truly a government that changed the agenda for a generation. But the government did not emerge out of the blue. Wartime experience was critical to the election result. The genius of Labour leaders was to capture the national mood, and at the same time lead that national mood. Labour was judged as the party best able to give legislative expression to popular hope. The country judged that the Conservatives, because of their historic failure to meet the challenges of the 1930s, could not deliver renewal in the 1940s. But in terms of its programme too, the 1945 government built on what had gone before. Earlier progressive social and economic reform laid the legislative and intellectual foundations. The debates of the 1930s helped shape the outlook of a generation of leaders. And wartime experience in government gave them the skills to implement their programme. They were elected ready to govern, and they did.

Our challenge is not to return to the 1940s but instead to take the values that motivated that government and apply them afresh to our time. I passionately want to lead a party which once again embodies the national mood for change and renewal.

The end of Labour's consensus

That links to my second theme, the challenge of modernisation today, which arises from the fact that, with the possible exception of 1964, Labour has been unable to recreate the strong political consensus of 1945. The truth that we must take seriously is that 1945 was the exception and not the rule. Labour in 1945 overcame, but did not resolve, fundamental issues of ideology and organisation facing the Labour Party. In wartime, these became obscured. But later they reasserted themselves. In the late 1970s and early 1980s they were almost fatal. Essentially both ideology and organisation became out of date. What Neil Kinnock, John Smith and I have sought to do is to cure those weaknesses and to transform the left-of-centre in British politics. By reason of the need to distinguish itself from the Liberal reformers, the Labour constitution identified itself with one particular strand of socialist thinking, namely state ownership. This means that its ideology came to be governed by too narrow a view of democratic socialism. Over time, Clause IV took on the status of a totem. Our agenda was misrepresented. And as statist socialism lost credibility, so did we lose support.

Further, the gap between our stated aims and policies in government fed the constant charge of betrayal – the view that our problem was that the leadership was too timid to tread the real path to true socialism. This did immense harm to the party. And it was to be compounded upon by our organisational weakness.

The party grew out of the trade unions' legitimate desire to defend their interests and their members in Parliament. As a result, Labour's organisation has traditionally been dominated by its large affiliated membership and a strictly activist-based structure of democracy. Of course, a party of ordinary working people should, by definition, have at its heart the interests of the majority. But producer interests have over the century become increasingly varied and diffuse. And in any event they need to be balanced by the needs of consumers. In terms of democratic organisation, as mass activism died and people stopped turning up in large numbers to union or party meetings, so the Party machine became a shell, prey to factionalism and sectarianism. It looked democratic but it wasn't. The key democratic link – which should be that between the Party and the real people it seeks to represent – disappeared.

Members of the 1970s' CLP general committee might say they represented their membership; union executive members might say they represented their members; but the truth was that they often didn't.

Building a new consensus
So the ideology was out of date; and yet the structure of the Party had no means of bringing that home. In the end, of course, the country

brought it home, by rejecting – repeatedly – the prospect of a Labour government. The task today is to reconstruct our ideology around the strength of our values and the way they are expressed. And then to create an organisation to match and reflect the ideology.

We are well on our way. The first came to fruition in the rewriting of Clause IV, in which far from escaping our traditions we recaptured them. The second is proceeding too. The ultimate objective is a new political consensus of the left-of-centre, based around the key values of democratic socialism and European social democracy, firm in its principles but capable of responding to changing times, so that those values may be put into practice and secure broad support to govern for long periods of time. To reach that consensus we must value the contribution of Lloyd George, Beveridge and Keynes and not just Attlee, Bevan or Crosland. We should start to explore our own history with fresh understanding and an absence of preconceptions.

July 1995 saw a Conservative Party afraid to ask and answer hard questions about itself, its character and its direction. The debate began, but was so painful it had to be abandoned. We should not flinch, and we need not do so, because we are so much stronger, so much more liberated by our voyage of rediscovery. Part of that rediscovery is to welcome the radical left-of-centre tradition outside of our own Party, as well as celebrate the achievements of that tradition within it. The strength of the latter was its attack upon the abuses of economic power, its commitment to social justice and its ability to mobilise the country for change. The strength of the former has been in its sensitivity to the abuse of political as well as economic power and its independent free thinking which has this century helped to promote our economic objectives. The task of the left-of-centre today is to put these two strengths together, led by Labour and providing the same broad consensus for change that a previous generation did in 1945.

I am not interested in governing for a term, coming to power on a wave of euphoria, a magnificent edifice of expectations, which dazzles for a while before collapse. I want to rebuild this Party from its foundations, making sure every stone is put in its rightful place, every design crafted not just for effect but to a useful purpose.

The lessons of 1945

There is, of course, dual significance in the year 1945: the end of the Second World War, and Labour's first absolute parliamentary majority. The two events are intimately connected because Labour's crushing victory was testimony to the fact that it embodied the hopes of war-torn Britain better than the Tories. Labour's vision chimed with the vision for which the British people had been fighting. Labour became the voice of the nation, in a sense never recognised as true before and rarely accepted as true since.

The 1945 election, and the government which followed, are therefore a source of immense pride for the Labour Party. By 1945, the people of Britain wanted national renewal: change from the depression years of the 1930s, change from the war years of the early 1940s. And they trusted Labour, whose leaders played a central part in the wartime coalition, to deliver that renewal. Labour promised to build a future for all the people. As Barbara Castle recently described it: 'We were washed into Westminster on a wave of popularity, acceptability, hope and faith that we would have a new society.'

It was not a raft of detailed policies that took the government to power, but a clear sense of purpose and direction. There was, of course, Beveridge, and the Labour plans for social security developed during the war. And the coalition government had passed the 1944 Education Act. But the debate on economic policy and the role of planning in the 1930s, though long gone, was rather confused. Other things were done on the hoof – for example, Aneurin Bevan and the structure of the health service. What the

1945 government did have, however was a very strong sense of direction based on core Labour values – fairness, freedom from want, social equality.

Renewal

In 1945, Labour was a patriotic party, as it is today. It embodied national purpose and personal advancement, nowhere more so than in its slogan, 'Now Let us Win the Peace'. The Second World War was a people's war. On the battlefield men of all classes fought together. On the home front, the evacuation of the cities brought people together in a way not seen before or since. To follow the people's war, Labour pledged to build a people's peace. It spoke for the people's vision of what Britain ought to be – a generous, brave, forward-looking bastion of decency and social justice. National unity and patriotic purpose were brought together to build a better society.

Labour put itself at the head of a movement for national renewal spanning classes, age groups and regions. Labour made gains right across the country. George Wallace, elected MP for Chislehurst – yes, Chislehurst in Kent – explains in Austin Mitchell's fascinating account of the 1945 election (published by the Fabian Society) that he ran into Ellen Wilkinson at the first meeting of the new PLP. 'You won then,' she said to him. 'What was the seat?' 'Chislehurst,' he replied. She said, 'My God, the revolution has arrived.'

What is more, Labour did not just promise change, it delivered it, combining idealism and practicality in equal measure. The achievements were immense:

- Labour engineered the transition from wartime to peacetime economy without a reversion to mass unemployment or the re-emergence of depressed areas;
- Labour implemented the Beveridge report, abolishing the hated means test, raising old age pensions from 10 shillings to

26 shillings a week, setting up a universal system of national insurance to cover sickness, unemployment and retirement, and supporting children and families with a welfare system that was at the time the envy of the world;

- Labour set up the NHS three years after its election, forty-seven years ago today. For the first time, the fear of illness was removed from the great mass of people. Defying the great Tory lie that equality meant levelling down, the government showed that socialism is about the abolition of second-class status, not attacking excellence but making it available to all;

- Overseas, Labour also made its contribution. Attlee's determination to grant independence to India signalled a readiness to reconsider the role of Empire, and Ernest Bevin's contribution was central to the Marshall Plan, to NATO and to the UN, which finally gave proper expression to the bonds of interdependence and mutuality that exist between peoples. Nor should we forget the role the Party played in helping socialist and progressive forces around the world: Denis Healey was not International Secretary for nothing.

By 1950, Sam Watson, the Durham Miners' leader, claimed at party conference: 'Poverty has been abolished. Hunger is unknown. The sick are tended. The old folks are cherished, our children are growing up in a land of opportunity.' The Tories were constantly on the defensive. They tried to bury the Beveridge report. They said full employment was impossible. They voted against the second and third readings of the NHS Bill. But the public mood turned against them. Labour did not just embody a new consensus: it helped to create it and sustain it.

In retrospect, of course, we can see that there were some mistakes and omissions. Peter Hennessy, a sympathetic biographer of that government, highlights three: a failure to recognise fully the realities of the new world order, manifested in the attitude of the government towards Europe; second, a reluctance to modernise the institutions of government itself – what Kenneth Morgan calls the Labour government's 'stern centralism'; and third, a tendency to look back on the problems of the 1930s, not forward to the challenges of the 1950s.

Unsympathetic biographers – Corelli Barnett leading amongst them – argue that by trying to build a New Jerusalem, Labour and Britain chose social comfort over economic gain. The reality is different. The 1945 government did pursue the goal of social justice. But it also laid enormous emphasis on economic modernisation. What is more, by pursuing social and economic goals together, it laid the basis for the most rapid period of economic growth in Britain's history. And because it got unemployment and poverty down, the government was good value. Little wonder a nine-year-old Neil Kinnock watched his grandfather weep as the news came through that Labour had lost the 1951 election.

The truth is that the 1945 government had intellectual vitality, moral courage and organisational effectiveness. It was a government that was willing to draw on the resources of the whole progressive tradition. The ideas of Keynes and Beveridge were the cornerstone of reform. Attlee proclaimed that 'the aim of socialism is to give greater freedom to the individual'. And the political philosopher T. H. Marshall avowedly linked the socialist project with its political ancestry. He divided the history of 300 years of political reform into three phases:

- the struggles for civil citizenship – liberty of the person, freedom of speech, thought and faith and the right to justice – in the eighteenth century;
- the campaigns for political citizenship – above all the right to vote – in the nineteenth century;

- and the enactment of social citizenship – above all minimum standards of economic welfare and social security – in the twentieth century.

Democratic socialism in Britain was indeed the political heir of the radical liberal tradition: distinctive for its own roots, principles and practices, but with recognisable affinity when put next to its progressive liberal cousin. What is more, the 1945 Labour Party backed up intellect with organisation. The party had 500,000 members in 1945.

By 1951 it had over a million. It appealed and gained support throughout the country. And Labour won in 1945 because it reached beyond its traditional base, especially in the south. The electoral map of 1945 is remarkably similar to that of the 1994 European elections. We won six of seven seats in Norfolk, seven of nine in Essex, four of five in Northamptonshire and two in Somerset.

Labour single-mindedly set out to reach beyond the traditional industrial areas, no one more so than Herbert Morrison who gave up safe Hackney and fought marginal Lewisham East. He won by 15,000 votes. Outer London swung dramatically to Labour. These were the new owner-occupied suburbs of Metroland and the Southern railway. As well as the industrial areas of London, Labour, in the form of Ashley Bramall, won Bexley in a by-election. That is Edward Heath's seat now. We won Enfield: Michael Portillo take note. And we gained Barnet – the home of Mrs Thatcher. None of these are Labour seats now.

Building on the lessons

We should therefore feel pride as we celebrate those achievements. But we should also feel humility. Our moment of greatest success remained just that – a moment. Since 1945, Labour in government has achieved a great deal, often in very difficult circumstances. These are real achievements. But looking back over the years since that great post-war government, it is clear that the coalition forged in 1945 has not been maintained: since 1951 we have been out of power for thirty-three of forty-four years. The 1964 government expanded education and created the Open University, reformed social legislation, kept unemployment down, spent more on education than defence and carried forward the attack on class barriers and prejudice started in 1945. In the 1970s, Labour dealt with the consequences of the world financial crisis of 1973, without the benefit of North Sea oil. It consolidated progress in the fields of pensions with the introduction of SERPs and women's rights with the passage of the Sex Relations Act. It passed the pioneering Race Relations Act, which still sets a standard for legislative action against racial discrimination.

But despite the high hopes, especially in Harold Wilson's first government, Labour did not succeed in establishing itself as a natural party of government. To create the conditions in which Labour is once again capable of leading a governing consensus – in which it is truly the 'people's party' – we have to learn the lessons of 1945. For me these are:

- the need for a clear sense of national purpose;
- the need to win the battle of ideas;
- the need to mobilise all the people of progressive mind around a party always outward-looking, seeking new supporters and members.

New Labour, eternal values

Since 1945, elections have been lost for reasons of bad luck, bad timing or bad policies. But the historical record demands something more than an election-by-election analysis of contingent factors. We need a systematic analysis. As early as 1952, Peter Shore was asking the right question: 'How is it that so large a proportion of the electorate, many of whom are neither wealthy or privileged, have been recruited for a cause which is not their own?'

That question is as relevant today as it was then. I believe it goes to the heart of what has been termed the 'progressive dilemma', defined by David Marquand as follows: 'The Labour Party has faced essentially the same problem since the 1920s: how to transcend Labourism without betraying the Labour interest; how to bridge the gap between the old Labour fortresses and the potentially anti-Conservative, but non-Labour hinterland; how to construct a broad-based and enduring social coalition capable not just of giving it a temporary majority in the House of Commons, but of sustaining a reforming government thereafter.'

One part of the explanation is obvious: our very success in 1945 forced the Conservative Party to adapt and change, to embrace the key components of the welfare state and the mixed economy. The 1945 government built a durable post-war settlement that forced the Tories to move onto our ground. The historian Peter Clarke puts it as follows: '[by the 1950s] much of the 1945 agenda was no longer radical and contentious; it had become part of the political furniture which both parties were now competing to rearrange rather than replace.' Even during Mrs Thatcher's counter-revolution in the 1980s, the Conservatives pulled back from a full-frontal assault on the enduring legacies of the 1945 settlement.

New Liberals

However, the record of Conservative adoption is only part of the story. The 'progressive dilemma' is rooted in the history of social and economic reform in Britain. Up to 1914, that history was defined by the Liberal Party's efforts to adapt to working-class demands. This involved the gradual replacement of the classical liberal ideology based on non-intervention and 'negative freedom' with a credo of social reform and state action to emancipate individuals from the vagaries and oppressions of personal circumstances. Following the growing assertiveness of trade unions from the 1860s and after the foundation the foundation of the Labour Representation Committee in 1900, working people were able to put new demands on the Liberal Party. These were the forces that were eventually to swamp the Liberals, but for a time they found political manifestation inside that Party in the rise of new Liberalism. Radical liberals saw that the electorate was growing and changing, and realised that liberalism could only survive if it responded to the new demands.

The intellectual bridgehead was established by Hobhouse and others. They saw the nineteenth-century conception of liberty as too thin for the purposes of social and economic reform, so they enlarged it. They realised that theoretical liberty was of little use if people did not have the ability to exercise it. So they argued for collective action, including state action, to achieve positive freedom, even if it infringed traditional *laissez-faire* liberal orthodoxy. They recognised that socially created wealth could legitimately be used for social purposes, even if this required change in the existing order of property rights. They did not call themselves socialists, though Hobhouse coined the term 'liberal socialism', but they shared the short-term goals of those in the Labour Party – itself not then an avowedly socialist party.

This became clear after the crushing defeat of the Balfour administration in 1905. The Liberal-led majority of 1906 to 1914 spanned a wide divergence of political views. On the Left, Labour MPs gave it their support. On the right, relics of Gladstonian liberalism, still espousing the agenda of the nineteenth-century liberal *laissez-faire*, were kept on board. But the intellectual energy came from the New Liberals. Their ideas drove the 1910 government, which legislated for reform of the House of Lords, improved working conditions, an embryonic welfare system and progressive taxation.

The new Liberals were people who were both liberals with a small 'l' and social democrats, also in the lower case, living on the cusp of a new political age, transitional figures spanning the period from one dominant ethic to another. All sought far-reaching social reform. However, the Liberal coalition disintegrated after the 1916 split, and by 1918 the Tories had captured Lloyd George and wiped out Asquith's Liberals. It was therefore the Labour Party which began to take the lead. But the ideas of the pre-war reformers lived on, sometimes in the Labour Party, sometimes in the Liberal Party, sometimes beyond party. J.A. Hobson was probably the most famous Liberal convert to what was then literally 'new Labour'. But Labour never fully absorbed the whole tradition, we had our own agenda.

Clause IV

Labour's ideological compass was set in 1918, when it adopted its first statement of objects. At the behest of Sidney Webb, the party established 'clear red water' between itself and the Liberals, in the form of Clause IV of the party constitution. Seventy years on, Clause IV has assumed a particular meaning, but at the time Sidney Webb saw the 'socialist clause' as a fudge. He would have been astonished to learn that Clause IV was still in existence seventy-five years later. He would have been amused that his clause had assumed totemic status on the left of the party. And he would have been appalled that the party's whole economic and social debate was subsumed for so long under the question of ownership.

The organisational structures of the party are also important, and I will address them soon. Quite naturally, as a party born out of the trade unions and formed largely to represent people at work, the trade unions had a major say in party structures. As the class contours of society changed, however, this has meant that the party has struggled against a perception that it had too narrow a base in its membership, finance and decision-making.

Social-ism

The phrase New Labour New Britain which the party is using today is therefore intended to be more than a slogan. It describes where we are in British politics today. It embodies a concept of national renewal led by a renewed Labour Party. It has three elements: ideology, organisation and programme. The ideological re-foundation of the party took place through the revision of Clause IV. The party clearly said that we are in politics to pursue certain values, not implement an economic dogma. Since the collapse of Communism, the ethical base of socialism is the only one that has stood the test of time. This socialism is based on the moral assertion that individuals are interdependent, that they owe duties to one another as well as themselves, that the good society backs up the efforts of the individuals within it, and that common humanity demands that everyone be given a platform on which to stand. It has objective basis too, rooted in the belief that only by recognising their interdependence will individuals flourish, because the good of each does depend on the good of all. This concept of socialism requires a form of politics in which we share responsibility both to fight poverty, prejudice and unemployment, and to create the conditions in which we can truly build one nation – tolerant, fair, enterprising, inclusive. That, fundamentally, was Attlee's kind of socialism, and it is also mine.

Once socialism is defined in this way – as social-ism – we can be liberated from our history and not chained by it. We can avoid the confusion of means and ends inherent in the 1918 definition of socialist purpose. Most important, by re-establishing our identity on our terms, we can regain the intellectual confidence to take on and win the battle of ideas. Because as I have said again and again since becoming leader, the choice is not between principle and power. That was the foolishness of the 1980s.

One member, one vote

But to be the people's party we must also look at the kind of party we are. The Party was born out of the desire to give working people a voice in the government of the country. That is why Labour was founded as the Labour Representation Committee. But the bedrock of the Party in the hopes and aspirations of trade unionists was quickly broadened to include people who joined out of belief in Labour's aims and values.

In organisational terms the consequences of the origins of the Party was the block vote, which sustained the leadership of the Party until the 1960s and 1970s, when the structure of accountability and organisation broke down. The Party lost contact with the electorate, and in the name of internal party democracy gave away its ultimate source of accountability – the people at large. That is why the change to One Member One Vote, and the changes in the organisation of the party conference are so important.

The nature of the party – who is in it, how their interests are articulated, how the decisions are made, the boundaries of what is possible and desirable, even how we behave towards each other – helps define the politics and the policies of the Party. That is why I attach such importance to mass membership. In 1945 we were truly representative of the country at large: we had candidates from all classes, all professions, all regions. George Orwell spoke of the 'skilled workers, technical experts, airmen, scientists, architects and journalists, the people who feel at home in the radio and ferro-concrete age' who would lead Labour's drive for change after the war. Today I want Labour to be a party which has in its membership the self-employed and the unemployed, small business people and their customers, managers and workers, home-owners and council tenants, skilled engineers as well as skilled doctors and teachers.

In addition to having more members, plans are in hand to give them greater say in conference decisions. We shouldn't forget that it was the unions themselves that have proposed gradually reducing the block vote. We want to repeat the success of the Clause IV consultation exercise, except this time on policy issues. We want the policy forum to establish itself as a platform for more open and constructive discussion than is possible on the floor of conference.

On the basis of values and organisation we can develop our programme. Socialists have to be both moralists and empiricists. Values are fundamental. But if socialism is not merely to be an abstract moralism, it has to be made real in the world as it is and not as we would like it to be. As Tony Wright put it in his book *Socialisms*: 'If a socialism without a moral doctrine is impossible, then a socialism without an empirical theory can become a mere fantasy.'

Our objectives

Our values do not change. Our commitment to a different version of society stands intact. But the ways of achieving that vision must change. The programme we are in the process of constructing entirely reflects our values. Its objectives would be instantly recognisable to our founders:

- to equip our country for massive economic and technological change;
- to provide jobs and security for all in this new world;
- to ensure that there are available to all strong public services that depend on the needs and not the wealth of those who use them;
- to attack poverty by reform of the welfare state and the labour market;
- to rebuild a sense of civic pride and responsibility in the world, not in isolation but as a leader among a community of nations.

114

What have changed are the means of achieving these objectives. Those should and will cross the old boundaries between left and right, progressive and conservative. They did in 1945. What marks us out are the objectives and the sense of unity and national purposes by which we are now driven.

On the economy, we have moved beyond the old battles between public and private sector. Instead we promote a modern industrial partnership between government and industry and at the workplace to achieve sustainable growth and high employment.

On welfare, the Labour objective is not to keep people on benefit, but to grant the financial independence that comes from employment. The world of work has changed since Beveridge – unemployment is often long term, the family is changing as women go out to work, and many pensioners live long enough to need care and not just income. We need a new settlement on welfare for a new age, where opportunity and responsibility go together.

On education, we seek excellence for all and not just a few, because Britain's problem has never been the education of an elite: quality education for all is our goal. An end to top-down bureaucracy. Schools should be free to run their own affairs. Local Education Authorities should be judged on whether they raise standards. And parents should have more say in the education of their children.

But beyond that we must tackle the third of schools that are poor or failing, changing from our outdated system of divided vocational and academic studies, and start to put in place the goal of lifelong learning that is crucial in a modern world. Schools need pressure and support, and under Labour they will get both.

On crime, hardly mentioned in the 1945 campaign – though who can doubt that the securities and solidarities of the post-war settlement contributed to the tranquillity of the post-war decades – we must recognise that it is traditional Labour voters who are most vulnerable to the terror of gangs and burglars and muggers. We all know some of the sources of anti-social behaviour: social decay, unemployment, lack of opportunity. But we know too that alienation is no excuse for crime, which is why Labour in government will be committed to attack crime itself and its causes.

On health, Labour's objective is a public health system that promotes good health and an NHS rebuilt as a people's service, free of market dogma, but also free of the old and new bureaucratic constraints, serving all the people, with doctors, nurses and administrators working as part of a unified system. That means GPs and health authorities teaming up to plan care, hospitals with operational freedom, and resources directed to meet need.

On the constitution, we face a massive task that the 1945 government did not address: to modernise our institutions of government to make them fit for the twenty-first century. There is no place for hereditary voting peers in the House of Lords. There should be no assumption of government secrecy, which is why a Freedom of Information Act is essential. And there should be no scope for the abuse of people's rights, which is why we are committed to a Bill of Rights. The trust that the British people had in the virtue of government fifty years ago does not exist today, and that is why we must reinvent government to reform Britain. Political renewal is an essential part of the economic and social renewal we all seek.

And on Europe, our objective must surely be international co-operation for mutual benefit. That benefit should come in the form of better economic performance, environmental improvement and secure defence. Labour will work for these goals, driven by the knowledge that the peoples of Europe prosper when they work together.

The long haul
I hope I have made it clear that I am in this for the long haul. We

were set up as a majority party in Britain, and the time has come to fulfil that destiny in government.

It is not to win an election, or even push through important changes after winning, or even force other parties to adapt to the political parameters that you establish. The 1945 government did these things: its great glory was that, unlike other progressive or left-of-centre governments this century, it did establish an enduring social and economic settlement. But the 1945 government did not presage with a further period of Labour rule.

Our task now is nothing less than national renewal, rebuilding our country as a strong and active civil society backing up the efforts of the individuals within it. That requires economic renewal, social renewal, and political renewal. But in setting out on our project, we should gain confidence from the government of 1945.

Confidence in our values. Confidence in our insights. Confidence in our ability not just to promise change but to deliver it. For that and many other reasons, I am delighted to honour the generation of 1945. They have set an example which it is an honour to follow.

'The power of the message'

New Statesman, 29 September 1995

By September 1995, Blair had established himself as a dynamic and bold leader of his Party. The vote on a revised Clause IV of the Labour Party constitution at a special conference in April had gone in his favour by a margin of nine to one. Through a series of ministerial resignations and scandals, coupled with parliamentary rebellions over Europe, John Major's government was being drained of authority. In this article for the New Statesman *published on the Friday before Labour's annual conference, Blair warns against complacency, and sets out his Party's programme.*

This week's Labour Party conference will be judged primarily by the public according to whether Labour has shown itself to be a party able to take the country forward. It will be judged by three other audiences however. First, by the delegates themselves, according to how far it has brought them into Labour's policy-making process. Second, by the Labour leadership, according to whether the Party has continued on the road to government. Third, by the Tories, according to whether Labour has inflicted any unnecessary wounds on itself. If we all keep those different judgements in our minds throughout the week, there should be a lot of disappointed Tories come Friday lunchtime, and a further reinvigorated Labour Party ready to build a new Britain.

The judgement that I personally shall make on Friday is whether we have been able to build on the success of new Labour over the past year by turning our attentions to building a programme to change Britain. It is new Britain that is our goal. New Labour is the means. Last year 'New Labour. New Britain' was our conference slogan. This year we must concentrate on showing clearly how we can make new Britain a reality.

Conference is also a time to look back. My judgement has always been that to renew from the dark days of 1983, Labour needs a quantum leap to become a serious party of government again. That process started under Neil Kinnock, continued under John Smith, and is now being taken further forward. Last year, I set us the major task of updating our ideology and improving our organisation so that, while remaining true to our principles, we revolutionised the manner in which they apply to the modern world.

The debate surrounding the revision of our constitution, announced at Blackpool last year, was a tremendous success for New Labour. The way the party conducted the debate was a sign of the strength, unity and maturity. Ideas were discussed. Issues raised. Members had their say. And at the special conference in April there was overwhelming support for change. The purpose of revision was simple: to state clearly and accurately what we stand for as a political party. It was a process not of destruction but of rebirth. The new statement says what we are – a democratic socialist party committed to common action for common good, determined to put power, wealth and opportunity in the hands of the many not the few, clear that rights are matched by responsibilities, and always seeking to extend social justice, economic prosperity, democracy and environmental protection to all the people.

The organisational changes have been equally important. We have increased membership by more than 120,000 in a year and it is now above 350,000. by the next election, more than half of our members will have joined since 1992. Those members are being given a direct say in the decisions of the party. They backed the change of Clause IV by nine to one. MPs are now elected by one member, one vote. Our relationship with the trade unions is being put on a new footing to reflect increased participation by ordinary trade unionists. The process reflects change that centre-left parties all over the world are undertaking.

The pace of change has been fast but the necessity for change cannot be underestimated. Without power, none of our hopes for Britain can be fulfilled. It is more than 25 years since Labour won 40 per cent of the vote. It is more than 21 years since we won an election. By 1996, we will have been out of power for longer than any other mainstream party of the left in the Western world. Our 1992 vote was actually lower than our 1979 vote. The swing required at the next election is larger than any required since 1945. And the Boundary Commission changes increased the swing required to 4.3 per cent. So the task is immense.

The task now is to gain the trust of the British people by presenting a programme for change that is radical, sensible, and in touch with their aspirations. Over the past year, we have laid strong foundations for our programme, with detailed policy documents on, among other things, health, education, the economy, crime, access to justice and the information superhighway. Some new key moves will be announced this week, and other areas will be developed throughout the next year. I want the party to show the same enthusiasm for debate and pragmatism over our policy programme as it showed last year over the proposed changes to Clause IV.

There is much to debate, but the themes of our programme for a new Britain are clear already. It should be based on measures to create lasting prosperity, a fair society and a new politics.

Our economic performance determines the way we can afford to live. Today, more than three years after the end of the last recession, we are suffering the effects of long-term neglect of economic fundamentals. Investment is sluggish. The housing market is flat. Very high levels of unemployment remain an economic burden and a social blight. To prepare for the new challenges of a vastly changed economic landscape, we need a new start.

Globalisation is changing the nature of the nation state as power becomes more diffuse and borders more porous. Technological change is reducing the power and capacity of government to control a domestic economy free from external influence. The role of government in this world of change is to represent a national interest, to create a competitive base of physical infrastructure and human skills. The challenge before our Party this year is not how to slow down the pace of change and so get off the world, but to educate and retrain for the next technologies, to prepare our country for new global competition, and to make our country a competitive base from which to produce the goods and services people want to buy.

The key to this is Labour's commitment to promoting long-term investment in order to secure growth and stability. For example, over the next year we will be examining the CBI's proposal to levy a lower rate on long-term share holdings. We will be looking at reforms of the takeover system, and how the public interest could better be served. And we will learn from best practice in the US where institutional investors are required to participate in decision-making about the composition of company boards and the appointment of non-executive directors.

A commitment to a fair society must be based on firm political ground. Over the past year we have been reclaiming ground we should never have lost to the Conservatives. Freedom. Responsibility. Family. Efficiency. These are Labour words and we should never have allowed them to be taken away. That is why it is right that tenants should be free from irresponsible behaviour by their neighbours. It is right that fathers retain responsibility for their children even after a divorce. And it is right that we attack waste to ensure that every penny of public money is well spent, because precisely the people who can least afford tax revenue to be wasted are those whom Labour was set up to represent.

This year we must build from that firm basis of values. It will require pragmatism and tough decisions. We will continue to develop plans to make welfare a springboard to work. And I am particularly keen to look at taking practical steps to lift school standards as a way of creating a fairer, more united society. David Blunkett will be looking in detail at the selection, training and monitoring of heads and teachers; at how best to extend under-fives' provision; at how to promote home-school contracts; and at how to augment the teaching profession by creating senior teachers from the best of the profession and associate teachers from the community. Labour's ambitions for national renewal also require a new relationship between government and citizens – a genuine reinvention of government. This means more openness, more decentralisation, more democracy, more checks on government power, and an end to sleaze. We have a vast programme of change already agreed that will represent a radical and lasting testament to a Labour government. It is important that we use this year to explain and promote these plans. It will be a busy conference and a busy year. We may not meet again before the election and I want all sections of the Party to be part of our campaign. I have lost track of the number of times that I have warned against complacency and indulgence since becoming leader. Taking victory for granted, or believing that opinion-poll leads allow us to take risks with the public's trust, would be catastrophic for Labour. It is what the Tories want us to do. The fight against complacency will go on until the election and after. Our success will be based on the power of our message. The Tories have betrayed the people because they have failed. The public knows that we have had the courage to change ourselves. We are in the process of showing that we have the ability to change Britain.

'Power with a purpose'

Renewal, October 1995

There is a world of difference between this article for Renewal *in October 1995 and the one Blair penned in 1993. In two years, Blair had been elected as Party leader, refashioned the Party's constitution, repositioned his Party's policies, and was being taken seriously as a future prime minister. This piece serves as a useful benchmark for Blair's progress to date, and an early guide to the key themes of the election campaign two years later.*

Labour's task at the end of the twentieth century is to find answers to two fundamental questions. First, how we cope with, and how we shape, the economic changes of the global economy to provide prosperity and security for all our people. Second, how we develop a modern form of social rules – a set of parameters and boundaries recognised and accepted by society as a whole and enforced to the benefit of all. A strong civic society must be able to achieve these ends.

This is a distinct Labour message because we understand the scale of change and are willing to organise our society to meet it. We recognise the need for a new moral purpose in politics and have the individual family and social values capable of sustaining it. The left recognises that you cannot build economic or social stability without social cohesion and that we must build a community where all citizens have a stake. To achieve this we must break down the barriers that hold people back. And finally, we must be outward-looking as a nation, not insular in addressing problems we face in common with other countries.

But the left-of-centre has to provide that it is up to the task. My leadership of the Party is based on the judgement that to become a series party of government again, the Labour Party needed not a serious of adjustments but a quantum leap. We had to reconnect our ideology and organisation so that, whilst remaining true to our principles, we updated completely the manner in which they applied to the modern world. In the last year we have made a lot of progress and I believe we are now beginning to reconnect with the British people in a way that we have not done for many years.

As I never tire of reminding people, there is still a very long way to go. And without power none of our dreams for Britain can be fulfilled. It is over twenty years since Labour won 40 per cent of the vote. It is more than twenty-one years since we won an election. By 1996 we will have been out of power for longer than any other mainstream party of the left in the Western world. Our 1992 vote was actually lower than our 1979 vote. And the swing required at the next election is larger than any required since 1945. So the task is immense.

Security in a changing world: a New Labour approach
Preparing the nation for economic change and re-establishing a sense of social order will require us to go beyond the old solutions of both the old left and new right which are quite simply not up to the task.

The old left solution of rigid economic planning and state control won't work. What is more, during the 1960s and 1970s the left developed almost in substitution for its economic prescriptions – which by then were failing – a type of social individualism that sometimes confused liberation from prejudice with a disregard for moral structures. It fought for racial and sexual equality, which was entirely right, but it appeared indifferent to the family and individual responsibility, which was wrong. Moreover, as the influence of some of the traditional supporters of the left in Labour and working-class organisation waned there was a real danger, occasionally realised, that single-issue pressure groups moved into the vacuum. I believe that this was an aberration. Look back to the first heyday of the left in the 1930s and 1940s and you will find heavy emphasis on responsibility, self-improvement and the family.

When we talk about strong families, responsibility and duty, being tough on crime, running an efficient economy, we are not aping the Tories but recapturing values that are rightfully ours. These things are what working-class Labour families up and down the country believe in. If these values are Tory values then no wonder we've lost the last four elections.

Similarly when I talk about being tough on crime and tough on the causes of crime, it is a message cheered to the echoes in housing estates across the land, where working people, often trapped in poverty or unemployment, are tormented by criminal behaviour, anti-social or violent neighbours, and drugs. It is to them we speak as much as to so-called Middle England.

When I talk of rights being accompanied by responsibilities, it is also a message that is common sense to traditional working-class families. And when I talk about the importance of strong families, I am talking about the foundation for a cohesive society and for strong communities. They are common sense Labour values and it is time we spoke up for them again.

The new right has equally failed to meet the fundamental challenge of providing security in a world of change. Though it asked some of the right questions in the 1980s about how we could be more enterprising as a nation, in the end it was a project more successful at destroying than creating. It failed to tackle investment in capacity and people and to cut long-term unemployment, just as it failed on education, the NHS, crime and welfare reform.

Socially, the Conservatives found few solutions to the social breakdown that they themselves had accelerated. The right developed a form of economic libertarianism that often lapsed into greed, selfishness and moral irresponsibility. The right's wish to abdicate its responsibility from preparing people for change is why it is incapable of meeting the challenges that people are facing.

We must move beyond the solutions of the old left and the new right. Forging this new agenda will take time. There are no easy solutions. But I believe it is only a reinvigorating left-of-centre that is capable of helping people cope with change.

First, the choice is not between resisting change and just letting it happen. Not between the state trying to run industry or some rather crude version of *laissez-faire* liberalism. Investing in education and skills; putting in place a system of lifelong learning; a partnership between public and private sector to renew a nation's infrastructure; backing for small business; ensuring the country is at the forefront of science and research; regenerating run-down inner-city areas and regions; above all creating the right framework for the harnessing and developing of new technologies; all require active government. That does not necessarily mean government from the centre. It may be a mix of public and private enterprise. It may not be government at all, but the private sector, given a strong competitive framework in which to exist, or the voluntary sector, a potential third force that can deliver services in a far more imaginative and creative way. But without a government that recognises the scale of the challenge and has some sense of urgency in acting to meet it, change will end up being perceived as an enemy and not a friend, a threat and not an opportunity.

Second, the left-of-centre is the true position of moral purpose today. The only way to rebuild social order is through strong values, socially shared, inculcated through individual and family. This is not some lurch into authoritarianism or an attempt to impose a regressive personal morality. It is, in fact, about justice and fairness. The strong and powerful can protect themselves. Those who lose most through the absence of rules are the weak and the vulnerable. The first casualties of social breakdown are often the poor and disadvantaged. That is why the left should treat it seriously.

Why is it the left that is best able to tackle the problem of social disorder? Because a society based on strong values has at its heart respect for others and mutual responsibilities. Obligation to more than oneself. Crude individualism of left or right won't work. The family is important because it is in the family that self-respect and respect for others are learned. It is in the family that that the limits of freedom are first experienced and the roots of responsibility put down. The family is the antithesis of narrow selfishness.

Of course, elements of the right, at least in theory, would assert notions of respect for others, but this is about more than not mugging your neighbour. It is where the traditional values of left, applied practically to the modern world, are our strength. The left can fashion a new moral purpose for a nation which combines individual and social responsibility and which can assert the importance of social rules and order, because through its belief in social justice and mutual respect it has some chance of achieving them. It has the moral authority to enforce the rules because it sets them within an active and strong community.

Attacking the establishment

I believe that many of those who supported the Tories in the 1980s were not really Tories but anti-establishment. But in reality many of the Tories wanted nothing more than to buy it out. The personnel has been changed slightly but the attitudes have not. Building a meritocracy is not about replacing a hereditary elite based on birth with a similar elite only this time based on wealth. It must be about giving more people the opportunities and chances to share in the nation's wealth and power.

The aim must be to break down the barriers so that every one of our citizens has the chances to get on and succeed. We are still a country riddled with old boy networks, cosy cartels, restrictive practices.

These are Labour's enemies. These are the people that hold the consumer to ransom and shut down opportunities for ordinary families. Our legal system is a nest of restrictive practices. The intake of Oxford and Cambridge from public schools has barely shifted in thirty years. Our education system is divided. We have hereditary peers voting on legislation in the House of Lords. And monopolies and cartels mean the privatised utilities, for example, seem to be run in the interest of directors and not consumers. We are light years away from being a true meritocracy – a country in which the talents of all can flourish.

New Labour

I have shown why I believe New Labour is the party most capable of meeting the new challenges that face us and providing the leadership the country needs. In short there are five key components to New Labour.

First, New Labour moves beyond the solutions of the old left and new right. We are a radical party that rejects some of the bureaucratic solutions of the old left, and the market dogma of the new right which has been shown not to work, and instead forges a new agenda around our core values and our beliefs in building a strong civil society. We believe in a partnership between public and private sectors, a better deal for consumers, an end to boom and bust, and making the use of new technology so that we provide the security and skills people need.

Second, New Labour distinguishes ends from means. That is what the change to Clause IV was all about. The commitment to wholesale nationalisation and an old-fashioned view of production have been replaced by a clear statement of the left-of-centre's values: power, wealth and opportunity for all, social justice, equality between people; democracy, respect for the environment; an international, not insular, view of Britain; support for family and community life. It is our values that form the basis of our socialism, not an economic prescription fashioned a century ago.

Third, New Labour reclaims the ground that we should never have let go of. Freedom. Responsibility. Family. Efficiency. These are Labour words and we should never have let the Tories take them from us. It is right that with opportunity comes responsibility. It is right that we are the party that supports the family.

Fourth, New Labour develops new ideas for the changing world. A global economy and a social revolution mean that we must find new thinking to address new problems. Welfare must adapt to new work patterns and for a new workforce. These important questions cannot be answered by the old ideologies. I have explained in this article why I believe only the left is able to meet these challenges.

Fifth, New Labour draws strength from the grassroots so that it is in touch with the people we seek to represent. The rise in membership of more than 120,000 has resulted in a new culture of openness. As the Clause IV vote in favour of change showed, grassroots members are in touch with mainstream opinion. By the next election more than half of our members will have joined since 1992. Those members are being given a direct say in the decisions of the Party. They backed the change to Clause IV by nine to one. MPs are now elected by one member one vote. Our relationship with the trade unions is being put on a new footing to reflect the participation of ordinary trade unionists on a basis in which no special favours are owed to anyone.

In short, my politics are simple, not complex. I believe you can have a country of ambition and aspiration with compassion and a sense of duty to others. The individual prospers best within a strong and decent, cohesive society. These are the real ends of the left-of-centre. The means of achieving them will, of course, vary from generation to generation and they should be pragmatically, not ideologically, driven.

Based on this central belief and the principles enshrined in our new constitution we are building a policy platform to address the need for security and social stability in a world of change. It is these key issues that this journal has begun to address and I hope will continue to explore in the coming months:

- partnership between a thriving private sector and public enterprise to prepare the country for economic change;
- partnership at work and an end to the old conflicts between management and workforce;
- a revolution in our country's education and skills;
- the reform of welfare to make it, as it should be, a platform of opportunity, not a recipe for dependency. Tackling the new challenges posed by the growing number of old people who will need both the security of a decent pension and affordable elderly care;
- public services that are accountable and decentralised while rejecting two-tierism and division;
- a programme to fight crime that recognises both prevention and punishment – tough on crime and tough on the causes of crime;
- democracy that is open, reformed and devolved;
- engaging constructively with Europe so that we can shape it to meet Britain's needs.

There will inevitably be overlap between right and left in the politics of the twenty-first century. The era of the grand ideologies, all-encompassing, all-pervasive, total in their solutions – and often dangerous – is over. In particular, the battle between the market and public sector is over. The value systems and the objectives will, of course, be different but there will be some policy convergence and we should be relaxed, not tribal, about that.

This should reflect itself in a more open, more pluralistic style of government, with a more healthy exchange of ideas. The lesson we learn from Labour's great reforming government of 1945 is that we need a broad coalition of support on the left. It was, after all, the Liberals Beveridge and Keynes who were two of the most influential drivers of post-war change. Just as it was the radical New Liberals at the beginning of the century who sought far-reaching social change.

I believe that the left-of-centre is beginning to be reborn in this country with a new purpose and a new vigour. We have a story to tell about the way in which we can shape change for the benefit of all our citizens, and the way in which we can provide stability and social order amidst upheaval. Our traditional values and instincts, now enshrined in our constitution, guide us while the means of achieving our goal of a strong civic society will change.

The process of change is not complete. It will continue. It reflects change that left-of-centre parties all over the world are undertaking.

It is this debate about the challenges of the coming century that should engage all of us on the left-of-centre. I welcome a debate on these key questions where the left should be providing the lead. *Renewal* is a journal that has recognised the need for modernisation from the beginning. It has been a valuable forum for debate. Its relaunch this month will, I hope, give it a new lease of life as a journal that will continue to think imaginatively and fearlessly, giving a platform to a wide range of views on the left. The left, I believe, is back in business – ready to provide the leadership this country needs. It must now show the confidence and open mindedness to map out this new course for Britain.

If we are given the chance to serve, I believe passionately that Britain will be a better place. We will no longer be settling for second best but be proud once again of our country. I believe that those who have felt excluded from the mainstream of society will be given the opportunity to get on, that the economy will be run in the interests of all, and that people will feel more secure, that their children are taught in better schools, the NHS is safe and not about to be sold off, and that our streets are safer to walk on. But, perhaps less tangibly, I believe that people will see Britain as a more tolerant, less divided, more outward-looking and optimistic country where all our citizens feel they have a future.

Labour Party conference speech
Brighton, 3 October 1995

In his second address as leader to the party faithful in October 1995 in Brighton, Blair uses the most overtly biblical language of any major address before or since: 'I am my brother's keeper. I will not walk by on the other side.' The theme for the speech – the young country – resonated with the times – the mid-nineties' Cool Britannia zeitgeist – and with Blair's own youthful exuberance. He jokes about the nicknames he has already earned – Bambi, Stalin – and about his famous photo opportunity with Kevin Keegan the previous autumn.

He also uses the public speaker's most trusted device: the anecdote, in this case about his walk down the Mall with the crowd calling 'Get the Tories out!' The section on tough choices – over university student funding, public sector pay, and tackling inflation – predicts accurately some of his government's later difficulties.

I know that for some New Labour has been painful. There is no greater pain to be endured in politics than the birth of a new idea. But I believe in it, and I want to tell you why. Socialism to me was never about nationalisation or the power of the state; not just about economics, or politics even. It is a moral purpose in life; a set of values; a belief in society, in cooperation, in achieving together what we are unable to achieve alone. It is how I try to live my life.

The simple truths: I am worth no more than anyone else. I am my brother's keeper. I will not walk by on the other side. We aren't simply people set in isolation from each other, face to face with eternity, but members of the same family, the same community, the same human race. This is my socialism. And the irony of our long years in opposition is that those values are shared by the vast majority of the British people.

I joined the Labour Party because it represented those values. But I felt something else: that, however great and timeless our values, our Party's politics, its structure and even its ideology no longer reflected those values in a way that brought them alive for the people. We were separated from the very people we said we represented. We called them 'our people' while forgetting who they were.

1983 was for me a watershed. Since then we have transformed our Party – our constitution rewritten; our relations with the trade unions changed; our Party organisation improved; political education on an unprecedented scale; new policy; breaking new ground.

But I didn't come into politics to change the Labour Party. I came into politics to change the country. And I honestly believe that if we had not changed, if we had not returned our Party to its values, freed from the weight of outdated ideology, we could not change the country. We could not win, and even if we did we would not have governed in the way Britain needs. For I do not want a one-term Labour government that dazzles for a moment then ends in disillusionment. I want a Labour government that governs for a generation and changes Britain for good.

It has been hard, I know. Hard for me sometimes – 1994 Bambi; 1995 Stalin. From Disneyland to dictatorship in twelve short months. I am not sure which one I prefer. Okay, I prefer Bambi. Honestly.

There have been some good moments. In 1995, for the first time since I became leader, my children were impressed by something I did. Did you really meet Kevin Keegan, Dad? Did you really do twenty-seven consecutive headers?

I have spent years being angry, passionate and indignant – about young people huddled in doorways, families made wretched by unemployment, the poor unable to make ends meet. I am fed up with anger. I tell you, they don't need our anger – they need action.

And they will get it not through the rage of opposition but through a Labour Party that has had the courage to take hard choices, get into government, and do something for them.

And let me tell you, the hard choices get harder in government:

- when we refuse to take risks with inflation because this country cannot be rebuilt on boom and bust, even to boost short-term unemployment;
- when we want more children at university but know that, though the student loan scheme will be replaced, we face hard choices about what its replacement will be;
- on public sector pay, when a Labour government, like any other, will have to say no as well as yes – even to people in this hall.

Hard choices are what good government is about.

I love my Party. I just hate it being in opposition. I love my country. And I hate what the Tories have done to it.

* * *

I want us to be a young country again. With a common purpose. With ideals we cherish and live up to. Not resting on past glories. Not fighting old battles. Not sitting back, hand on mouth, concealing a yawn of cynicism, but ready for the day's challenge. Ambitious. Idealistic. United. Where people succeed on the basis of what they give to their country, rather than what they take from their country. Saying not 'this was a great country' but 'Britain can and will be a great country again'.

* * *

The coming election is not a struggle for political power. It is a battle for the soul of our nation.

During the 1995 VJ Day celebrations, I was on a platform with Tory ministers. As we walked down the Mall, there were thousands of people, holding their Union Jacks, and it soon became clear – to the horror of the Tories – that many of them were Labour supporters. They were waving and shouting and urging me to 'get the Tories out'. These people love this country. It is because they love this country that they look to Labour to change it. This is the patriotic party because it is the people's party.

As the Tories wave their Union Jacks I know what so many people will be thinking. I know what people will want to say to those Tories. It is no good waving the fabric of our flag when you have spent sixteen years tearing apart the fabric of our nation, tearing apart the bonds that tie communities together and make us a united kingdom, tearing apart the security of those people, clutching their Union Jacks, swelling with pride at their victory over tyranny, and yelling at me to 'get those Tories out', because they want security, because they want to leave a better world for their children and their grandchildren than they created for themselves and because they know the Tories cannot supply it.

Decent people. Good people. Patriotic people. When I hear people urging us to fight for 'our people', I want to say: these are our people. They are the majority. And we must serve them, and build that new Britain, that young country, for their children and their families. I make them this promise: I will do all I can to get the Tories out. And I will devote every breath that I breathe, every sinew of my body, to ensuring that their grandchildren do get to live in that new Britain in a new and better world.

The prize is immense. It is new Britain. One Britain: the people united by shared values and shared aims, a government governing for all the people, the party founded by the people back, truly as the people's party. New Labour. New Britain. The Party renewed, the country reborn.

John Smith memorial lecture
London, 7 February 1996

The furthest reaching and most enduring of the changes Labour made in its first term in office is the programme of constitutional reform. The government established a parliament for Scotland, an assembly for Wales, city government for London, and tackled the hereditary peers in the House of Lords.

In this lecture, delivered in London in February 1996 to commemorate John Smith, Blair maps out the rationale for constitutional reform. This selection includes the opening section and the final section, where Blair quotes Thomas Jefferson. The central section, not published here, was a detailed argument in favour of reforms to local government, including elected city mayors, devolved government for London, Scotland and Wales, reform of the Lords, and freedom of information. Blair makes a direct appeal to the Liberal Democrats to cooperate on the reform agenda. It contains many pledges delivered; it also contains some – a referendum on reform of the electoral system for the House of Commons, and a 'new politics' – for which we are still waiting.

I cannot believe that we are so lacking in courage or are so complacent that we cannot rise to the challenge of renewing our democracy. Of course, there are crucial points of implementation that can be returned to, in detail, at the appropriate time before the election. But let us first agree the terms of this debate: change or no change. And let those who form the latter camp, opposing all change, justify their position as a matter of principle and not avoid it by skirmishing in the thicket of detail.

It follows from this that I do not regard changing the way we are governed as an afterthought, a detailed fragment of our programme. I regard it as an essential part of new Britain, of us becoming a young, confident country again.

My vision is this:

- an economy in which we are enhancing opportunity for people in a new global market of massive economic and technological change;
- a society that is one nation, in which all are included;
- a politics in which we are giving power back to the people.

A stake in the economy, a stake in society, a stake in the political system.

And I will work with all those of goodwill who believe in the need for political change. If the political debate were not so narrow and crabbed by the onslaught of the pre-election struggle, then I believe there are Conservatives who would support at least some of the changes we propose. For this agenda to have legitimacy it must have consent on the broadest possible basis. Already the Liberal Democrats have said they will work with us to secure it – indeed in some respects they want to go further – and I welcome that. Let the new way of governing be accompanied by a new politics and if there are areas of profound disagreement let them be confronted honestly.

A large part of the Tory case will be to say: all politicians are the same. Dragged down themselves, they believe it is in their interest to drag us all down ... But we should not let cynicism drive out real debate about the condition of Britain. We are offering a different and new type of politics. We believe in it and our commitment to share power and hand it back to the people is our earnest expression of it. So what is the task we have set ourselves? Our ambition is to create a young Britain with a new politics which treats people as full citizens, gives them greater power over government.

* * *

The Tories oppose all measures to give people a real stake in our democracy. They want to keep power for the few not the many – for the centre, for the unelected and for hereditary peers.

New Labour wants to give power to the people. To be a government working in partnership with the people, which gives them freedom, choice and responsibility and where the country is more united, more open and more confident about the future than it has been in decades.

That is the choice and this is the future we want to build in the name of John Smith.

I conclude with the words of Thomas Jefferson: 'Men, by their constitutions, are naturally divided into two parties. One – those who fear and distrust the people, and wish to draw all powers from them into the hands of the higher classes. Two – those who identify themselves with the people, have confidence in them, cherish and consider them as the most honest and safe depository of the public interests. In every country these two parties exist, and in everyone where they are free to think, speak and write, they will declare themselves.'

I know which was the party of John Smith and I am proud to follow in his footsteps.

Foreword to *The Personal World: John Macmurray on Self and Society*

by Philip Conford (Floris Books), 1996

At Oxford University in the early seventies, Tony Blair found inspiration, not from Marx or Mao, but John Macmurray. Blair came to the ideas of this slightly obscure Scottish Christian philosopher via his mentor Peter Thomson.

Macmurray's central thesis is that individuals thrive only in the context of a strong and mutually reinforcing society, and that individuals can take responsibility for their own destiny and the shape of their own society. From Macmurray flows Blair's acceptance of Christian Socialism, and from there his dedication to Labour politics, in its ethical, communitarian incarnation.

In July 1994, just after his election to the Labour leadership, Blair told the Scotland on Sunday *newspaper, 'If you really want to understand what I'm all about you have to take a look at a guy called John Macmurray. It's all there.'*

In this introduction to a new edition of Macmurray's writings in 1996, Blair sets a test for philosophy: 'It must either increase an understanding of the world or our ability to change it. At best it can do both. This is a test John Macmurray passes with flying colours.'

John Macmurray is not one of the twentieth century's most famous philosophers. This is surprising. Actually his work is more accessible, better written and above all far more relevant than most of what I and many others studied as hallowed texts at university.

In the end, it is probable that his scope was too ambitious, too definitive for the narrow discipline of academic philosophers. For that reason alone, he is worth reading.

I also find him immensely modern. Not that all his thoughts and judgements did not betray the marks of his time. But rather, he was modern in the sense that he confronted what will be the critical political question of the twenty-first century: the relationship between individual and society. The first half of the twentieth century saw the creation of the great institutions of the collective will – the welfare state and government. The second half saw a reaction to them in the name of the individual who, partly through the power of government, had become more prosperous, was a taxpayer and developed a more individualised set of economic and social attitudes.

Now the task is to construct a new settlement for individual and society today. We have reached the limits of a narrow selfish individualism, but have learnt the mistakes that collective power can make. We desire social stability and know there is an active role for government – the market is not master – but we want it for today, when culture, lifestyle, and personal finances have been transformed.

Macmurray offers two insights. First, he places the individual firmly within a social setting – we are what we are, in part, because of the other, the 'You and I'. We cannot ignore our obligations to others as well as ourselves. This is where modern political notions of community begin.

Secondly, by rooting his vision in the personal world and in intention, he rejects simple determinism. The personal is not submerged in the social or organic.

In religious terms, also, it is easy to see his influence in a whole generation of Christian philosophers. For him, spirituality was based in this world; it was not an abstraction from it. Again, for many young people today, who search for spiritual meaning but who shrink from the notion it can be found in retreat from reason, Macmurray has much to say.

For philosophy to be at all relevant, it must either increase an understanding of the world or the ability to change it. At best, it can do both. This is a test John Macmurray passes with flying colours. I hope more people discover him.

Introduction to *What Needs to Change*

ed. Giles Radice (HarperCollins), 1996

This introduction to a collection of essays by Charles Handy, Patricia Hewitt, David Puttnam, David Marquand, Michael Young and Peter Hennessy amongst others published in 1996 is possibly the most cogent explanation of Blair's definition of socialism as a set of ethics and values. It also defines the difference between Labour and Conservative values, and looks at why Labour failed in the 1970s and 1980s. It concludes with a call to arms for intellectuals to breathe new life into Labour's project.

Blair describes the classic New Labour synthesis: 'ambition is matched by compassion, success by social justice, and rewards by responsibility' and cites the belief of John Smith that radical politics is about developing 'the extraordinary potential of ordinary people'.

Blair's essay appeared just months before Labour's first landslide election victory, at a time of intellectual confidence, excitement and anticipation for Labour's supporters.

I said in my 1995 party conference speech that I wanted to see Britain become a 'young country' again. I meant that instead of trading off our past, we needed to develop the energy, the enthusiasm and the ideas to match the challenges of the future. We need to be proud of our history, but not bound by it; judicious in embracing new ideas, but open to new thinking; above all, aware that we live in a radically changed world from that left by our grandparents, we need to construct a new and radical politics to serve the people in the new century ahead.

My vision is of a Britain that is truly one nation, where we work together to prepare ourselves for massive economic and technological change; to extend opportunity in a world of deep insecurity; to create a genuine civic society where everyone has a stake, where everyone has a responsibility, and where power is pushed down towards the people instead of being hoarded centrally; and to secure our place in the world as a nation cooperating with others in Europe and elsewhere.

I emphasise the idea of Britain as one nation. Without social justice, there will be no modernisation, without mutuality and solidarity there will be no prosperity; without shared values there will be no progress; without responsibility there is no society. A high level of social cohesion is not just urgent in itself; it is essential for an efficient and prosperous economy, which is why we have to bring together a drive for economic efficiency with that for social justice.

Labour is the only party with the aim of doing this. But I have believed for some time that only a changed Labour Party could do it. That is why the first year of my leadership was dominated by modernising the Labour Party; only then could it be the vehicle for modernising Britain. Already much has been done. Our constitution has been rewritten; our relations with the trade unions have been changed; our democratic structures have been renewed. We are opening up the Party so that members can have a much greater part in policy-making. Many more people have been attracted to join and the Party is in touch with the voters.

In 1945, Labour was truly representative of the nation as a whole. In 1964, it summoned up a spirit of national progress. Today, I want the Party to capture the spirit of national renewal. We need new thinking because the old, all-embracing ideologies have given way to a more complex, uncertain world. Labour is now in a position to offer that leadership. We have as members the self-employed and the unemployed, small business people and their customers, managers and workers, home owners and council tenants, skilled engineers as well as skilled doctors and teachers. In touch with the communities we want to serve, we can articulate the realities of daily life, and show how it can be improved.

My politics is in essence quite simple: it is rooted in my values. Values provide a compass with which to navigate one's way through the political jungle. They help define the objectives and character not only of political parties but also of society.

My value system is based on a belief about individuals and the society in which they live. It is only in a strong and active community that the individual thrives. People must have a stake in society – the essence of social justice. They need to work together for what they cannot achieve alone. And they should all fulfil responsibilities to the wider community. These are the principles of practical and popular socialism championed by Keir Hardie and Clement Attlee. And they are the source of Labour's enduring appeal.

I have always thought that its underlying system of values was one of the Labour Party's greatest strengths. It is what makes many people join the Party in the first place. The rejection of injustice, the commitment to solidarity and democracy, the embrace of mutual responsibility motivate members of the Labour Party and resonate in the country. The modernisation of Labour has been in part about trying to get the Party back to those traditional values and removing from it the dead weight of an ideology which had very little to do with its basic purpose.

What happened to the Labour Party in the late 1970s and early 1980s is that its intellectual temple was stormed and captured by a generation of politicians and academics who thought that values and concepts like community and social justice were too weak to guide the party. Since the 1950s, left and right, in the Party and in politics more generally, were defined by the battle for state control of industry. As a result, the Party went through a period when, because for many it justified itself solely in terms of nationalisation, it became divorced from the people it claimed to represent and at the same time subjected itself to continual debate about betrayal. Tragically, it turned its back on an entire strain of thinking within the Labour Party – the tradition of ethical socialism. Yet it is socialism as ethics which has stood the test of time: if it teaches us nothing else, experience in Eastern Europe should teach us that.

With the revision of Clause IV, the Labour Party has reclaimed its basic values. We say that socialism is based on the moral assertion that individuals are interdependent, that they owe duties to one another as well as themselves, and that power, wealth and opportunity should be held by the many, not the few. This moral credo shows itself in our practical commitment to a mixed economy, with public and private sectors both working in the public interest, a fair society that is judged by the condition of the weak as well as the strong, a more democratic politics that diffuses power, and a realisation that we must conserve the environment for the benefit for future generations. I sum it up by saying that we need a society in which ambition is matched by compassion, success by social justice, and rewards by responsibility.

For all the so-called radicalism of the Thatcherites, they wanted not to break up the establishment but to buy it out. Their recipe has not worked. They have cut public spending on investment, but the result is higher taxes to pay for higher spending on the costs of economic failure. They have privatised utilities, but created powerful and unaccountable private monopolies in the process. They said markets would overcome the failures of government, but they created the most centralised and heavy-handed state in peacetime history.

Radical politics, by contrast, is about giving many more people the opportunity to share in the nation's wealth and power. In John Smith's words, it is about developing 'the extraordinary potential of ordinary people'. Labour has always succeeded when it has been the party of popular aspiration and opportunity. In the end, the Tories remain the party of privilege, and as long as that basic dividing line exists, we will be speaking to the needs of the majority in Britain.

The best politics always aspires to the creation of a country which feels itself as a cohesive and united unit, where there is a strong sense of purpose and justice and where people have obligations to each other as well as to themselves.

For far too long we have defined ourselves as a nation not by what unites us but by what divides us. We have a class-ridden and unequal society; a social fabric which is tattered and torn; and a politics where centralisation and secrecy drive out democracy and accountability. The majority of Britons are insecure and unsure of their future. We still have two education systems – one public, one private. We have what amounts to a new 'underclass', cut off and alienated from society.

Part of our job is to ensure that the people frozen out of Tory Britain are brought in from the cold, their talents used, their potential developed. But citizenship is about duties as well as rights. The freedoms won by ordinary people over the past one hundred years are what make this a civilised society today. T. H. Marshall described the process as the century-by-century accretion of civil, political and social rights. The assumptions of hierarchy, deference, and status are broken down, and progress to full citizenship is gradually achieved. But full citizenship requires that people take on new responsibilities too.

That is why I talk of the need to build a new social order in which there is respect for both rights and responsibilities. Not the old social order of hierarchy and repression, but a new one that combines freedom and responsibility in a modern way. In the 1970s and the early 1980s, the left sometimes spoke as though it was possible to divorce rights from responsibilities. It was in a way a social forerunner of the economic individualism of the new right. It rightly fought for racial and sexual equality but it appeared to ignore individual responsibility and the need for family stability. I believe that was an aberration.

When we talk about strong families, responsibility and duty we are not aping the Tories but recapturing values in which our forebears and supporters believe. Similarly, when we talk about being tough on crime and tough on the causes of crime, it is a message warmly welcomed in housing estates across the land, where people, often trapped by poverty and unemployment, are tormented by criminal behaviour, antisocial or violent neighbours, and drugs. This is not a Tory agenda, but a Labour one. And in a world of massive change – economic, social, political – it is more important than ever, because, without it, people become the victims of change, not masters of it.

The Conservatives have failed to provide security for this new world. In fact, they have fought to use insecurity as the only spur for progress. Their economic liberalism has often lapsed into greed, selfishness and moral irresponsibility, while much of what they have done in power has actually helped accelerate social breakdown.

The only way to rebuild social order and stability is through strong values, socially shared, inculcated through individuals, family, government and the institutions of civil society. This is not a lurch into authoritarianism or an attempt to impose a regressive morality. It is, in fact, about justice and fairness, freedom and responsibility. The strong and powerful can protect themselves. Those who lose most through absence of rules are the weak and vulnerable. Unless we act together, the rewards will be hoarded at the top.

It was always short-sighted of the Labour Party to allow the Conservatives to wrap themselves in the national flag and to monopolise and distort the idea of patriotism. Now they run the government not for the nation but in the narrow interests of their party, as their behaviour over the Nolan Committee report on corruption in Parliament, their policy over the European Union and their partisan 1995 Queen's Speech demonstrate.

In 1945 and in 1964 Labour was the party which brought the nation together and gave it a sense of purpose. In the Party's publication *The Spirit of 1945*, there was a letter from a colonel writing home at the end of the war. He predicted that the Labour Party would win by a landslide because, in contrast to the Tories who represented only the 'moneyed interests', Labour was for the 'common man'. It is this idea of the Labour Party as the party of the people, as an inclusive, one-nation party, reaching out to people and bringing them together which is so relevant today.

The concept of one nation is powerfully patriotic. When Michael Portillo exploited the professionalism and bravery of the SAS and tried to whip up anti-European feelings at the Conservative Party conference in October 1995, he revealed not patriotism but xeno-phobic nationalism. Not surprisingly it was deeply resented by many people in the armed forces. Patriotism is about pride in British achievements, in the National Health Service, in the sciences and the arts as well as in the professionalism of our forces, but it is also about a belief in the capacity of the British people to improve themselves and be a force for good, by deed and example, in the wider world. The carer who gives up her time to look after elderly people, the committed teacher who improves standards at school, the devoted civil servant who provides a service to the public, the business executive who wins export orders by developing new products – that too is patriotism. A country with high ambitions and high ideals for itself but also outward-looking and tolerant of others: that is patriotism for the new millennium.

Today's Labour Party – 'New Labour' – is the heir to a proud tradition in the Party's history. The 1945 government combined practicality and idealism in equal measure. It changed Britain in a way that was relevant to the post-war world. It was 'new' Labour. In

1964, Harold Wilson was a moderniser, as his speeches and programmes demonstrate. But despite the considerable achievements of that government he was unable to carry through his project in full. The Wilson government did not fully succeed in modernising the economy or establishing Labour as the natural party of government. Without change within the Party there was bound to be a tension between what he wanted to do and the culture and politics of the Party that had to do it. The modernising edge was blunted.

In the 1990s, a renewed Labour Party is in a much stronger position to lead national renewal. I would highlight four key issues that will be of lasting importance to this country: the creation of a stakeholder economy based on the contribution of the many and not the few; the rebuilding of social cohesion and social justice; the dismantling of unaccountable power, vested interests and class hierarchies; and a new role for Britain in the wider world, and in Europe in particular.

Our economic performance determines the way we can afford to live. But today, four years on from the last recession, we are suffering from the long-term neglect of economic fundamentals. The failure of economic management has caused the Tory government's failure on employment, spending and tax. We have slipped from thirteenth to eighteenth in the world prosperity league because of our failure to modernise and invest.

I believe in a 'stakeholder economy' in which everyone has the opportunity to succeed and everyone has the responsibility to contribute. It is based on the idea that unless we mobilise the efforts and talents of the whole population, we will fail to achieve our economic potential, and continue to fall behind. A stakeholder economy is one in which opportunity is extended, merit rewarded and no group of individuals locked out.

In a global economy, transformed by a revolution in the way we work and communicate, the opportunities are great but so are the risks. If a few prosper but the majority suffer, then the country will fail to stem its economic decline. The old ways will not work, and we should not be afraid of new ways of looking at things. The stakeholder economy is a new way for the left-of-centre to look at the creation of wealth rather than just its distribution. It is an economic rationale for a fairer and stronger society. For Labour, it provides a unifying theme for the policies which we have already got, and a framework for thinking about policy development in the future.

A stakeholder economy has as its foundation the economic stability that is necessary to plan and invest. That is why we are committed to balancing the government books over the cycle, and borrowing only for investment. It requires more investment and better investment – notably capital spending through public–private partnership to regenerate our infrastructure, investment by industry, funded by patient and committed provision of capital from the financial sector, and we need to make the most of new technology, not just because industries like telecommunications and media are the industries of the future, but because all organisations can become more productive using the enormous advances in technology.

Our greatest investment should be in education and skills. We have always offered high-class education to those at the top, but education and training for the majority have been inadequate. The rise in higher education participation is a welcome first step, though we need a more equitable and secure funding regime for the future. But in truth, the knowledge race has only just begun. There are 60 million undergraduates in India; South Korea has 80 per cent of eighteen-year-olds reaching university entrance standard; and yet in Britain millions have trouble with basic reading and writing. To develop the capabilities of our people, we will need to combine reform and vision in education. Reform means a new combination of pressure and support in schools, so children and teachers are stretched to achieve all they can and give all they can. The best local authorities are already pioneering personalised learning in primary schools, weekend schools, new links with the world of work. We need to build on them but we need a national lead as well. Hence Labour's proposals for wiring up schools, libraries and hospitals, and for developing plans to give every child access to a laptop computer. We also need to open up the world of learning to more people already in work. We are well on the way to the development of Individual Learning Accounts and we are proposing a University for Industry – exciting initiatives for the information age.

With investment and education comes partnership at work – industrial relations that help employers and employees join their common interests and resolve their differences. The foundation of that partnership must be minimum standards of pay and conditions. But it means too a culture of respect, trust, cooperation and team-working between government and business in regional development, infrastructure, science and innovation and technology.

The second pillar is the rebuilding of social cohesion in Britain. The counterpart of a stakeholder economy is a stakeholder society. Social justice is inconceivable while millions of people have no stake in society. That is why we have placed such stress on tackling unemployment, and especially long-term unemployment, which is the cause of social decay and disintegration in many communities. Our objective is not to keep people on benefit but to give people the financial independence that comes from having a job. The world has changed enormously since the Beveridge Report of 1942, which formed the basis of our social security legislation – unemployment is often long term, women go out to work, part-time work must be properly recognised. We need a new settlement on work and welfare for a new age, where opportunity and responsibility go together. If we can substantially reduce unemployment we will bring hope to the unemployed but also relief to those left paying for it.

One nation also means building security for a new age. In relation to pensions for example, the old assumption that all pensioners were penniless without state help is obviously wrong. The rise of second and third private pensions needs to be recognised. That is why we are looking at the Commission on Social Justice's innovative idea of a Minimum Pension Guarantee for pensioners that integrates tax and benefits and effectively abolishes the stigmatising and ineffective means test.

But security is not just about old age and unemployment. It is about freedom from the fear of crime, and freedom from the fear that if one becomes ill the health service will not be in a position to provide the necessary care. Crime has always been a Labour issue. Apart from anything else, it is often Labour voters who are the most persistent victims of crime. That is why it is so ironic that the Conservatives claimed to be the party of law and order. They have always offered more in the way of rhetoric than solutions.

On health, the challenge is slightly different. Labour is justly proud of the NHS. It is the most visible symbol of popular socialism. Under the Tories it is directly threatened. Privatisation is not just on the agenda. It is happening. Academics who saw merit in some of the government's reforms also say that the private finance initiative may be the backdoor route to large-scale privatisation of clinical services. Labour has to counter the Tories by making health a major issue at the next election, and also by promoting our own ideas for reform, detailed in a policy paper agreed at the 1995 conference. The NHS may have been battered in the Tory years, but it has survived. Labour's job will be to revive it for the next century, devolving power downwards to hospitals and doctors and nurses but setting it within a service that is cooperating and not competing as if it were a commercial enterprise operating in the marketplace.

The third area is political reform and modernisation, to make our government fit for the twenty-first century. If we want to create an active civil society, the system of government has to be one that shares power and responsibility with the people. Centralised government, such as we have in Britain, is inefficient, unjust and fails to give people power over their lives. Decentralisation of government is essential if power, wealth and opportunity are to be in the hands of the many rather than the few. Devolving power and democratising power is an idea whose time has come.

There is no place for hereditary voting in the House of Lords. There should be no assumption of government secrecy, which is why a Freedom of Information Act is essential. We have made clear our proposals for a Scottish Parliament and a Welsh Assembly. London, our great capital, will be run by a directly elected authority like any other capital. If, in time, the regions of England want a greater say in their health, education, police and transport, then that too can come. And there should be no scope for the abuse of people's rights, which is why we are committed to the incorporation of the European Convention on Human Rights into British law. The trust that people had in government fifty years ago no longer exists, which is why political renewal is integral to economic and social renewal.

One of the keys will be the rebirth of accountable local government. The concentration of power in Whitehall has been one of the most harmful consequences of the sixteen years of Tory rule. But despite the pressures on them, many Labour local councils have pioneered excellent innovations in service delivery, and at the same time turned themselves into the catalysts of local renewal, working with the business sector, voluntary organisations and the local community to improve the economic and social environment. The good work they have done – from job creation and economic development, to education reform, to leisure and other public services –

will be an enormous source of expertise and good practice for a future Labour government.

Institutional reform will not revive faith in politics in and of itself, but it will help. To be fair, disillusion with politics is not just a British phenomenon, but a more generalised one. People have learnt not to trust their leaders; they have come to think politicians are in it for what they can get out of it. We want to change this.

It is crucial for the Labour Party to build up trust and then retain it. That is why it is so important only to promise what we can deliver. People often say to me that we must seek to generate excitement with big promises. But that is a recipe for disillusion in government. I want a government that lasts because it is in tune with the people, and because the people understand the priorities and strategies of their government. The reason why we changed the policy on the minimum wage, so that it would be set with reference to the state of the labour market and not according to a preset formula, is that we needed a policy that could be carried out for the good of the country. This policy we now have is the one we shall be proud to adopt in government. The same applies to our position on tax and spending, and also on regional government.

Radical policies require patient politics. The last thing the British people want is for me to say 'vote Labour' because of this and that and then on the Friday afterwards to go back on what I have said. That is why I take an unashamedly long-term view of political strategy as well as economic and social change.

The climate of optimism, the belief that we can do better as a nation will, I hope, give those who may have become disillusioned over the last sixteen years a new lease of life. One of the tasks for the Party in the run-up to the election and beyond is to start building a common thread between the ideas of academics, thinkers and intellectuals on what Labour is trying to do. I believe Labour's project is exciting and relevant. But it needs to be built, developed, carried forward into new areas. That requires constant engagement in the battle of ideas.

One of the most corrosive aspects of political debate is the use of negative campaigning which makes a rational discussion of serious issues difficult and, to some extent, inhibits our relations with academic thinkers. If somebody connected with the Labour Party writes or says something controversial, then the Tories will misrepresent it, especially during the election campaign, as Labour Party policy. But despite this, we need to address the fact that for far too long the left has been on the defensive, partly because it confused medium-term policy prescriptions with underlying values and partly because it lost its intellectual self-confidence under the onslaught of the Thatcherite right. But there is now an emerging common agenda, shared by many thinking people, around two points which I made earlier: first, that we have to navigate our way through a world of great economic, social and political change, and this makes new demands on the policies as well as the style of government; and second, that, unless we can unify our country, we will not be able to modernise it in the way that international and domestic change demands. Renewal and cohesion go together; they are two sides of the same coin.

The role of intellectuals and thinkers is crucial to changing the political climate. It is in fact critical to the regeneration of politics. I want Labour to be able to draw on a coalition of thinkers, including people outside the Party. We should never forget that the 1945 Labour government's programme was based on a broad centre-left tradition of ideas. In the 1990s, we should be similarly eclectic. The Labour Party has shown that it is back in business and ready to provide the leadership this country needs. We must show the confidence and open-mindedness to join together with others to map out a new course for Britain.

This book is an important part of the process. The insights of the contributions brought together in this volume are testimony to the rebirth of confidence and new thinking on the left-of-centre of British politics. It is reflected in the enormous interest in New Labour around the world. There is a great opportunity in Britain today to show that there is an alternative to the divisive and inefficient remedies of the new right, and I am determined that we seize it.

'The Stakeholder Society'

Fabian Review, February 1996

'Stakeholding' was a short-lived buzz-phrase in the New Labour lexicon, appearing in the mid-90s, being the subject of some debate amongst commentators and economics such as John Kay and Will Hutton, and vanishing soon after. The phrase appeared in a speech by Blair in January 1996 in Singapore, and this article in Fabian Review *in February 1996 is taken from it. The article focuses on economics, and the need for a high-tech economy, backed by a high-skill workforce, and a new partnership between government and business. It contains the basic principles of Blair and Gordon Brown's approach to macroeconomics, which owe much to the economic programme of Bill Clinton, and his advisers such as Robert Reich.*

It is assumed whenever a politician visits one of the so-called 'Asian Tigers' that it is to study the reasons for their success with a view to implementing them back home. And indeed, some lessons can be learnt, such as high levels of savings and investment and a commitment to education and infrastructure. But many of these lessons would be learnt studying success stories in individual companies in Britain and Europe.

The rates of growth the Asian Tigers have achieved are indeed remarkable. But they owe much to the stage of development of these economies. There are some experts who see some of the Eastern European economies averaging 4 per cent to 7 per cent growth over the next decade. Japan enjoyed such growth until relatively recently. At an earlier period of history Britain enjoyed extraordinary levels of growth. The difference is that in the old days it took much longer to achieve them.

Some have claimed the success of the South-East Asian economies can be explained by deregulation and it is true that in today's global market an open economy is a precondition of efficiency. But again, you could equally point to the levels of long-term investment, often wildly in excess of those of the developed Western economies. Or some say that it is the low levels of public spending; then others will point out that in certain economies, such as Singapore, though public spending is low, compulsory private saving is often high. And over the past few years in some of the Tigers, such as Taiwan, public spending has been increasing.

There is, however, another way of regarding the issue of South-East Asia and the Pacific Rim. We tend, explicitly or implicitly, to regard these thriving economies as a threat. But they are also a huge opportunity. British business has much to gain from a dynamic and increasingly prosperous Asia. New markets are opened. New services are required in finance, retail and distribution. Capital projects are multiplied. This is provided that British industry and the British economy are geared to rising to the challenge. Though we are doing well in some sectors, the truth is that we could and must do much better.

I want Britain to be one of the really dynamic economies of the twenty-first century. It is sobering to think that just over a century ago we were at the top of the league of prosperous nations, thirteenth in 1979, and today eighteenth. Yet our people, by their intelligence, grit and creativity were still a people unrivalled anywhere in the world. We must develop that ability and so make ourselves world leaders again.

The key words are investment, quality and trust. In a speech in Japan in January, I set out our belief in the need to invest in people and capacity to build a strong economy. I referred to our proposals on industry, for public–private partnership, infrastructure, technology, science, small businesses and above all education and skills.

The reason for investment is to create long-term strength. The better our capacity, the more up-to-date our plant and technology, the higher grade our skills, the stronger the product will be. When very low labour cost countries can outbid us at the lower end of the market we must be moving up continually to higher value-added products. That comes through quality. We will not sell our goods and services by being the cheapest, important though cost is. We will sell them by being the best.

The easy way to competitiveness has been seen as devaluation. Since 1979 the pound has virtually halved in relation to the Deutschmark. But it is not competitiveness that lasts, unless it is backed up by an improvement in quality. In an age of customised design, articulate and careful consumers, it is through highly value-added products of quality that we will score. The best British companies know this and are doing it. But to build lasting prosperity it is not enough merely for individual companies to be engaged. The creation of an economy where we are inventing and producing goods and services of quality needs the engagement of the whole country. It must become a matter of national purpose and national pride. We need to build a relationship of trust, not just within a firm but within a society. By trust, I mean the recognition of a mutual purpose for which we work together and in which we all benefit. It is a 'Stakeholder Economy' in which opportunity is available to all, advancement is through merit and from which no group or class is set apart or excluded. This is the economic justification for social cohesion, for a fair and strong society, a traditional commitment of left-of-centre politics but one with relevance today, if it is applied anew to the modern world.

We know the pace of and effect of global markets and technological change. Jobs can be rendered obsolete, even whole industries. The world of work has been transformed. There is a revolution happening in media, communications and information. There is a real risk that, in this era of change, some prosper but many are left behind, their ambitions laid waste.

We need a country in which we acknowledge an obligation collectively to ensure each citizen gets a stake in it. One-nation politics is not some expression of sentiment, or even of justifiable concern for the less well off. It is an active politics, the bringing of a country together, a sharing of the possibility of power, wealth and opportunity. The old means of achieving that on the left was through redistribution in the tax and benefit regime. But in a global economy, the old ways won't do. Of course, a fair tax system is right. But really a life on benefit – dependent on the state – is not what most people want. They want independence, dignity, self-improvement, a chance to earn and get on. The problems of low pay and unemployment must be tackled at source.

The economics of the centre and centre-left today should be geared to the creation of the Stakeholder Economy which involves all our people, not a privileged few, or even a better off 30 or 40 or 50 per cent. If we fail in that, we waste talent, squander potential wealth-creating ability and deny the basis of trust upon which a cohesive society, one nation, is built. If people feel they have no stake in a society, they feel little responsibility towards it and little inclination to work for its success.

The implications of creating a Stakeholder Economy are profound. They mean a commitment by government to tackle long-term and structural unemployment. The development of an underclass of people, cut off from society's mainstream, living often in poverty, the black economy, crime and family instability, is a moral and economic evil. Most Western economies suffer from it. It is wrong, and unnecessary and, incidentally, very costly.

Reform of the welfare state must be one of the fundamental objectives of an incoming Labour government. Our welfare state, begun by Lloyd George and Churchill, then a Liberal, and carried through by the 1945 Labour government, is one of our proudest creations. But it suffers today from two important weaknesses: it does not alleviate poverty effectively; and it does not properly assist the growth of independence, the move from benefit to work. Too many people go on to benefit to stay there. The result is that it neither meets sufficiently its founding principle, nor is it cost-effective.

For Singapore the Central Provident Fund has worked well. But I stress that, though of course Chris Smith will examine carefully the CPF system, we cannot transplant one system in one country to another country with a different system born in very different circumstances. But where there are lessons to be learned we will learn them and it is surely right, for example, to look at a better balance between savings, investment and security in the modern world.

The Stakeholder Economy has a stakeholder welfare system. By that I mean that the system will only flourish in its aims of promoting security and opportunity across the life-cycle if it holds the commitment of the whole population, rich and poor. This requires that everyone has a stake. The alternative is a residual system just for the poor. After the Second World War, the route to this sort of commitment was seen simply as universal cash benefits, most obviously child benefits and pensions. But today's demands and changed lifestyles require a more active conception of welfare based on services as well as cash, childcare as well as child benefit, training as well as unemployment benefit.

Secondly, our education system must be guaranteed to serve all our people, not an elite. Britain has extraordinary talent in science, research and innovation, though occasionally we do not develop it the way we should. But we need the commitment to excellence at the top to permeate all the way down. This is not just about spending money. Recently, Sir Geoffrey Holland, the former permanent secretary at the Department of Education, now Vice Chancellor at Exeter University, gave one of the most powerful and persuasive speeches about education that I have ever heard. He argued that there was room for a 30 per cent improvement in the education system within existing budgets, not least by building the system so as to include people rather than exclude them and by developing genuine leadership at all levels of the system.

Third, we must ensure the new technologies, with their almost limitless potential, are harnessed and dispersed amongst all our people. Knowledge and technology can combine today as never before to educate, liberate and expand horizons. A class divide in technology in the information age would be a disaster and it must be avoided.

Fourth, we must build the right relationship of trust between businesses and government. For far too long, relations have been dogged by the fear of business that government wants to take it over and government's fear that business left to its own devices will not be socially responsible. In reality, in a modern economy, we need neither old style *dirigisme* nor rampant *laissez-faire*. There are key objectives on which business and government can agree and work together to achieve. This 'enabling' role of government is crucial to long-term stability and growth.

The same relationship of trust and partnership applies within a firm. Successful companies invest, treat their employees fairly and value them as a resource not just of production but of creative innovation. The debate about corporate governance in Britain is still in its infancy and has largely been focused on headline issues like directors' pay and perks. We cannot by legislation guarantee that a company will behave in a way conducive to trust and long-term commitment. But it is surely time to assess how we shift the emphasis in corporate ethos – from the company being a mere vehicle for the capital market to be traded, bought and sold as a commodity – towards a vision of the company as a community or partnership in which each employee has a stake, and where a company's responsibilities are more clearly delineated.

Finally, stakeholders in a modern economy will today, more frequently than ever before, be self-employed or in small businesses. We should encourage this, diversify the range of help and advice for those wanting to start out on their own and again use the huge potential of the developing technology to allow them to do so successfully. They may work alone or in small units but they are part of the larger economic picture.

This brings me back to the Asian Tigers. One feature of them, discerned for example by Dr Fukuyama (an economist of the right who is nonetheless concerned at the selfish individualism of parts of Western society), is their high level of social cohesion. This may be based on value systems either different or inappropriate for Western economies. But the broad notion of a unified society with a strong sense of purpose and direction can be achieved in different ways for different cultures and nations.

And it is really a matter of common sense. Working as a team is an effective way of working, or playing a sport, or running an organisation. My point is that a successful country must be run in the same way. That cannot work unless everyone feels part of the team, trusts it and has a stake in its success and future.

This is where a new economics of the centre and left-of-centre must go, an open economy working with the grain of global change, disciplined in macroeconomic and fiscal policy yet distinguished from the *luissez-faire* passive approach of the right by a willingness to act to prepare the country for this change, and a commitment to ensure that its benefits are fairly distributed and all our citizens are part of one nation and get the chance to succeed. That is the real way to combine efficiency and equity in a modern age.

Labour Party conference speech
Blackpool, 1 October 1996

This was Blair's last Labour Party conference speech before the 1997 general election, and he delivered a majestic speech, filled with uplifting oratory. The early parts dissect the Tory record in office and repeat the slogans of the coming campaign, particularly 'enough is enough'. Blair also coins his famous sound bite: 'Ask me my three main priorities for government, and I tell you: education, education, education.'

But in this latter section, Blair makes a sweeping tour d'horizon of British history, invoking everyone from the Old Testament prophets, to anti-slave trade campaigner William Wilberforce, to veteran trade union leader Jack Jones, to the generation which won the Second World War, to the cause of progress. Blair uses the rhetorical device of epizeuxis, repetition for emphasis, on phrases such as 'coming home'.

Blair borrows heavily from the England football team song 'Three Lions' which had been a huge hit in the summer of 1996 during the European championships. In a populist passage he transposes 'football's coming home' for 'Labour's coming home'. Luckily for all concerned, he refrained from singing it.

The peroration has echoes of Oliver Cromwell's demand to the Rump Parliament in 1653: 'Depart, I say, and let us have done with you. In the name of God, go!'

And yes, we are a democratic socialist party. It says so in the new Clause IV in words which I drafted and the party overwhelmingly supported. But it stands in a tradition bigger than European social democracy, bigger than any –ism. Bigger than any of us. It stands in a tradition whose flame was alive in human hearts long before the Labour Party was thought of. A tradition far above ideology but not beyond ideals. We are not a sect or a cult. We are part of the broad movement of human progress. The marriage of ambition with justice, the constant striving of the human spirit to do better and to be better. It is that which separates us from Conservatives.

It was there when the ancient prophets of the Old Testament first pleaded the cause of the marginal, the powerless, the disenfranchised. There when Wilberforce fought the slave trade against the vested interests of Tory money. There when the trade union movement began as an instrument against abuse in the workplace. There when Jack Jones went to fight in the Spanish Civil War for another people's freedom out of nothing more than the goodness of his heart. There when we said, having conquered the evil of Hitler, that the welfare state must be built so that the destitution of the 1930s never returned. It is here now in this room, as we build around the Labour Party the new force for progress in Britain's politics to bring in the new age of achievement for our nation.

One thousand days to prepare for a thousand years. Consider a thousand years of British history and what it tells us. The first parliament in the world. The industrial revolution ahead of its time. An empire, the largest the world has ever known. The invention of virtually every scientific device of the modern world. Two world wars in which our country was bled dry, in which two generations perished, but which in its defeat of the most evil force ever let loose by man showed the most sustained example of bravery in human history.

Our characteristics? Common sense. Standing up for the underdog. Fiercely independent. But the outstanding British quality is courage. Not just physical bravery. The courage to think anew. To break convention when convention is holding us back. To innovate whilst others conform. To do it our way.

I say to the British people. Have the courage to change now. We are coming home to you. We are back as the people's party; and that is why people are coming back to us.

* * *

I don't care where you're coming from; it's where your country's going that matters. If you believe in what I believe in, join the team. Labour has come home to you. So come home to us. Labour's coming home. Seventeen years of hurt. Never stopped us dreaming. Labour's coming home. As we did in 1945. I know that was then, but it could be again. Labour's coming home.

* * *

One thousand days to prepare for a thousand years. Not just turning a page in history, but writing a new book. Building on the greatness of our nation through the greatness of its people. No more squandering the nation's assets. No more sleaze. No more cash for questions. No more lies. No more broken promises. I say to the Tories: enough is enough. Enough. Be done. Be done. The glory days of Britain are not over. But the Tory days are. Let us call our nation to its destiny. Let us lead it to our new Age of Achievement and build for us, our children, and their children, a Britain, united to win in the new millennium.

Part three:
Blair the Prime Minister

Speech welcoming Bill Clinton to address the British Cabinet

29 May 1997

Tony Blair led the Labour Party to a stunning landslide victory in the May 1997 General Election.

A strong sense of kinship developed between the US Democrats under Bill Clinton and New Labour under Blair. Election strategists from the UK and USA made reciprocal study tours following the 1992 UK general election and the 1992 US elections, and policy wonks forged close ties. It was not surprising that Clinton visited the new British Prime Minister within a month of his 1997 victory; in return, the President was afforded the honour of an address to the British Cabinet at Downing Street. On this visit, the Clintons and Blairs dined together at Pont de la Tour, a fashionable restaurant by Tower Bridge. With these words, Blair welcomed his political ally and friend to the Cabinet Room at Downing Street.

Mr President, we are absolutely delighted to have you here and it is a very great day for us for the President of the United States to come in and address our Cabinet.

We know that you have been very busy over the past few days, we have been at some of the meetings together – the European Union and US Summit of course, and then the NATO/Russia agreement, which we congratulate you on formulating, the Founding Act, which will be very important in bringing peace to the world, and also of course the other meetings that have taken place commemorating the Marshall Plan. And we were particularly delighted, incidentally, that you mentioned yesterday, the contribution of Ernest Bevin to that plan, which was a very, very considerable achievement from an earlier Labour government.

I would just like to say one or two words right at the very beginning. First of all, to welcome you and say how delighted we are to have you here, and to say that I hope that this does usher in a new time of understanding and cooperation between our two countries that have such strong bonds of history and of heritage together.

I think you, like me, have always believed that Britain does not have to choose between its strong relationship in Europe and its strong transatlantic relationship with the United States of America; strong in Europe and strong with the United States. I think the one strength deepens the other. And a Britain that is leading in Europe is a Britain capable of ever closer relations also with the United States of America. And we will obviously be wanting to discuss today many of the issues that concern Europe and the United States, the issues of enlargement and NATO. We will obviously be discussing Bosnia and Northern Ireland as well.

But in particular I want to say how absolutely delighted I am, on a personal level, to welcome you here. Because we believe that the courage and strength and leadership that you have shown in the United States has brought enormous benefits, not just to your own country, but the world and we are delighted to see you here.

Statement by the Prime Minister following the death of Diana, Princess of Wales

31 August 1997

On the morning of Sunday 31 August 1997, the death of Diana, Princess of Wales, in a car crash in Paris had been confirmed. Blair, riding high in the polls, caught the public mood of shock and grief perfectly in his short statement to the media.

The phrase 'people's princess' was suggested by Alastair Campbell. Blair delivered these words on his way to St Mary's Church in Trimdon in his constituency.

I am utterly devastated. The whole of our country, all of us, will be in a state of shock and mourning. Diana was a wonderful, warm and compassionate person who people, not just in Britain, but throughout the world, loved and will mourn as a friend. Our thoughts and prayers are with her family, in particular with her two sons, and with all of the families bereaved in this quite appalling tragedy.

I feel like everyone else in this country today – utterly devastated. Our thoughts and prayers are with Princess Diana's family – in particular her two sons, two boys – our hearts go out to them. We are today a nation, in Britain, in a state of shock, in mourning, in grief that is so deeply painful for us.

She was a wonderful and warm human being. Though her own life was often sadly touched by tragedy, she touched the lives of so many others in Britain – throughout the world – with joy and with comfort. How many times shall we remember her, in how many different ways, with the sick, the dying, with children, with the needy, when, with just a look or a gesture that spoke so much more than words, she would reveal to all of us the depth of her compassion and her humanity? How difficult things were for her from time to time, surely we can only guess at – but the people everywhere, not just here in Britain but everywhere, they kept faith with Princess Diana, they liked her, they loved her, they regarded her as one of the people. She was the people's princess and that's how she will stay, how she will remain in our hearts and in our memories for ever.

Speech on Her Majesty the Queen and Prince Philip's Golden Wedding Anniversary

20 November 1997

Blair, who wrote in Marxism Today *in 1990 that 'a modern society requires a modern constitution', marked the golden wedding anniversary of the Queen and Prince Philip with a generous and congratulatory speech. Whatever private views on the Monarchy Blair may have, as Prime Minister he has been wholly supportive during some difficult times for the Royal Family.*

Your Majesty, Your Royal Highness, distinguished guests. I am honoured to be your Prime Minister and to say to you today on behalf of the whole of the British nation: congratulations to you and to Prince Philip on the occasion of your fiftieth Wedding Anniversary – you have our loyalty, our love and our heartfelt thanks for all your years of devotion to us.

Her Majesty's closing words to me at Buckingham Palace on Tuesday at the end of our meeting were: 'Don't be too effusive, please.'

Sorry, Ma'am, but I am from the Disraeli school of prime ministers in their relations with the Monarch. But I can do it with feeling because it's true.

I am the tenth prime minister of Queen Elizabeth II's reign. So she has pretty much the measure of us by now. It is more than a little awesome for me to think that the same weekly audiences I have were once enjoyed by Churchill and Macmillan, people who to me seem figures of history.

I know I speak for the former prime ministers present here today – Sir Edward Heath, Lord Callaghan, Lady Thatcher and John Major – when I say how invaluable and pleasurable those weekly audiences are. This is for two reasons.

First, if she will forgive me, though she is the Queen, and the essence of dignity, it is a dignity that is very much down to earth.

Unstuffy, unfussy and unfazed by anything. With a keen sense of humour and a mean ability for mimicry. There are only two people in the world to whom a prime minister can say what he likes about Cabinet colleagues. One's the wife, the other's the Queen. It is to them we can express the full extent of our affection for ministers.

But the other reason prime ministers enjoy the audience is one I confess I didn't really believe until I became Prime Minister.

For reasons not simply to do with her experience, though of course that helps, she is an extraordinarily shrewd and perceptive observer of the world. Hers is advice worth having. At the time of the Commonwealth Heads of Government Meeting in Edinburgh, she helped me through it with the breadth of her knowledge of the countries, but with more than that – with her feel for the culture and spirit of the Commonwealth people.

The work the Queen does in the Commonwealth is one of the great unsung stories of our time. She travels there incessantly, and, as in India recently, her visits become the occasion of massive business and commercial success for Britain.

They revere her as Head of the Commonwealth. The affection is clear and mutual. When Fiji rejoined us this year and their prime minister addressed the heads of government, it was plain that a major motivation for Fiji was to be reunited with the Queen.

You are a symbol of unity in a world of insecurity, of continuity in a world where nothing stays the same. In Britain, people often just don't know how many miles you travel up and down the land, the places you visit, the people you meet. It is hard work. But in each place and with each person, you bring enormous pleasure and joy; for each one, a memory never forgotten.

You and Prince Philip. For it is a partnership. He works in his own right across a huge range of charities and organisations and he is also there by the Queen's side, her support and steadfast companion. Thank you, sir, for all you have done to make the Queen's reign a success.

Of course, like any family, you have had your ups and downs – Your share of tragedy and sorrow, as well as joy. You spoke in 1992 of the *annus horribilis* you had endured. This year, too, the tragedy of the death of Diana, Princess of Wales, has put you and those closest to you through a terrible test. I know from the conversations we had during those days how deeply you felt those events for yourself, Prince Charles and the boys. I know too, contrary to some of the hurtful things that were said at the time, how moved you were by the outpouring of grief which followed, as in the security and sanctity of your own home you sought as a family to help the boys.

I believe that, for both you and Prince Philip, life's chief imperative, what keeps you going, is a simple concept: duty. Duty leading to service.

Despite your position or perhaps because of it, it cannot always be easy. But you do it – the unenjoyable as well as the enjoyable – because it is your duty.

I make a lot of this being a modern country. I am the youngest of your prime ministers. But contrary to myth, modernity and tradition can and do live happily together. The best of modernity builds on the best of tradition. A strong and flourishing Monarchy can play the same full part in a new modern Britain as it has in the past. My generation pays tribute to you today with every bit as much force as older generations do. For the Queen stands for those values of duty and service that are timeless, as relevant now as ever. I wasn't born when you were married. I was three weeks old at your Coronation. As a young boy in short trousers, I stood and waved my flag as I saw you first in Durham City back in the early 60s. I am proud as proud can be to be your Prime Minister today offering this tribute on behalf of the country. You are our Queen. We respect and cherish you. You are, simply, the best of British. So may I invite all of our guests to join me in wishing you and Prince Philip many further happy years together, with the assurance of the united affection of your people, here and throughout the Commonwealth.

Ladies and Gentlemen, Her Majesty the Queen and Prince Philip.

'Why the Dome is good for Britain'

Speech to a business breakfast at London's Royal Festival Hall,
24 February 1998

Blair's government had two choices in 1997 when considering what to do with the programme they inherited from the Tories for a Millennium Dome in Greenwich, east London. They could cut their losses and scrap the scheme, or throw their full weight behind it. After serious opposition from some Cabinet ministers, Blair opted for the latter option. This speech is filled with uncharacteristic hyperbole and phrases which came back to haunt Blair's government when the Dome failed to meet expectations.

Picture the scene. The clock strikes midnight on December 31, 1999. The eyes of the world turn to the spot where the new millennium begins – the Meridian Line at Greenwich. This is Britain's opportunity to greet the world with a celebration that is so bold, so beautiful, so inspiring that it embodies at once the spirit of confidence and adventure in Britain and the spirit of the future in the world. This is the reason for the Millennium Experience. Not a product of imagination run wild, but a huge opportunity for Britain. It is good for Britain. So let us seize the moment and put on something of which we and the world will be proud.

Then we will say to ourselves with pride: this is our Dome, Britain's Dome, and believe me, it will be the envy of the world.

It does not surprise me that the cynics have rubbished the idea. They are in good company. They are part of an inglorious strand of British history: like those who said St Paul's would be a calamity, that the 1851 exhibition would have no visitors and that the 1951

Festival of Britain would never be finished on time.

It's easy to say don't do something. To say it won't be done on time. That it costs too much. That no one will visit it. It takes little courage to say no to a new idea.

But just suppose we gave in to the cynics and snipers. Suppose for a second we allowed pessimism to drive out ambition. Suppose we tore down the masts, suppose we said no to the jobs and the tourists, suppose we sacked the builders, returned the land to its previous contaminated state, suppose we dismissed Britain's finest designers, musicians, directors and singers, suppose we told Richard Rogers not to build his great building in this country but to move it elsewhere, then when the eyes of the world fell on Greenwich people would see a derelict site and a signpost in the ground reading: Britain – year 2000. Nothing done. Wouldn't those same cynics feel just a bit unsettled? Wouldn't they feel that Great Britain had missed an opportunity?

Today I say to the British people new Britain is a place for daring and boldness, for striving for excellence. Greenwich is the place the millennium begins. If it was Paris Mean Time, don't you think the French would put on a show? If it was Berlin Mean Time don't you think the Germans would do likewise? When I was last in the United States people were already talking about how Britain would be the focus of the world's attention in the year 2000. So let's get behind Greenwich and the Millennium Experience. Nowhere is doing anything like it. It promises to be the most fantastic day out in the world.

In June when the government decided to go ahead with the Dome I set down five clear criteria.

First, the content should inspire people. Today you will judge for yourself what I believe are truly wonderful designs and ideas for the Dome's contents.

Second, it should have national reach. The Millennium Challenge will offer a series of activities involving the whole nation in the run-up to the millennium. It will touch every part of the country.

Third, the management of the project should be first rate. Indeed we have in place a superb team at the Millennium Company – and have signed up the best creative talents in Britain to work on the contents.

Fourth, that it should not call on the public purse. This project is on budget. It is not costing any taxpayers' money. It is costing just £400 million of lottery money and the rest of the costs are coming from sponsorship, ticket sales, merchandising, licensing rights. It will turn in a profit for Britain. There are estimates already of tourism to the value of £500 million to £1 billion in value. It is just 20 per cent of the money being spent on the millennium. The great majority of the lottery's Millennium Commission money – £1.5 billion in fact – is going on spectacular projects around the country like £15 million for the Lowry centre in Salford, £46 million for the Millennium Stadium at Cardiff Arms Park, £27 million for the National Discovery Park in Liverpool, £23 million for the National Space Centre in Leicester, £41 million for the Bristol 2000 project, £37 million for the Eden Project in Cornwall, £27 million for the International Centre for Life in Newcastle, £23 million for the Hampden Park Stadium in Glasgow, £33 million for a new University for the Highlands and Islands and £43 million for a national cycle network of 2,785 miles of cycle routes throughout the United Kingdom. Just some of the superb projects – educational, environmental, entertaining – that get less attention than the Millennium Dome but will be of huge benefit to the British people.

Fifth, there should be a lasting legacy. The Dome itself will last for decades to come after the year 2000. It will become an international landmark. There will be lasting benefit to Greenwich.

I am confident that all five of these conditions are not just being met but have made great progress.

And the whole government is behind the Dome in what is a remarkable team effort. Peter Mandelson has given the project a real sense of purpose and direction. John Prescott has given unwavering support for the Dome and led the push to get transport for the Dome – river and underground – delivered on time. He has also led the way in building a millennium village, a remarkable development beside the Dome – high-tech, environmentally friendly regeneration that will bring jobs and prosperity to the area. David Blunkett is ensuring that education is at the heart of the Dome's contents. We will ensure that school parties get cheaper tickets to the Dome. Chris Smith has given shape to the wider millennium celebrations. Margaret Beckett supported by Sir Robert May, the Chief Scientific Officer, is working with the Millennium Company on the Dome's science content.

I am confident about Britain's preparations for the millennium.

And the reason for that is that we are tapping in to the creative talents of the British people. We are by nature adventurous, innovative, pioneering, creative. And as we approach the millennium we can boast that we have a richness of talent in this country that is unparalleled: the finest artists, authors, architects, musicians, designers, animators, software makers, scientists. We are leading the world in creativity. So why not put it on display? Why not shout about it? The Dome will be a celebration of the best of Britain.

But the millennium will be more than simply the Dome. There is a national programme for volunteering, for community cooperation, for celebrating the values that the millennium represents, values that represent the best of humanity in the 2000 years since the birth of Christ.

It will bring the nation together in a common purpose – to make a difference. It will unite the nation. It will be a meeting point of people from all backgrounds. It will be an event to lift our horizons. It will be a catalyst to imagine our futures.

In this experience I want people to pause and reflect on this moment, about the possibilities ahead of us, about the values that guide our society.

The Dome's content will contain a rich texture of feelings: spiritual, emotional, fun. It will combine the best of other attractions in a unique experience. Exhilarating like Disney World – yet different. Educational and interactive like the Science Museum – yet different. Emotional and uplifting like a West End musical – yet different. It will be shaped by the people. Visitors from all round the world will have the time of their lives.

The Cabinet thought long and hard and talked long and hard about whether to go ahead with the Dome. One of the clinching arguments for me came when both John Prescott and Jack Straw talked about their memories, deep and personal, of the Festival of Britain. It clearly made a huge impact on them. I want every child in Britain to be part of the Millennium Experience. This will be a celebration for the whole country. I want today's children to take from it an experience so powerful and memories so strong that it gives them that abiding sense of purpose and unity that stays with them through the rest of their lives. Their experience is part of the Millennium Experience.

Last Thursday I saw for myself the developing ideas for the content. And they are truly spectacular. They draw on the talents of Britain's finest creative brains. They will use the smartest new technology and brainpower. They will draw too on the strengths and innovation of business.

For this is a celebration that is good for British business. The Millennium Experience is a chance to demonstrate that Britain will be a breeding ground for the most successful businesses of the twenty-first century.

The twenty-first century company will be different. Many of Britain's best known companies are already redefining traditional perceptions of the role of the corporation. They are recognising that every customer is part of a community, and that social responsibility is not an optional extra.

These companies are establishing themselves as leaders in new markets of innovation in education, in environmental responsibility and in concern for the social well-being of customers. The companies that have confirmed their investment in the Millennium Dome today reflect those values.

Today we can announce just the beginning of a raft of new sponsors for the Dome with some of the finest companies getting behind the project: the first four founding partners, British Telecom, Manpower, Tesco and Sky, have led the way, all making contributions of at least £12 million in value to the project. But we have also had substantial commitment from BAA and British Airways and the backing of the National Lottery outlets to make Millennium Dome tickets accessible in all parts of the country. The Corporation of the City of London too are committed to substantial backing when matched by money from City businesses and institutions and I welcome the Lord Mayor's presence today as evidence of their support. These businesses are showing the world that Britain is the natural home of the twenty-first century company.

Other companies that believe they too are twenty-first century companies rising to the challenge of the new millennium will want to join this project.

You'll make up your own minds, but I believe that anyone interested in Britain's future will share my view that this is going to be a huge asset for the country as a symbol of British confidence, as a monument to our creativity, and as a fantastic day out.

The bandwagon is beginning to roll. The benefits to Britain are huge. And come December 31, 1999, at a historic moment in time, Greenwich will be the most exciting place in the world to be.

Arrival ceremony at the White House
5 February 1998

*After Bill Clinton's successful visit to London, the honour was recipro-
cated in February 1998. Blair's words at the White House, 'Today, in
the face of Saddam Hussein, we must stand together once more. We
want a diplomatic solution to the crisis. But the success or failure of
diplomacy rests on Saddam. If he fails to respond, then he knows that
the threat of force is there, and it is real', seem very prescient.*

Mr President, I was honoured to accept your invitation to make an
official visit to Washington, and I am delighted to be here.

Your visit to London last year was without doubt a highlight of
the early months of my premiership. Perhaps more important, your
visit to Northern Ireland in 1995 was a highlight of the struggle of
that Province for peace. Then, I was leader of the opposition. Today,
as Prime Minister, I know and value your concern, and your
support, as we work towards a lasting and peaceful settlement. We
value too the determination you have expressed once more to bring
to justice those responsible for the Lockerbie bombing.

On so many issues we think alike. We are in politics for the same
things: because we want to modernise our countries in preparation
for the new millennium; because we believe in freedom, in fairness;
because we want greater prosperity for our people, a better standard
of living for what you call middle America, and I call middle Britain
– the majority of hardworking decent people who play by the rules.

Bill Clinton has in his time said some very kind things about me.
Let me say something about Bill Clinton. He said what he wanted to
deliver, and he is delivering. He never said it would be easy, but he

stuck to his guns. He never promised miracles, but he has delivered progress for the people who elected him.

Bill Clinton has been here for six years. In Britain, we are a new government, at the beginning of our journey. There will be tough times and tough decisions for us too. But we too are determined to deliver for our people, and to fulfil the promises we made to them.

It is an ambitious project because it seeks to reach out beyond the old boundaries of left and right, which the people found to be irrelevant long before the politicians did. Ours is the politics of the radical centre, managing economic and social change rather than allowing it to manage us.

As the next few days unfold, I know that the ties between us will strengthen further. More important, the bonds between our countries will strengthen.

We have stood together before in the face of tyranny. Today, in the face of Saddam Hussein, we must stand together once more. We want a diplomatic solution to the crisis. But the success or failure of diplomacy rests on Saddam. If he fails to respond, then he knows that the threat of force is there, and it is real.

We must also work together to move forward the Middle East Peace Process. There are few more important tasks for international diplomacy in the next few months.

In the next three days, we will spend many hours together, and discuss many issues. We do so with a shared language, shared values, a shared determination to stand up for what is right.

We do so confident of strengthening the bonds that tie us together, and building a new transatlantic relationship founded on the successful modernisation of our two countries – a new and modern relationship for a new century.

The Third Way:
new politics for the new century

Fabian Society pamphlet, 1998

The 'Third Way' was an attempt led by academics and politicians in the late nineties to define progressive politics in Europe, the USA and beyond. At this time, with the Democrats in the White House and New Labour in Downing Street, it seemed that a new progressive hegemony might be forged. The Third Way created much academic discussion, led by Anthony Giddens at the London School of Economics and others. In the opening section of this Fabian pamphlet Blair places his socialism in a broader international context, and demands 'permanent revisionism' for Labour's policies. In this latter theme, Blair echoes Tony Crosland, Hugh Gaitskell, and the Labour revisionists of the 1950s.

I have always believed that politics is first and foremost about ideas. Without a powerful commitment to goals and values, governments are rudderless and ineffective, however large their majorities.

Furthermore, ideas need labels if they are to become popular and widely understood. The 'Third Way' is to my mind the best label for the new politics which the progressive centre-left is forging in Britain and beyond.

The Third Way stands for a modernised social democracy, passionate in its commitment to social justice and the goals of the centre-left, but flexible, innovative and forward-looking in the means to achieve them. It is founded on the values which have guided progressive politics for more than a century – democracy, liberty, justice, mutual obligation and internationalism. But it is a *third* way because it moves decisively beyond an old left preoccupied by state control, high taxation and producer interests; and a new right treating public investment, and often the very notions of 'society' and collective endeavour, as evils to be undone.

My vision for the twenty-first century is of a popular politics reconciling themes which in the past have been wrongly regarded as antagonistic – patriotism *and* internationalism; rights *and* responsibilities; the promotion of enterprise *and* the attack on poverty and discrimination. The left should be proud of its achievements in the twentieth century, not least universal suffrage, a fairer sharing of taxation and growth, and great improvements in working conditions and in welfare, health and educational services. But we still have far to go to build the open, fair and prosperous society to which we aspire.

The Third Way is not an attempt to split the difference between right and left. It is about traditional values in a changed world. And it draws vitality from uniting the two great streams of left-of-centre thought – democratic socialism and liberalism – whose divorce this century did so much to weaken progressive politics across the West. Liberals asserted the primacy of individual liberty in the market economy; social democrats promoted social justice with the state as its main agent. There is no necessary conflict between the two, accepting as we do now that state power is one means to achieve our goals, but not the only one and emphatically not an end in itself.

In this respect that Third Way also marks a third way *within* the left. Debate within the left has been dominated by two unsatisfactory positions. The fundamentalist left has made nationalisation and state control an end in itself, hardening policy prescription into ideology. Radicalism was judged by the amount of public ownership and spending. In opposition was a moderate left which too often either accepted this basic direction while arguing for a slower pace of change or ignored the world of ideas. Revisionists periodically tried to change the agenda, but their success was limited. The Third Way is a serious reappraisal of social democracy, reaching deep into the values of the left to develop radical new approaches.

A decade ago, the right had a virtual monopoly of power in the democratic West. In America, across Europe, even in Scandinavia, the right was in power, apparently impregnable. Today, the position is transformed. In most of the European Union the centre-left is in office. While learning lessons about efficiency and choice, particularly in the public sector, we argue as confidently as ever that the right does not have the answer to the problems of social polarisation, rising crime, failing education and low productivity and growth.

Yet the left is not returning to the old politics of isolationism, nationalisation, bureaucracy and 'tax and spend'. We are acting afresh. Across Europe, social democratic governments are pioneering welfare state reform, tackling social exclusion, engaging in new partnerships, and establishing a stable economic basis for long-term stability and investment.

I want this pamphlet to explain the Third Way to a larger audience. It does not seek to paint a full canvas: all successful, dynamic political projects are 'work in progress', and our work is at an early stage. But it is important to take the debate forward from what the Third Way *isn't* to what it should become. For me the debate starts with the core values on which the progressive centre-left is founded.

Values

My politics are rooted in a belief that we can only realise ourselves as individuals in a thriving civil society, comprising strong families and civic institutions buttressed by intelligent government. For most individuals to succeed, society must be strong. When society is weak, power and rewards go to the few, not the many.

Values are not absolute, and even the best can conflict. Our mission is to promote and reconcile the four values which are essential to a just society which maximises the freedom and potential of all our people – equal worth, opportunity for all, responsibility and community.

Equal worth

Social justice must be founded on the equal worth of each individual, whatever their background, capability, creed or race. Talent and effort should be encouraged to flourish in all quarters, and governments must act decisively to end discrimination and prejudice. Awareness of discrimination is, rightly, being heightened over time. The attack on racial discrimination now commands general support, as does the value of a multicultural and multi-ethnic society. A new awareness is growing of the capacity of, for example, disabled and elderly people, as they assert their own rights and dignity. The progressive left is on their side, recognising that despite two centuries of campaigning for democratic rights, we have a long way to go before people are recognised for their abilities.

Opportunity for all

The new constitution of the Labour Party commits us to seek the widest possible spread of wealth, power and opportunity. I want to highlight opportunity as a key value in the new politics. Its importance has too often been neglected or distorted. For the right, opportunity is characteristically presented as the freedom of individuals from the state. Yet for most people, opportunities are inseparable from society, in which government action necessarily plays a large part. The left, by contrast, has in the past too readily downplayed its duty to promote a wide range of opportunities for individuals to advance themselves and their families. At worst, it has stifled opportunity in the name of abstract equality. Gross inequalities continue to be handed down from generation to generation, and the progressive left must robustly tackle the obstacles to true equality of opportunity. But the promotion of equal opportunities does not imply dull uniformity in welfare provision and public services. Nor does the modern left take a narrow view of opportunities: the arts and the creative industries should be part of our common culture.

Responsibility

In recent decades, responsibility and duty were the preserve of the right. They are no longer; and it was a mistake for them to ever become so, for they were powerful forces in the growth of the Labour movement in Britain and beyond. For too long, the demand for rights from the state was separated from the duties of citizenship and the imperative for mutual responsibility on the part of individuals and institutions. Unemployment benefits were often paid without strong reciprocal obligations; children went unsupported by absent parents. This issue persists. Our responsibility to protect the environment, for instance, is increasingly pressing. So is the responsibility of parents for their children's education. The rights we enjoy reflect the duties we owe: rights and opportunity without responsibility are engines of selfishness and greed.

Community

Human nature is cooperative as well as competitive, selfless as well as self-interested; and society could not function if it was otherwise. We all depend on collective goods for our independence; and all our lives are enriched   or impoverished – by the communities to which we belong. In deciding where to act on behalf of the national community, whether as regulator or provider, governments must be acutely sensitive not to stifle worthwhile activity by local communities and the voluntary sector. The grievous twentieth-century error of the fundamentalist left was a belief that the state could replace civil society and thereby advance freedom. The new right veers to the other extreme, advocating wholesale dismantling of core state activity in the cause of 'freedom'. The truth is that freedom for the many requires strong government. A key challenge of progressive politics is to use the state as an enabling force, protecting effective communities and voluntary organisations and encouraging their growth to tackle new needs, in partnership as appropriate.

These are the values of the Third Way. Without them, we are adrift. But in giving them practical effect, a large measure of pragmatism is essential. As I say continually, what matters is what works to give effect to our values. Some commentators are disconcerted by this insistence on fixed values and goals but pragmatism about means. There are even claims that it is unprincipled. But I believe that a critical dimension of the Third Way is that policies flow from values, not vice versa. With the right policies, market mechanisms are critical to meeting social objectives, entrepreneurial zeal can promote social justice, and new technology represents an opportunity, not a threat.

Our values define our enemies. Cynicism and fatalism, prejudice and social exclusion: these are the enemies of talent and ambition, of aspiration and achievement. Cynicism, claiming that politics and public service cannot improve the quality of our lives. Fatalism, that says global markets have wrested the economy beyond our influence. Prejudice, denying equal worth and encouraging snobbery and xenophobia. Social exclusion, limiting or denying opportunities on a scale unacceptable in a fair and open society.

What of policy? Our approach is 'permanent revisionism', a continual search for better means to meet our goals, based on a clear view of the changes taking place in advanced industrialised societies.

'Building for the long term'

Progress, December 1998

Progress was established by Labour modernisers in 1995 as a vehicle for the Blairite message. In the run-up to the 1997 election it organised seminars and weekend schools to allow Party members to meet and discuss policy issues. Since 1997, Progress has organised some major conferences at which senior politicians have made speeches. Backing up this network is Progress *magazine, which is sent to Party members and subscribers. This article in* Progress *covers the economic prospects for Labour's first term, and demonstrates that Labour had already made some real strides after just eighteen months in office.*

Britain's economy will face a challenging time over the next year. I am not going to pretend everything will be rosy, but nor are the clouds as black as some people are trying to paint.

No country, despite what the Tories appear to think, can be immune to the financial and economic turmoil which started in the Far East and has now spread through every continent. One quarter of the world is already in recession. World growth rates have been slashed by almost a half. So growth in Britain will be lower next year than expected six months ago.

But thanks to the steps this New Labour government has taken, our economy is in far better shape than in the past to weather these global economic storms.

We saw the damage that the Tory policies of boom and bust caused this country twice in the last eighteen years. Hundreds of thousands of people lost their homes, millions their jobs. Record unemployment, sky-high interest rates, inflation out of control.

We were powerless to do anything about it when we were in opposition. But as soon as we came into government, we started to put in place policies to end this disastrous stop–go cycle and build a stable economy capable of sustained and steady growth.

Tough targets were set for inflation. The Bank of England was given independence to take politics out of interest rates. We announced we would tackle the huge borrowing of the Tories by keeping to strict spending limits for the first two years.

These were hard choices but the rewards are now being seen. Inflation is now on target. Despite the world slowdown and the fact that a quarter of the world economies are now contracting, Britain's economy is forecast to continue growing next year, with higher growth resuming in the following years.

Borrowing has been reduced by £20 billion and we are on course this year to repay debt, saving interest charges in the future. And, because of our prudent decisions, the economic downturn will not stop our plans to spend an extra £40 billion in our schools and hospitals over the next three years – the biggest ever investment. Gordon Brown has made clear this investment is not just affordable but vital to a modern and decent country. He was also able to go further by making an immediate extra investment of £250 million in our health service this winter.

I know the devastating impact of job losses on those affected and their communities. After all, Fijitsu is in my constituency. So I am not the slightest bit complacent. We will give all the help we can to those whose jobs are under threat. But I also want those job losses to be put in perspective. Unemployment did rise in October. But the figures also show there are over 400,000 more people in work now than at the election. And youth unemployment is at its lowest level since 1976.

There is one other important way our policies are paying dividends. Long-term interest rates are at their lowest for thirty-five years because Britain now has, at last, a government seen as serious about inflation. This has also allowed interest rates already to be cut twice to 6.75 per cent.

During the last slowdown under the Tories, interest rates had to stay at 15 per cent for over a year, and at 10 per cent or more for four whole years.

But that's the remarkable thing about the Tories. They seem to have forgotten their own record, the misery they caused, the two deepest recessions since the war, or the way they deliberately played politics with inflation before the last election.

They haven't changed. They demand spending to be cut but won't say which schools or hospitals should lose the extra investment we promise. They call for us to scrap the New Deal, the minimum wage or the Working Families Tax Credit. Policies which will not only help make Britain a fairer country but also which will make us more prosperous.

We are building for the long term, to equip Britain for the challenges of the new century. This means making use of our country's best resource – the talents and energy of our people. Around 160,000 young people are taking part in the New Deal. More than 50,000 are already in jobs or training within the first six months of the New Deal running nationally. Our policies to make work pay will also help our country make better use of everyone's talents.

It is one of the ways we are battling to close the productivity gap with our competitors. British business remains 40 per cent less competitive than their US counterparts and 20 per cent less than French and German firms. By investing more in schools and skills, in our vital infrastructure, in research, in developing British ideas here at home, we can close that gap to make Britain far more prosperous.

We are steering a course for stability in an unsettled world. We won't deny short-term difficulties but nor will we be diverted from policies for long-term strength.

Introduction to *God's Politicians*
by Graham Dale (HarperCollins), 2000

Graham Dale's history of the Christian Socialist contribution to the Labour Party ends with a section on Tony Blair, the latest, but by no means the first, Christian Socialist to lead to the Labour Party. Blair provides the foreword to the book, published in 2000. He returns to his familiar theme of politics as a moral activity and the need to put beliefs into action, and asks for his government to be judged by its deeds.

I am pleased to provide the foreword to this book celebrating the 'Christian contribution to 100 years of Labour'. The Labour Party has always included people of different faiths as well as people with no religious faith and this diversity is its strength. Christianity is one of the many forces that have influenced Labour during its first hundred years and is not a faith the Party claims a monopoly on – Christians have served and continue to serve in other political parties. However, as this book shows, many Christians have played a significant role in the development of the Labour Party and it is appropriate that we acknowledge the impact these people have had.

The Labour Party and the nation are indebted to people whose Christian faith motivated their political service; individuals who were outraged by the social injustice they saw all around them and believed it was their duty to stand up for the downtrodden; individuals who wanted to show compassion towards their neighbours and saw the Labour Party as a means by which this could be done; individuals who saw a connection between the values of Christ and the values of socialism, and who chose to work out these connections in the rough and tumble of party politics.

It was the Christian values of these people that informed their political thinking. They believed in community, in equality and in individual responsibility. Their beliefs forced them to take political action when faced with the great need around them – the need for jobs, the need for homes or the need for healthcare. They believed that legislation, not charity, was needed to transform the inadequate present into a better future. In 1906 the Labour Party had just thirty MPs, eighteen of whom were Nonconformists, so it is easy to understand why some say Labour owes more to Methodism than to Marx. But there were Anglicans and Catholics too, people from other faiths and people of no religious faith, all of whom united around their belief that politics had a moral purpose. For all these people the Labour Party was a means through which their values could be put into action, and this is the nub of the issue. Neither faith nor politics can be simply about believing – it must be about action. Religious beliefs and political beliefs will achieve nothing until people are prepared to act on those beliefs. It is on what politicians do and not just what they believe that they are judged. Just as it is on what this Labour government has done – on jobs, on education, on the NHS and on the national minimum wage – that it too will be judged.

I warmly commend this account of the men and women who built the Labour Party and whose faith informed their political action: from Keir Hardie (a Nonconformist), often described as the father of the Party, through to Arthur Henderson (a Methodist), who gave the Party its original Clause IV; John Wheatley (a Roman Catholic), who gave the nation its first housing programme and Ellen Wilkinson (a Methodist), who walked with the men of Jarrow in their dignified protest for work; George Lansbury (an Anglican), a Labour leader and pacifist who argued with Hitler, and Stafford Cripps (an Anglo-Catholic), a Labour chancellor who helped secure Russian support in the fight against Hitler; and more recently Harold Wilson (a Congregationalist), who caught the mood of the nation in the 1960s and John Smith (a Presbyterian) whose untimely death denied him his request of 'a chance to serve'. It is to recognise people like these, both these recorded here and others unknown, that this book has been written. We are grateful to them for the service they have provided to their Party and to this country.

Touchstone issues memo
29 April 2000

In April 2000, a leaked memorandum appeared in the newspapers penned by Blair, and focusing on the so-called touchstone issues which connect with the voters. The Sun ran the story under the headline 'Rattled'. The memo covers crime, asylum, families, and defence which Blair describes as 'There are a clutch of issues – seemingly disparate – that are in fact linked. We need a strategy that is almost discrete, focused on them. They are roughly combining "on your side" issues with toughness and standing up for Britain.'

Within a few months Blair's government was rocked by a crisis in the farming sector caused by foot-and-mouth disease in cattle, which resulted in Blair delaying the 2001 general election. Within twenty months, the terrorist attacks on the World Trade Center and the Pentagon made Blair's memo on the challenges facing his government seem almost trivial.

There are a clutch of issues – seemingly disparate – that are in fact linked. We need a strategy that is almost discrete, focused on them.

They are roughly combining 'on your side' issues with toughness and standing up for Britain.

They range from: the family – where, partly due to MCA (Married Couple Allowance) and gay issues, we are perceived as weak; asylum and crime, where we are perceived as soft; and asserting the nation's interests where, because of the unpopularity of Europe, a constant barrage of small stories beginning to add up on defence and even issues like Zimbabwe, we are seen as insufficiently assertive.

All this, of course, is perception. It is bizarre that any government I lead should be seen as anti-family. We are, in fact, taking very tough measures on asylum and crime.

Kosovo should have laid to rest any doubts about our strength in defence. But all of these things add up to a sense that the government – and this even applies to me – are somehow out of touch with gut British instincts.

The Martin case – and the lack of any response from us that appeared to empathise with public concern and then channel it into the correct course – has only heightened this problem.

We need a thoroughly worked-out strategy stretching over several months to regain the initiative in this area.

Each of these issues should be analysed and the correct policy response drawn up. Then each should be dealt with, but with a message which ties it all together.

This is precisely the sort of thing AC (Alastair Campbell, Tony Blair's press secretary) and CF (Lord Charles Falconer, Cabinet Office Minister) should do if a new system is put in place which frees up their time.

My thoughts are:

(i)   Possibly on the Martin case, asking a senior judge to look at changing the sentencing law, i.e. to allow lesser sentences than life. We also need a far tougher rebuttal or alternatively action, re the allegations that jurors were intimidated.

(ii)   On asylum, we need to be highlighting removals and decisions plus if the April figures show a reduction, then a downward trend. Also if the benefits bill really starts to fall, that should be highlighted also. Plus some of the genuine asylum claims being given some publicity.

(iii)   On crime, we need to highlight the tough measures: compulsory tests for drugs before bail; the PIU (Performance

Innovation Unit) report on the confiscation of assets; the extra number of burglars jailed under the 'three strikes and you're out'.

Above all, we must deal now with street crime, especially in London.

When the figures are published for the six months to April, they will show a small – 4 per cent – rise in crime. But this will almost certainly be due to the rise in levels of street crime – mobile phones, bags being snatched. This will be worst in London.

The Met Police are putting in place measures to deal with it; but, as ever, we are lacking a tough public message along with the strategy. We should think now of an initiative, e.g. locking up street muggers. Something tough, with immediate bite which sends a message through the system.

Maybe, the driving licence penalty for young offenders. But this should be done soon and I, personally, should be associated with it.

(iv) On defence, we need to make the CSR (Comprehensive Spending Review) work for defence. Big cuts and you can forget any hope of winning back ground on "standing up for Britain".

(v) On the family, we need two or three eye-catching initiatives that are entirely conventional in terms of their attitude to the family. Despite the rubbish about gay couples, the adoption issue worked well. We need more. I should be personally associated with as much of this as possible.

TB, 29 April 2000.

'Faith in politics'
Speech to the Christian Socialist Movement, 29 March 2001

This keynote address to a multi-faith conference organised by the Christian Socialist Movement, to which Blair belongs, was made in the run-up to the 2001 general election. Blair used it as a platform to recite some of government's successes – on education, poverty, families and international debt relief – but also made some broader points about the role of faith groups in society, and his own convictions. He says: 'equal worth, responsibility, community – these values are funda- mental to my political creed.'

I am delighted to be with you this morning.

As a member of CSM, I am proud of the long and strong tradition of Christian Socialism within the Labour Party. But the Christian faith is not and should never be the monopoly of any one political party or section of the community. An abhorrence of prejudice based on race, class, gender or occupation is fundamental to the Gospels. It is what draws so many Christians into politics, across the political spectrum.

I am also delighted to see here today representatives from many other faith communities. Our major faith traditions – all of them more historic and deeply rooted than any political party or ideology – play a fundamental role in supporting and propagating values which bind us together as a nation.

The first National Holocaust Day, two months ago, was a testament to this fundamental unity. Religious leaders and political leaders joined together in honouring the sacredness of life, the equal worth of all, the importance of inclusion, and the responsibility of each individual and each community to uphold these values and never to forget the evil of which human societies are capable.

This year's census will, for the first time, contain a voluntary question about religion. Some will be surprised that this is necessary, at a time when many have been saying that religion and spirituality are in decline.

But I sense that the conventional wisdom is no longer the reality in modern Britain. I sense a new and vital energy about the practice of faith in the UK. A new and vital energy within the churches and other faith groups about engagement in the communities within which you work and have your being. And a new appreciation of the valuable work done by countless ministers of religion and their congregations, day in day out.

Today's theme of 'faith in politics' is, at the most basic level, about the importance of values in politics and public life. Politics without values is sheer pragmatism. Values without politics can be ineffective. The two must go together. So faith in politics isn't only about the relationship between faith and politics.

It is also about having faith in the political process itself and its capacity to achieve a better society. In an age of cynicism about politics, this cannot be emphasised too strongly.

Our values are clear. The equal worth of all citizens, and their right to be treated with equal respect and consideration despite their differences, are fundamental. So too is individual responsibility, a value which in the past the left sometimes underplayed. But a large part of individual responsibility concerns the obligations we owe to one another. The self is best realised in community with others. Society is the way we realise our mutual obligations – a society in which we all belong, no one left out. And Parliament and government, properly conceived, are the voice and instrument of the national community.

Equal worth, responsibility, community – these values are fundamental to my political creed.

They play a large part in faiths represented here today. You seek to realise them not just in the practice of your faith, but in your community and voluntary activity, extending far beyond the confines of your regular congregations.

I will say something about this voluntary activity later. But let me first address the critical issue of translating values into policies.

Policy is of course the business of politics. And it is not an easy business. In working out the best way forward it is not always simple to determine the right balance between the values of equal worth, community and individual responsibility.

For example, every issue in the reform of the welfare state involves judgements about what the individual can rightly expect of society, and what society can rightly expect of the individual.

The purpose of society is to empower the individual; to enable them to fulfil not just their economic potential but their potential as citizens. This is a contract between us all, based on mutual responsibility.

When we say that everyone able to do so has a clear responsibility to find a job and look after their family, we don't therefore say that government has no role. On the contrary, with policies such as the New Deal, the minimum wage and the Working Families Tax Credit, society through government is harnessing national resources to see that work pays, that job seekers get the support they need to find jobs, and that those with family responsibilities get the extra help they require without having to go back on to benefit. That approach explains why unemployment today is below a million for the first time in a quarter of a century.

A sharper focus on individual responsibility is going hand in hand with a great improvement in the support provided by government. Responsibility from all – security and opportunity for all. Not an idle slogan, but the only way forward as we break the old culture which left generations of families trapped in unemployment and poverty.

It is also the reason for investing in children. We are committed to abolishing child poverty in twenty years and reducing it by a quarter by 2004. Tax and benefits changes made since 1997 are lifting a million children out of poverty.

Education is critical. Children only get one chance of a decent education and too many have been failed in the past. When we came to office, barely half of eleven-year-olds were up to standard in basic literacy and numeracy. Now, thanks to smaller class sizes and the literacy and numeracy strategies, the proportion has risen to nearly three-quarters. All children are of equal worth. We want all children to have the opportunities and aspirations which only a minority possessed in the past.

And we can't separate the welfare of children from the families in which they are brought up. As I said in welcoming National Marriage Week, 'I fully support marriage and see it and family life as the foundation of a strong and stable society. The government's primary concern is with the stability of relationships where children are involved, and we recognise that this stability is most easily found within marriage.'

These are obligations we recognise within our nation, based on our values. But the nation itself is part of a broader community of nations.

Churches and other faith groups make a major contribution in delivering healthcare and education to the poorest in developing countries. I pay tribute to the work of the faith communities and their leaders, through Jubilee 2000, in highlighting the scale and urgency of the issues we face as members of an international community with obligations to its least advantaged.

Since the end of the millennium year, Britain has been deriving no profit from any debt repayments from the world's most heavily indebted poor countries. We have already agreed either to cancel their debts, or to place repayments in trust, ready for the day when the money can be used to tackle poverty. And we are encouraging other countries and the multilateral institutions to follow our lead.

I know that for many responding to the CSM's Faith in Politics enquiry, progress on debt relief has been especially welcomed. Many have also welcomed the fact that, after eighteen years of decline, the proportion of Britain's GDP committed to overseas aid is rising again. Between 1997 and 2004 the aid budget will increase by 45 per cent in real terms. By the final year it is set to total £3.6 billion, the largest UK aid budget ever.

But there is much more to do. We need more development aid from everyone in the international system; and we need to ensure that it is used more effectively. We need better terms of trade for poor countries and policies to help them attract greater flows of private investment. We need policies to tackle corruption and to promote effective governance and human rights. We need a stronger voice for poor countries within international institutions, and action to protect the environment. And we need increased investment in education and health.

For me these are basic issues of justice, and the government is active on all these fronts. The international development targets are clear: to halve the proportion of the world's population living in extreme poverty; to get all primary age children into school; to reduce infant and child mortality by two-thirds; and to ensure sustainable development plans are in place in every country to reverse the loss of environmental resources. We are committed to achieving all these targets by 2015.

Let me particularly highlight the health issue. Earlier this month Gordon Brown and Clare Short underlined our commitment to a major new global health fund to tackle the three diseases – HIV-AIDS, tuberculosis and malaria – which kill 6 million people a year, most of them in the poorest countries of sub-Saharan Africa. With some countries facing HIV infection rates of between 25 and 35 per cent, there is a real threat that we could see a reversal of the development gains made in Africa in the last half-century.

Together with the Italian and Canadian governments and the European Commission, we are promoting the idea of a new global health fund to combat the diseases of poverty. I have set up a dedicated team to look at how such a fund could work and I hope to have specific proposals to put to colleagues in the G8 in the summer.

In all these areas – poverty, children, education, international development – we have made a start. But we have so much more to do to live up to our values, and we will not be satisfied until we have achieved far more.

Let me turn now to local communities and the role of churches and other faith groups. Community action has always been a central mission of the churches and other faith groups. Looking outwards to the needs of others, beyond your own immediate members, is a prime expression of your beliefs and values. And in carrying out this mission you have developed some of the most effective voluntary and community organisations in the country.

In many cases you meet urgent social needs directly. In others you work in partnership with central and local government to give a special character to the delivery of public services which the state funds and would otherwise have to provide directly. In both these areas you make a unique contribution.

Education is a prime example of this second activity. Church schools are a true partnership between the churches and the government. They are a pillar of our national education system, valued by very many parents for their faith character, their moral emphasis, and the high quality of education they generally provide. Since 1997 we have been glad to form partnerships with other faith groups to provide state-funded schools.

It is misguided and outdated to suggest that there is a straight choice between voluntary activity and state activity. The two should go together. And where the two do go together – the government fully recognising its obligations, looking to the voluntary sector as partner not substitute – the impact is far greater than government acting on its own. We see this in countless charities, schools, health projects, youth work, provision for the elderly, the homeless, work with offenders and ex-offenders, local regeneration schemes and many other social activities.

Faith groups are among the main sponsors and innovators of voluntary activity in all these areas. Community by community, you are engaged directly. You know the terrain. You have committed volunteers, and often an infrastructure invaluable for delivering projects speedily and effectively. And you do this because of your faith, not in isolation from it, a point that government – central and local – must always appreciate.

My message today is therefore simple. Your role in the voluntary sector, working in partnership with central and local government, is legitimate and important. And where you have the desire and ability to play a greater role, with the support of your communities, we want to see you do so. But again I emphasise, we want you as partners, not substitutes.

We want to take this partnership forward wherever we can.

We are supporting an increase in the number of church and other faith schools, where you wish to sponsor them and there is local support. We are giving new community-based initiatives like Sure Start – for the under-threes in vulnerable areas – a specific brief to form partnerships with local voluntary and faith organisations.

We are launching today Experience Corps, a national organisation with £19 million of funding over three years to promote volunteering by the over-50s in each locality.

Experience Corps will operate through an independent company chaired by Sally Greengross. It will work in partnership with public and voluntary sector organisations, including faith-based groups, to create and fill new volunteering opportunities for the over-50s nationwide.

There is far more we can do in partnership if we create the right opportunities.

This is why, from next week, we will pay for most of the cost of VAT on repair and refurbishment work carried out on listed buildings in the faith sector. You can now spend less on repairing the church roof and more on other priorities.

It is why we support the work of the multi-faith Inner-Cities Religious Council, with full ministerial involvement, in developing your role in urban regeneration.

It is why we are pioneering a new Community Investment Tax Credit, to improve incentives for the private sector to support voluntary and faith-based community enterprise.

It is why we are glad to see the Local Government Association addressing the issue of faith group participation in locally funded voluntary activity, which we hope will lead to a strong endorsement of the further role you can play in partnership with local government.

To back this up we intend to pilot projects with local regeneration partnerships to see how obstacles to faith community involvement can be overcome in practice.

We are also glad to announce, after consultation with the churches and other faith communities, that a successor to the inter-faith Lambeth Group, set up to prepare for the millennium, will now look at how government consults and interfaces with faith communities across the range of our shared interests. This has my personal backing, and we stand ready to give whatever support is necessary to the Group and the proposals it ultimately makes.

Let me end by returning to faith and values.

All your local and social activity is driven by your values and beliefs and the spiritual dimension of your faith.

In a world of uncertainty, rapid change and technological transformation, I believe these underpinning values are becoming more not less relevant. I spend a lot of my time visiting schools and talking to young people. I don't find any shortage of ideals or values. On the contrary, as Chief Rabbi Jonathan Sacks put it recently, our teenagers are very much the 'we' generation, not the 'me' generation.

It is the 'we generation' that we want to shape tomorrow. And if we remain true to our values, they will have the opportunities and institutions to do so.

General Election victory statement
8 June 2001

The Labour Party won the June 2001 general election with a landslide victory, making Tony Blair the first Labour Prime Minister to lead the party into two full parliamentary terms. But the election victory was not celebrated by cheering crowds waving Union Jacks as in 1997. The election turnout fell to 58 per cent, a new low, and there was little excitement about the election. There was a more muted feel to the victory, and this statement delivered to the media in Downing Street reflects the businesslike mood.

I've just returned from Buckingham Palace from my audience with the Queen. I want to say what an enormous privilege and honour it is to be entrusted with the government of this country. And I am deeply conscious of that privilege and honour at this time. I would like to congratulate all the Members of Parliament from whatever political party who've been elected to the House of Commons. I would like also to say this word about my opponent in the election, Mr Hague. Even though, obviously, I've profoundly disagreed with many of the things he may have said during the course of this campaign I thought he showed extraordinary stoicism and resilience in very difficult circumstances. And I said to him in the early hours of this morning I wish him well, I wish him the very best of luck in the future.

It has been a remarkable and historic victory for my party but I am in no doubt at all as to what it means. It is a mandate for reform and for investment in the future and it is also very clearly an instruction to deliver. I've learnt many things over the past four years as Prime Minister. I've learnt, I hope, from the mistakes as well the good things but above all else I've learnt of the importance of establishing the clear priorities of government. Of setting them out clearly for people and then focusing on them relentlessly whatever events may come and go. And I believe that there is an even greater obligation on us, on me, after re-election to tell people very clearly what are the difficult choices and challenges we face and how we work our way through them. And that I will try to do.

So in the course of the campaign that we've just had I set out in a series of speeches the changes that I believe the country needs to see. On the foundation of a strong economy we need to keep it strong, we need to make sure that mortgages and inflation are as low as possible. But then on top of that we need to start building the economy of the future based on skill and talent and education and the application of technology. Knowing that for this country in the future the forces of global competition and technological change mean that we can only compete on the basis of skill and ability, not low wages.

And then we have the importance, the critical importance, of investment in and reform of our public services, most particularly our National Health Service, our education system and our transport system. And again here I have no doubt at all from talking to people, from meeting them, from hearing their concerns over the past few weeks that they may applaud the direction in which we wish to go but they want us to do it as fast and as profoundly as we possibly can. And that, again, is an obligation we must discharge. In our welfare system we need change too, we need to separate very clearly those who cannot work who need security and protection and must have it. And those who can work but at present don't who we must try to help off a life on benefit and in to productive work.

Then there is the reform of our Criminal Justice System. There is no issue that touches our citizens more deeply than crime and law and order on our streets. And we need to make the changes there so that we have a Criminal Justice System that punishes the criminal but also offers those convicted of crime a chance to rehabilitate and get their way out of the life of crime.

And finally in respect of Europe and the wider world we need to make changes there too so that we are engaged, exerting influence, having the self-belief not to turn our back on the world or retreat into isolationism.

And these changes will not be easy but Britain is a very special country and its people are a very special people. And our very best quality is our ability, when we need to do so, to face up to and overcome the challenge of change. And all those changes are for one purpose, and that again is a purpose I've tried to set out in the few weeks of this campaign and will try to set out again in the years to come. And the purpose of each and every change that we make must be this, to create a society which is a genuine, open, meritocratic nation. Where we lay to one side the old adage about knowing your place and where the only place that any man, woman or child knows is the place that their talents take them. Where we create a country genuinely where not just a few people at the top but everyone, every one of our citizens, gets the chance to fulfil their true potential.

I believe in the last four years we have laid foundations, I believe our victory in this election shows that the British people understand we have laid foundations but now is the time to build upon them. Thank you.

Statement in response to terrorist attacks in the United States

11 September 2001

Blair was about to deliver a speech to the Trades Union Congress in Blackpool when he was told about the attacks on the World Trade Center and the Pentagon. He travelled immediately to London and convened the COBRA committee – Britain's emergency high command. This statement, delivered to the media towards the end of 11 September 2001, has two key messages: that the UK government had taken immediate precautionary action, including suspending flights over London and stepping up security at government buildings, and secondly, that the British government would stand 'shoulder to shoulder' with the Americans. Few could argue that Blair failed to live up to this last promise.

The full horror of what has happened in the United States earlier today is now becoming clearer. It is hard even to contemplate the utter carnage and terror which has engulfed so many innocent people. We've offered President Bush and the American people our solidarity, our profound sympathy, and our prayers. But it is plain that citizens of many countries round the world, including Britain, will have been caught up in this terror.

I have just chaired an emergency meeting of the British government civil contingencies committee, and I would like to explain some of the measures that we have agreed to take here. There are a range of precautionary measures. We have stepped up security at airports to the highest levels. No flights will take off from the United

Kingdom for which we cannot apply the highest standards of security for air crew and passengers. Private flights have been stopped except where specifically authorised. Flight paths into London have been changed, so there will be no civil over-flights of central London.

Security has been increased across the full range of government buildings and military premises. The police across the whole of the UK are on full alert. All our defence facilities round the world have been moved to high alert to ensure the protection of British service personnel. Advice is being given to major financial and business institutions about appropriate security measures. A number of other security measures have been taken, and of course we are in close touch with US, European and other allies, and are co-operating with them on issues of security. All relevant ministers remain in communication, and the committee – the civil contingencies committee – will meet again tomorrow at 8am.

Obviously some of these measures, not least the effect upon airports, will lead to some disruption, and I hope people understand that. But other than the specific measures we have taken, or that we have advised others to take, business and everyday life can continue as normal. As for those that carried out these attacks, there are no adequate words of condemnation. Their barbarism will stand as their shame for all eternity.

As I said earlier, this mass terrorism is the new evil in our world. The people who perpetrate it have no regard whatever for the sanctity or value of human life, and we, the democracies of the world, must come together to defeat it and eradicate it. This is not a battle between the United States of America and terrorism, but between the free and democratic world and terrorism. We, therefore, here in Britain stand shoulder to shoulder with our American friends in this hour of tragedy, and we, like them, will not rest until this evil is driven from our world.

Statement on military action in Afghanistan

7 October 2001

Twenty-six days after the terrorist attacks in New York, Washington and Pennsylvania, the United States and Britain, backed by a broad international coalition, launched a military assault on the Taliban regime in Afghanistan. Blair delivered this statement to the media at Downing Street as the first reports of the aerial bombardment of targets in Afghanistan started to appear. He is keen to mention humanitarian aid for the Afghan people, and the need to tackle the drugs trade. Blair's statement followed that of George W. Bush, speaking in Washington.

As you will know from the announcement by President Bush military action against targets inside Afghanistan has begun. I can confirm that UK forces are engaged in this action. I want to pay tribute if I might right at the outset to Britain's armed forces. There is no greater strength for a British Prime Minister and the British nation at a time like this than to know that the forces we are calling upon are amongst the very best in the world.

They and their families are, of course, carrying an immense burden at this moment and will be feeling deep anxiety as will the British people. But we can take pride in their courage, their sense of duty and the esteem with which they're held throughout the world.

No country lightly commits forces to military action and the inevitable risks involved but we made it clear following the attacks upon the United States on September 11 that we would take part in action once it was clear who was responsible.

There is no doubt in my mind, nor in the mind of anyone who has been through all the available evidence, including intelligence material, that these attacks were carried out by the al Qaeda network masterminded by Osama bin Laden. Equally it is clear that his network is harboured and supported by the Taliban regime inside Afghanistan.

It is now almost a month since the atrocity occurred, it is more than two weeks since an ultimatum was delivered to the Taliban to yield up the terrorists or face the consequences. It is clear beyond doubt that they will not do this. They were given the choice of siding with justice or siding with terror and they chose to side with terror.

There are three parts all equally important to the operation of which we're engaged: military, diplomatic and humanitarian. The military action we are taking will be targeted against places we know to be involved in the operation of terror or against the military apparatus of the Taliban. This military plan has been put together mindful of our determination to do all we humanly can to avoid civilian casualties.

I cannot disclose, obviously, how long this action will last but we will act with reason and resolve. We have set the objectives to eradicate Osama bin Laden's network of terror and to take action against the Taliban regime that is sponsoring it. As to the precise British involvement I can confirm that last Wednesday the US government made a specific request that a number of UK military assets be used in the operation which has now begun. And I gave authority for these assets to be deployed. They include the base at Diego Garcia, reconnaissance and flight support aircraft and missile firing submarines. Missile firing submarines are in use tonight. The air assets will be available for use in the coming days.

The United States are obviously providing the bulk of the force required in leading this operation. But this is an international effort:

as well as the UK, France, Germany, Australia and Canada have also committed themselves to take part in the operation.

On the diplomatic and political front in the time I've been Prime Minister I cannot recall a situation that has commanded so quickly such a powerful coalition of support and not just from those countries directly involved in military action but from many others in all parts of the world. The coalition has, I believe, strengthened not weakened in the rwenty-six days since the atrocity occurred. And this is in no small measure due to the statesmanship of President Bush to whom I pay tribute tonight.

The world understands that whilst, of course, there are dangers in acting, the dangers of inaction are far, far greater. The threat of further such outrages, the threat to our economies, the threat to the stability of the world.

On the humanitarian front we are assembling a coalition of support for refugees in and outside Afghanistan which is as vital as the military coalition. Even before September 11 four million Afghans were on the move. There are two million refugees in Pakistan and one and a half million in Iran. We have to act for humanitarian reasons to alleviate the appalling suffering of the Afghan people and deliver stability so that people from that region stay in that region.

So we are taking action therefore on all those three fronts: military, diplomatic and humanitarian. I also want to say very directly to the British people why this matters so much directly to Britain. First let us not forget that the attacks of September 11 represented the worst terrorist outrage against British citizens in our history. The murder of British citizens, whether it happens overseas or not, is an attack upon Britain. But even if no British citizen had died it would be right to act.

This atrocity was an attack on us all, on people of all faiths and people of none. We know the al Qaeda network threaten Europe, including Britain, and, indeed, any nation throughout the world that does not share their fanatical views. So we have a direct interest in acting in our own self-defence to protect British lives. It was also an attack (indistinct) just on lives but on livelihoods. We can see since 11 September how economic confidence has suffered with all that means for British jobs and British industry. Our prosperity and standard of living, therefore, require us to deal with this terrorist threat.

We act also because the al Qaeda network and the Taliban regime are funded in large part on the drugs trade. Ninety per cent of all the heroin sold on British streets originates from Afghanistan. Stopping that trade is, again, directly in our interests.

I wish to say finally, as I've said many times before, that this is not a war with Islam. It angers me, as it angers the vast majority of Muslims, to hear bin Laden and his associates described as Islamic terrorists. They are terrorists pure and simple. Islam is a peaceful and tolerant religion and the acts of these people are wholly contrary to the teachings of the Koran.

These are difficult and testing times, therefore, for all of us. People are bound to be concerned about what the terrorists may seek to do in response. I should say there is at present no specific credible threat to the UK that we know of and that we have in place tried and tested contingency plans which are the best possible response to any further attempts at terror.

This, of course, is a moment of the utmost gravity for the world. None of the leaders involved in this action want war. None of our nations want it. We are a peaceful people. But we know that sometimes to safeguard peace we have to fight. Britain has learnt that lesson many times in our history. We only do it if the cause is just but this cause is just. The murder of almost seven thousand innocent people in America was an attack on our freedom, our way of life, an attack on civilised values the world over. We waited so that those responsible could be yielded up by those shielding them. That offer was refused. We now have no choice so we will act. And our determination in acting is total. We will not let up or rest until our objectives are met in full.

Labour Party conference speech

Brighton, 3 October 2001

The Guardian's *Michael White called Blair's speech to the 2001 Labour Party conference in Brighton 'almost certainly the most powerful speech of his career'. It came just days after the horrors of 9/11, and reflects Blair's realisation that global politics had changed for good ('The kaleidoscope has been shaken'). There is no party political knockabout or any sideswipes at his opponents. This speech addresses the fundamental questions of geopolitics: terrorism, genocide, poverty, war, and regional instability. At times, Blair seems to echo the Victorian imperialists Gladstone and Palmerston in his conviction that Britain can be a force for good in the world. This speech contains the philosophical basis for Blair's actions in taking Britain to war in Afghanistan and Iraq, and, more than any other of his conference speeches, is his own words.*

In retrospect, the millennium marked only a moment in time. It was the events of September 11 that marked a turning point in history, where we confront the dangers of the future and assess the choices facing humankind.

It was a tragedy. An act of evil. From this nation goes our deepest sympathy and prayers for the victims and our profound solidarity with the American people.

We were with you at the first. We will stay with you to the last.

Just two weeks ago, in New York, after the church service I met some of the families of the British victims.

It was in many ways a very British occasion. Tea and biscuits. It was raining outside. Around the edge of the room, strangers making small talk, trying to be normal people in an abnormal situation.

And as you crossed the room, you felt the longing and sadness; hands clutching photos of sons and daughters, wives and husbands; imploring you to believe them when they said there was still an outside chance of their loved ones being found alive, when you knew in truth that all hope was gone.

And then a middle-aged mother looks you in the eyes and tells you her only son has died, and asks you: why?

I tell you: you do not feel like the most powerful person in the country at times like that.

Because there is no answer. There is no justification for their pain. Their son did nothing wrong. The woman, seven months pregnant, whose child will never know its father, did nothing wrong.

They don't want revenge. They want something better in memory of their loved ones.

I believe their memorial can and should be greater than simply the punishment of the guilty. It is that, out of the shadow of this evil, should emerge lasting good: destruction of the machinery of terrorism wherever it is found; hope amongst all nations of a new beginning where we seek to resolve differences in a calm and ordered way; greater understanding between nations and between faiths; and above all justice and prosperity for the poor and dispossessed, so that people everywhere can see the chance of a better future through the hard work and creative power of the free citizen, not the violence and savagery of the fanatic.

I know that here in Britain people are anxious, even a little frightened. I understand that. People know we must act but they worry what might follow.

They worry about the economy and talk of recession. And, of course there are dangers; it is a new situation. But the fundamentals of the US, British and European economies are strong. Every reasonable measure of internal security is being undertaken.

Our way of life is a great deal stronger and will last a great deal longer than the actions of fanatics, small in number and now facing a unified world against them. People should have confidence.

This is a battle with only one outcome: our victory, not theirs.

* * *

This is an extraordinary moment for progressive politics.

Our values are the right ones for this age: the power of community, solidarity, the collective ability to further the individual's interests.

People ask me if I think ideology is dead. My answer is: in the sense of rigid forms of economic and social theory, yes.

The twentieth century killed those ideologies and their passing causes little regret. But, in the sense of a governing idea in politics, based on values, no. The governing idea of modern social democracy is community. Founded on the principles of social justice. That people should rise according to merit, not birth; that the test of any decent society is not the contentment of the wealthy and strong, but the commitment to the poor and weak.

But values aren't enough. The mantle of leadership comes at a price: the courage to learn and change; to show how values that stand for all ages can be applied in a way relevant to each age.

Our politics only succeed when the realism is as clear as the idealism.

This Party's strength today comes from the journey of change and learning we have made.

We learnt that however much we strive for peace, we need strong defence capability where a peaceful approach fails.

We learnt that equality is about equal worth, not equal outcomes.

Today our idea of society is shaped around mutual responsibility;

a deal, an agreement between citizens, not a one-way gift from the well-off to the dependent.

Our economic and social policy today owes as much to the liberal social democratic tradition of Lloyd George, Keynes and Beveridge as to the socialist principles of the 1945 government.

Just over a decade ago, people asked if Labour could ever win again. Today they ask the same question of the opposition. Painful though that journey of change has been, it has been worth it, every stage of the way.

On this journey, the values have never changed. The aims haven't. Our aims would be instantly recognisable to every Labour leader from Keir Hardie onwards. But the means do change.

The journey hasn't ended. It never ends. The next stage for New Labour is not backwards; it is renewing ourselves again. Just after the election, an old colleague of mine said: 'Come on, Tony, now we've won again, can't we drop all this New Labour and do what we believe in?'

I said: 'It's worse than you think. I really do believe in it.'

* * *

America has its faults as a society, as we have ours.

But I think of the Union of America born out of the defeat of slavery.

I think of its constitution, with its inalienable rights granted to every citizen still a model for the world.

I think of a black man, born in poverty, who became chief of their armed forces and is now secretary of state Colin Powell and I wonder frankly whether such a thing could have happened here.

I think of the Statue of Liberty and how many refugees, migrants and the impoverished passed its light and felt that if not for them, for their children, a new world could indeed be theirs.

I think of a country where people who do well don't have questions asked about their accent, their class, their beginnings but have admiration for what they have done and the success they've achieved.

I think of those New Yorkers I met, still in shock, but resolute; the firefighters and police, mourning their comrades but still head held high.

I think of all this and I reflect: yes, America has its faults, but it is a free country, a democracy, it is our ally and some of the reaction to September 11 betrays a hatred of America that shames those that feel it.

So I believe this is a fight for freedom. And I want to make it a fight for justice too. Justice not only to punish the guilty. But justice to bring those same values of democracy and freedom to people round the world.

And I mean: freedom, not only in the narrow sense of personal liberty but in the broader sense of each individual having the economic and social freedom to develop their potential to the full. That is what community means, founded on the equal worth of all.

The starving, the wretched, the dispossessed, the ignorant, those living in want and squalor from the deserts of Northern Africa to the slums of Gaza, to the mountain ranges of Afghanistan: they too are our cause.

This is a moment to seize. The kaleidoscope has been shaken. The pieces are in flux. Soon they will settle again. Before they do, let us reorder this world around us.

Today, humankind has the science and technology to destroy itself or to provide prosperity to all. Yet science can't make that choice for us. Only the moral power of a world acting as a community can.

'By the strength of our common endeavour we achieve more together than we can alone.'

For those people who lost their lives on September 11 and those that mourn them, now is the time for the strength to build that community. Let that be their memorial.

The Courage of Our Convictions
Fabian Society pamphlet, 2002

In September 2002, ahead of a difficult Labour Party conference, with revolts promised on public sector reform, Blair published a Fabian Society pamphlet containing his views. The pamphlet appeared against a backdrop of growing criticism about the scale and pace of improvements to the health, education and transport systems, and disquiet over some aspects of the government's plans.

Here is the opening section of the pamphlet, which makes the case for reform, and seeks to explain to Labour voters and those working in the public services, why reform is necessary.

The progressive prize

New Labour's purpose is not simply to amend a few policies or to manage the country more efficiently. It is to set a new course for Britain in the twenty-first century. Central to this goal is the transformation of our public services.

We reject the pessimists and the Tories who believe our public services cannot be improved upon and increasing investment would only be pouring money into a bottomless pit. Their option is privatised services for the better off and cheap 'safety net' public services for the poor with dismantled protection for those who work in them. It is a future of extremes in which the divide between rich and poor grows as the middle class opts out systematically from public provision. The goal is a smaller state with an ever decreasing share of national income invested in public services.

It is why they spend so much time denigrating our public services, refusing to acknowledge progress, desperate to demoralise those who use them. What they want to do do is to undermine the notion of universal public service, paid for through taxes and based on need, not ability to pay.

We reject also the view, held by some on the left, that a Labour government's role is simply to defend existing services, not to extend choice or accountability but simply pour in more money. They share – although they would never admit it – the right's pessimistic view that our public services cannot fully meet people's needs and aspirations. They believe – wrongly in my view – that the best way to defend those working in the public service and to secure their futures is to defend the status quo and veto reform. This approach urges higher public spending to address the worst shortcomings of current provision, but would leave arcane structures in the public sector largely unchanged.

Radical investment and reform

New Labour, in contrast, is confident in our public services and public servants. Our vision is rooted in strong public services that extend social justice in a dynamic market economy through investment in the talents of every individual, not just an elite.

We believe public services are both a ladder of opportunity and a source of security in a global economy, helping our citizens to negotiate unpredictable change. So we are prepared not only to inject greater investment into public services, but to ensure they can play their full part in building a fairer society, to reform the systems and structures of those services for the modern era.

The opportunity for the centre-left in British politics to shape the destiny of the country has never been greater. But if the right is able to claim, through our inability to reform these institutions or promote choice for the individual citizen, that public services are inherently flawed, we will see support for them wither and the clamour for private provision increase. It will mean a further assault on the public realm and a devastating attack on our most cherished ideals.

By contrast, if we are bold enough in our mission to reform we will rehabilitate public services after two decades of neglect, and mark not merely a new advance for progressive politics, but the extension of opportunity and social justice in our society. This represents a great and precious moment for Britain.

We recognise we cannot achieve this alone. To be strong incumbents supporting the public sector while also acting as agents of change is an inherently difficult task. It requires a government able to learn and renew as it governs. We must improve the partnership with the people who work in our public services and those who use them. The political and intellectual resources to sustain a progressive government extend well beyond our own party confines, and we need to exploit those resources more effectively.

On 4 June 1945, two days before the D-Day landings, Churchill invited Ernie Bevin to accompany him to Portsmouth to say farewell to some of the troops. 'They were going off to face this terrific battle', Bevin recounted, 'with great hearts and great courage. The one question they put to me as I went through their ranks was: "Ernie, when we have done this job for you are we going back on the dole?" Both the Prime Minister and I answered, "No, you are not."'

The people of 1945 wanted a government that could fulfil their hopes of work and dignity in old age, of decent life-chances for their children. Half a century later in a time of peace and prosperity we again have the chance to advance decisively the interests of working people and their families in Britain.

Only by meeting this urgent challenge of revitalising our public services can we realise Labour's historic values. Strong public services have always defined New Labour's purpose, infused our ambition, and fuelled our optimism about what we can achieve for

Britain in the twenty-first century. It would be a betrayal of our Party's past achievements and values if we were to falter in the task of reform. For reform is the surest route to social justice.

Iraq debate speech to the House of Commons

18 March 2003

When Tony Blair rose to make this speech on the eve of the war in Iraq to a full, noisy and expectant House of Commons chamber, he did not know whether he would still be Prime Minister by nightfall. Faced with a major rebellion by Labour backbenchers opposed to military action against Saddam Hussein, Blair needed not just to win the argument, but to win the vote in the House of Commons. If he had failed to do so, it seems likely that he would have handed his letter of resignation to the Queen.

Blair, deploying all of his skills as a barrister, detailed Iraq's breaches of UN resolutions, the cat-and-mouse interplay between Saddam Hussein and the UN weapons inspectors, and, most controversially, the threat posed by Iraq's weapons of mass destruction.

Blair won the vote, and within weeks British and American troops were in action in Iraq.

I beg to move the motion standing on the order paper in my name and those of my Right Honourable friends.

At the outset I say: it is right that this House debate this issue and pass judgement. That is the democracy that is our right but that others struggle for in vain. And again I say: I do not disrespect the views of those in opposition to mine.

This is a tough choice. But it is also a stark one: to stand British troops down and turn back; or to hold firm to the course we have set. I believe we must hold firm.

The question most often posed is not: why does it matter? But: why does it matter so much? Here we are: the government with its most serious test, its majority at risk, the first Cabinet resignation over an issue of policy. The main parties divided. People who agree on everything else disagree on this and, likewise, those who never agree on anything finding common cause.

The country and Parliament reflect each other: a debate that, as time has gone on, has become less bitter but not less grave.

So: why does it matter so much?

Because the outcome of this issue will now determine more than the fate of the Iraqi regime and more than the future of the Iraqi people, for so long brutalised by Saddam. It will determine the way Britain and the world confront the central security threat of the twenty-first century; the development of the UN; the relationship between Europe and the US; the relations within the EU and the way the US engages with the rest of the world.

It will determine the pattern of international politics for the next generation.

But first, Iraq and its WMD. In April 1991, after the Gulf War Iraq was given fifteen days to provide a full and final declaration of all its WMD.

Saddam had used the weapons against Iran, against his own people, causing thousands of deaths. He had had plans to use them against allied forces. It became clear after the Gulf War that the WMD ambitions of Iraq were far more extensive than hitherto thought. This issue was identified by the UN as one for urgent remedy. UNSCOM, the weapons inspection team, was set up. They were expected to complete their task following the declaration at the end of April 1991.

The declaration when it came was false – a blanket denial of the programme, other than in a very tentative form. So the twelve-year game began.

The inspectors probed. Finally in March 1992, Iraq admitted it had previously undeclared WMD but said it had destroyed them. It gave another full and final declaration. Again the inspectors probed but found little.

In October 1994, Iraq stopped cooperating with UNSCOM altogether. Military action was threatened. Inspections resumed. In March 1995, in an effort to rid Iraq of the inspectors, a further full and final declaration of WMD was made. By July 1995, Iraq was forced to admit that too was false.

In August they provided yet another full and final declaration. Then, a week later, Saddam's son-in-law, Hussein Kamal, defected to Jordan. He disclosed a far more extensive BW programme and for the first time said Iraq had weaponised the programme; something Saddam had always strenuously denied. All this had been happening whilst the inspectors were in Iraq. Kamal also revealed Iraq's crash programme to produce a nuclear weapon in 1990.

Iraq was forced then to release documents which showed just how extensive those programmes were. In November 1995, Jordan intercepted prohibited components for missiles that could be used for WMD. In June 1996, a further full and final declaration was made.

That too turned out to be false. In June 1997, inspectors were barred from specific sites. In September 1997, another full and final declaration was made. Also false. Meanwhile, the inspectors discovered VX nerve agent production equipment, something always denied by the Iraqis. In October 1997, the US and the UK threatened military action if Iraq refused to comply with the inspectors. But obstruction continued.

Finally, under threat of action, in February 1998, Kofi Annan went to Baghdad and negotiated a memorandum with Saddam to allow inspections to continue.

They did. For a few months. In August, cooperation was suspended. In December the inspectors left. Their final report is a withering indictment of Saddam's lies, deception and obstruction, with large quantities of WMD remained unaccounted for.

The US and the UK then, in December 1998, undertook Desert Fox, a targeted bombing campaign to degrade as much of the Iraqi WMD facilities as we could.

In 1999, a new inspections team, UNMOVIC, was set up. But Saddam refused to allow them to enter Iraq.

So there they stayed, in limbo, until after Resolution 1441 when last November they were allowed to return.

What is the claim of Saddam today? Why, exactly the same claim as before: that he has no WMD. Indeed we are asked to believe that after seven years of obstruction and non-compliance finally resulting in the inspectors leaving in 1998, seven years in which he hid his programme, built it up even whilst inspection teams were in Iraq, that after they left he then voluntarily decided to do what he had consistently refused to do under coercion.

When the inspectors left in 1998, they left unaccounted for:

- 10,000 litres of anthrax;
- a far-reaching VX nerve agent programme;
- up to 6,500 chemical munitions;
- at least 80 tonnes of mustard gas, possibly more than ten times that amount;
- unquantifiable amounts of sarin, botulinum toxin and a host of other biological poisons;
- an entire Scud missile programme.

We are now seriously asked to accept that in the last few years, contrary to all history, contrary to all intelligence, he decided unilaterally to destroy the weapons. Such a claim is palpably absurd.

Resolution 1441 is very clear. It lays down a final opportunity for Saddam to disarm. It rehearses the fact that he has been, for years, in material breach of seventeen separate UN Resolutions. It says that this time compliance must be full, unconditional and immediate. The first step is a full and final declaration of all WMD to be given on 8 December. I won't go through all the events since then – the House is familiar with them – but this much is accepted by all members of the UNSC.

The 8 December declaration is false. That in itself is a material breach. Iraq has made some concessions to cooperation but no one disputes it is not fully co-operating. Iraq continues to deny it has any WMD, though no serious intelligence service anywhere in the world believes them.

On 7 March, the inspectors published a remarkable document. It is 173 pages long, detailing all the unanswered questions about Iraq's WMD. It lists twenty-nine different areas where they have been unable to obtain information.

For example, on VX it says: 'Documentation available to UNMOVIC suggests that Iraq at least had had far-reaching plans to weaponise VX ...

'Mustard constituted an important part (about 70 per cent) of Iraq's CW arsenal ... 550 mustard filled shells and up to 450 mustard filled aerial bombs unaccounted for ... additional uncertainty with respect of 6,526 aerial bombs, corresponding to approximately 1,000 tonnes of agent, predominantly mustard.

'Based on unaccounted for growth media, Iraq's potential production of anthrax could have been in the range of about 15,000 to 25,000 litres ... Based on all the available evidence, the strong presumption is that about 10,000 litres of anthrax was not destroyed and may still exist.'

On this basis, had we meant what we said in Resolution 1441, the Security Council should have convened and condemned Iraq as in material breach.

What is perfectly clear is that Saddam is playing the same old games in the same old way. Yes, there are concessions. But no fundamental change of heart or mind.

But the inspectors indicated there was at least some cooperation; and the world rightly hesitated over war. We therefore approached a second Resolution in this way.

We laid down an ultimatum calling upon Saddam to come into line with Resolution 1441 or be in material breach. Not an unreasonable proposition, given the history. But still countries hesitated: how do we know how to judge full cooperation?

We then worked on a further compromise. We consulted the inspectors and drew up five tests based on the document they published on 7 March. Tests like interviews with thirty scientists outside of Iraq; production of the anthrax or documentation showing its destruction.

The inspectors added another test: that Saddam should publicly call on Iraqis to cooperate with them. So we constructed this framework: that Saddam should be given a specified time to fulfil all six tests to show full cooperation; that if he did so the inspectors could then set out a forward work programme and that if he failed to do so, action would follow.

So clear benchmarks; plus a clear ultimatum. I defy anyone to describe that as an unreasonable position. Last Monday, we were getting somewhere with it. We very nearly had majority agreement and I thank the Chilean President particularly for the constructive way he approached the issue.

There were debates about the length of the ultimatum. But the basic construct was gathering support. Then, on Monday night, France said it would veto a second Resolution whatever the circumstances. Then France denounced the six tests. Later that day, Iraq rejected them. Still, we continued to negotiate.

Last Friday, France said they could not accept any ultimatum. On Monday, we made final efforts to secure agreement. But they remain utterly opposed to anything which lays down an ultimatum authorising action in the event of non-compliance by Saddam. Just consider the position we are asked to adopt. Those on the Security Council opposed to us say they want Saddam to disarm but will not countenance any new Resolution that authorises force in the event of non-compliance.

That is their position. No to any ultimatum; no to any Resolution that stipulates that failure to comply will lead to military action.

So we must demand he disarm but relinquish any concept of a threat if he doesn't. From December 1998 to December 2002, no UN inspector was allowed to inspect anything in Iraq. For four years, not a thing. What changed his mind? The threat of force. From December to January and then from January through to February, concessions were made. What changed his mind? The threat of force. And what makes him now issue invitations to the inspectors, discover documents he said he never had, produce evidence of weapons supposed to be non-existent, destroy missiles he said he would keep? The imminence of force.

The only persuasive power to which he responds is 250,000 allied troops on his doorstep. And yet when that fact is so obvious that it is staring us in the face, we are told that any Resolution that authorises force will be vetoed.

Not just opposed. Vetoed. Blocked. The way ahead was so clear. It was for the UN to pass a second Resolution setting out benchmarks for compliance; with an ultimatum that if they were ignored, action would follow.

The tragedy is that had such a Resolution been issued, he might just have complied. Because the only route to peace with someone like Saddam Hussein is diplomacy backed by force.

Yet the moment we proposed the benchmarks, canvassed support for an ultimatum, there was an immediate recourse to the language of the veto.

And now the world has to learn the lesson all over again that weakness in the face of a threat from a tyrant is the surest way not to peace but to war.

Looking back over twelve years, we have been victims of our own desire to placate the implacable, to persuade towards reason the utterly unreasonable, to hope that there was some genuine intent to do good in a regime whose mind is in fact evil. Now the very length of time counts against us. You've waited twelve years. Why not wait a little longer?

And indeed we have.

[Resolution] 1441 gave a final opportunity. The first test was 8 December. He failed it. But still we waited. Until 27 January, the first inspection report that showed the absence of full cooperation. Another breach. And still we waited.

Until 14 February and then 28 February with concessions, according to the old familiar routine, tossed to us to whet our appetite for hope and further waiting. But still no one, not the inspectors nor any member of the Security Council, not any half-way rational observer, believes Saddam is cooperating fully or unconditionally or immediately.

Our fault has not been impatience.

The truth is our patience should have been exhausted weeks and months and years ago. Even now, when if the world united and gave him an ultimatum: comply or face forcible disarmament, he might just do it, the world hesitates and in that hesitation he senses the weakness and therefore continues to defy.

What would any tyrannical regime possessing WMD think viewing the history of the world's diplomatic dance with Saddam? That our capacity to pass firm resolutions is only matched by our feebleness in implementing them.

That is why this indulgence has to stop. Because it is dangerous. It is dangerous if such regimes disbelieve us. Dangerous if they think they can use our weakness, our hesitation, even the natural urges of our democracy towards peace, against us. Dangerous because one day they will mistake our innate revulsion against war for permanent incapacity; when in fact, pushed to the limit, we will act. But then when we act, after years of pretence, the action will have to be harder, bigger, more total in its impact. Iraq is not the only regime with WMD. But back away now from this confrontation and future conflicts will be infinitely worse and more devastating.

But, of course, in a sense, any fair observer does not really dispute that Iraq is in breach and that 1441 implies action in such circumstances. The real problem is that, underneath, people dispute that Iraq is a threat; dispute the link between terrorism and WMD; dispute the whole basis of our assertion that the two together constitute a fundamental assault on our way of life.

There are glib and sometimes foolish comparisons with the 1930s. No one here is an appeaser. But the only relevant point of analogy is that, with history, we know what happened. We can look back and say: there's the time; that was the moment; for example, when Czechoslovakia was swallowed up by the Nazis – that's when we should have acted.

But it wasn't clear at the time. In fact at the time, many people thought such a fear fanciful. Worse, put forward in bad faith by warmongers. Listen to this editorial – from a paper I'm pleased to say with a different position today – but written in late 1938 after Munich when, by now, you would have thought the world was tumultuous in its desire to act.

'Be glad in your hearts. Give thanks to your God. People of Britain, your children are safe. Your husbands and your sons will not march to war. Peace is a victory for all mankind. And now let us go back to our own affairs. We have had enough of those menaces, conjured up from the Continent to confuse us.'

Naturally should Hitler appear again in the same form, we would know what to do. But the point is that history doesn't declare the future to us so plainly. Each time is different and the present must be judged without the benefit of hindsight.

So let me explain the nature of this threat as I see it.

The threat today is not that of the 1930s. It's not big powers going to war with each other.

The ravages which fundamentalist political ideology inflicted on the twentieth century are memories.

The Cold War is over. Europe is at peace, if not always diplomatically. But the world is ever more interdependent. Stock markets and economies rise and fall together. Confidence is the key to prosperity. Insecurity spreads like contagion. So people crave stability and order. The threat is chaos. And there are two begetters of chaos. Tyrannical regimes with WMD and extreme terrorist groups who profess a perverted and false view of Islam.

Let me tell the House what I know. I know that there are some countries or groups within countries that are proliferating and trading in WMD, especially nuclear weapons technology.

I know there are companies, individuals, some former scientists on nuclear weapons programmes, selling their equipment or expertise.

I know there are several countries – mostly dictatorships with highly repressive regimes – desperately trying to acquire chemical weapons, biological weapons or, in particular, nuclear weapons capability. Some of these countries are now a short time away from having a serviceable nuclear weapon. This activity is not diminishing. It is increasing.

We all know that there are terrorist cells now operating in most major countries. Just as in the last two years, around twenty different nations have suffered serious terrorist outrages. Thousands have died in them.

The purpose of terrorism lies not just in the violent act itself. It is in producing terror. It sets out to inflame, to divide, to produce consequences which they then use to justify further terror.

Round the world it now poisons the chances of political progress: in the Middle East; in Kashmir; in Chechnya; in Africa. The removal of the Taliban in Afghanistan dealt it a blow. But it has not gone away.

And these two threats have different motives and different origins but they share one basic common view: they detest the freedom, democracy and tolerance that are the hallmarks of our way of life. At the moment, I accept that association between them is loose. But it is hardening. And the possibility of the two coming together – of terrorist groups in possession of WMD, even of a so-called dirty radiological bomb – is now, in my judgement, a real and present danger.

And let us recall: what was shocking about 11 September was not just the slaughter of the innocent; but the knowledge that had the terrorists been able to, there would have been not 3,000 innocent dead, but 30,000 or 300,000 and the more the suffering, the greater the terrorists' rejoicing.

Three kilograms of VX from a rocket launcher would contaminate a quarter of a square kilometre of a city. Millions of lethal doses are contained in one litre of Anthrax. 10,000 litres are unaccounted for.

September 11 has changed the psychology of America. It should have changed the psychology of the world. Of course, Iraq is not the only part of this threat. But it is the test of whether we treat the threat seriously. Faced with it, the world should unite. The UN should be the focus, both of diplomacy and of action. That is what 1441 said. That was the deal. And I say to you to break it now, to will the ends but not the means, that would do more damage in the long term to the UN than any other course.

To fall back into the lassitude of the last twelve years, to talk, to discuss, to debate but never act; to declare our will but not enforce it; to combine strong language with weak intentions, a worse outcome than never speaking at all.

And then, when the threat returns from Iraq or elsewhere, who will believe us? What price our credibility with the next tyrant? No wonder Japan and South Korea, next to North Korea, have issued such strong statements of support.

I have come to the conclusion after much reluctance that the greater danger to the UN is inaction: that to pass Resolution 1441 and then refuse to enforce it would do the most deadly damage to the UN's future strength, confirming it as an instrument of diplomacy but not of action, forcing nations down the very unilateralist path we wish to avoid.

But there will be, in any event, no sound future for the UN, no guarantee against the repetition of these events, unless we recognise the urgent need for a political agenda we can unite upon.

What we have witnessed is indeed the consequence of Europe and the United States dividing from each other. Not all of Europe – Spain, Italy, Holland, Denmark, Portugal – have all strongly supported us. And not a majority of Europe if we include, as we should, Europe's new members who will accede next year, all ten of whom have been in our support.

But the paralysis of the UN has been born out of the division there is. And at the heart of it has been the concept of a world in which there are rival poles of power. The US and its allies in one corner. France, Germany, Russia and its allies in the other. I do not believe that all of these nations intend such an outcome. But that is what now faces us.

I believe such a vision to be misguided and profoundly dangerous. I know why it arises. There is resentment of US predominance. There is fear of US unilateralism. People ask: do the US listen to us and our preoccupations? And there is perhaps a lack of full understanding of US preoccupations after 11 September. I know all of this.

But the way to deal with it is not rivalry but partnership. Partners are not servants but neither are they rivals. I tell you what Europe should have said last September to the US. With one voice it should have said: we understand your strategic anxiety over terrorism and WMD and we will help you meet it. We will mean what we say in any UN Resolution we pass and will back it with action if Saddam fails to disarm voluntarily; but in return we ask two things of you: that the US should choose the UN path and you should recognise the fundamental overriding importance of restarting the MEPP, which we will hold you to.

I do not believe there is any other issue with the same power to reunite the world community than progress on the issues of Israel and Palestine. Of course there is cynicism about recent announcements. But the US is now committed, and, I believe, genuinely to the Roadmap for peace, designed in consultation with the UN. It will now be presented to the parties as Abu Mazen is confirmed in office, hopefully today.

All of us are now signed up to its vision: a state of Israel, recognised and accepted by all the world, and a viable Palestininan state.

And that should be part of a larger global agenda. On poverty and sustainable development. On democracy and human rights. On the good governance of nations.

That is why what happens after any conflict in Iraq is of such critical significance. Here again there is a chance to unify around the UN. Let me make it clear.

There should be a new UN Resolution following any conflict providing not just for humanitarian help but also for the administration and governance of Iraq. That must now be done under proper UN authorisation. It should protect totally the territorial integrity of Iraq.

And let the oil revenues – which people falsely claim we want to seize – be put in a trust fund for the Iraqi people administered through the UN.

And let the future government of Iraq be given the chance to begin the process of uniting the nation's disparate groups, on a democratic basis, respecting human rights, as indeed the fledgling democracy in Northern Iraq – protected from Saddam for twelve years by British and American pilots in the No Fly Zone – has done so remarkably.

And the moment that a new government is in place – willing to disarm Iraq of WMD – for which its people have no need or purpose – then let sanctions be lifted in their entirety.

I have never put our justification for action as regime change. We have to act within the terms set out in Resolution 1441. That is our legal base.

But it is the reason, I say frankly, why if we do act we should do so with a clear conscience and strong heart. I accept fully that those opposed to this course of action share my detestation of Saddam. Who could not? Iraq is a wealthy country that in 1978, the year before Saddam seized power, was richer than Portugal or Malaysia.

Today it is impoverished, 60 per cent of its population dependent on Food Aid. Thousands of children die needlessly every year from lack of food and medicine. Four million people out of a population of just over 20 million are in exile.

The brutality of the repression – the death and torture camps, the barbaric prisons for political opponents, the routine beatings for anyone or their families suspected of disloyalty are well documented.

Just last week, someone slandering Saddam was tied to a lamp post in a street in Baghdad, his tongue cut out, mutilated and left to bleed to death, as a warning to others. I recall a few weeks ago talking to an Iraqi exile and saying to her that I understood how grim it must be under the lash of Saddam.

'But you don't', she replied. 'You cannot. You do not know what it is like to live in perpetual fear.' And she is right. We take our freedom for granted. But imagine not to be able to speak or discuss or debate or even question the society you live in. To see friends and family taken away and never daring to complain. To suffer the humility of failing courage in face of pitiless terror. That is how the Iraqi people live. Leave Saddam in place and that is how they will continue to live.

We must face the consequences of the actions we advocate. For me, that means all the dangers of war. But for others, opposed to this course, it means – let us be clear – that the Iraqi people, whose only true hope of liberation lies in the removal of Saddam, for them, the darkness will close back over them again; and he will be free to take his revenge upon those he must know wish him gone.

And if this House now demands that at this moment, faced with this threat from this regime, that British troops are pulled back, that we turn away at the point of reckoning, and that is what it means – what then?

What will Saddam feel? Strengthened beyond measure. What will the other states who tyrannise their people, the terrorists who threaten our existence, what will they take from that? That the will confronting them is decaying and feeble.

Who will celebrate and who will weep?

And if our plea is for America to work with others, to be good as well as powerful allies, will our retreat make them multilateralist? Or will it not rather be the biggest impulse to unilateralism there could ever be? And what of the UN and the future of Iraq and the MEPP, devoid of our influence, stripped of our insistence?

This House wanted this decision. Well, it has it. Those are the choices. And in this dilemma, no choice is perfect, no cause ideal. But on this decision hangs the fate of many things.

I can think of many things, of whether we summon the strength to recognise the global challenge of the twenty-first century and beat it, of the Iraqi people groaning under years of dictatorship, of our armed forces – brave men and women of whom we can feel proud, whose morale is high and whose purpose is clear – of the institutions and alliances that shape our world for years to come.

To retreat now, I believe, would put at hazard all that we hold dearest, turn the United Nations back into a talking shop, stifle the first steps of progress in the Middle East, leave the Iraqi people to the mercy of events on which we would have relinquished all power to influence for the better.

Tell our allies that at the very moment of action, at the very moment when they need our determination that Britain faltered. I will not be party to such a course. This is not the time to falter. This is the time for this House, not just this government or indeed this Prime Minister, but for this House to give a lead, to show that we will stand up for what we know to be right, to show that we will confront the tyrannies and dictatorships and terrorists who put our way of life at risk, to show at the moment of decision that we have the courage to do the right thing. I beg to move the motion.

Speech to the US Congress
18 July 2003

Tony Blair became only the third British prime minister, after Clement Attlee and Margaret Thatcher, to address the Congress of the United States of America. It was a grand piece of political theatre, with persistent standing ovations throughout the speech. Blair's sweeping themes of democracy, globalisation, and the war on terrorism, and the eloquent language he uses, make this address to Congress one of the great political speeches of the age. This is my favourite Tony Blair speech.

Mr Speaker, Mr Vice President, Honourable Members of Congress. Thank you most sincerely for voting to award me the Congressional Gold Medal. But you, like me, know who the real heroes are: those brave servicemen and women, yours and ours, who fought the war, and risk their lives still.

Our tribute to them should be measured in this way: by showing them and their families that they did not strive or die in vain but that, through their sacrifice, future generations can live in greater peace, prosperity and hope.

Let me also express my gratitude to President Bush. Through the troubled times since September 11 changed the world, we have been allies and friends. Thank you, Mr President, for your leadership.

I feel a most urgent sense of mission about today's world. September 11 was not an isolated event, but a tragic prologue. Iraq, another act; and many further struggles will be set upon this stage before it's over.

There never has been a time when the power of America was so necessary; or so misunderstood; or when, except in the most general sense, a study of history provides so little instruction for our present day.

We were all reared on battles between great warriors, between great nations, between powerful forces and ideologies that dominated entire continents. These were struggles for conquest, for land or money. The wars were fought by massed armies. The leaders were openly acknowledged: the outcomes decisive. Today, none of us expect our soldiers to fight a war on our territory. The immediate threat is not war between the world's powerful nations. Why? Because we all have too much to lose.

Because technology, communication, trade and travel are bringing us ever closer. Because in the last fifty years countries like ours and mine have trebled their growth and standard of living. Because even those powers like Russia, China or India can see the horizon of future wealth clearly and know they are on a steady road towards it. And because all nations that are free value that freedom, will defend it absolutely but have no wish to trample on the freedom of others.

We are bound together as never before.

This coming together provides us with unprecedented opportunity but also makes us uniquely vulnerable.

The threat comes because, in another part of the globe, there is shadow and darkness, where not all the world is free, where many millions suffer under brutal dictatorship; where a third of our planet lives in a poverty beyond anything even the poorest in our societies can imagine; and where a fanatical strain of religious extremism has arisen, that is a mutation of the true and peaceful faith of Islam and because in the combination of these afflictions, a new and deadly virus has emerged.

The virus is terrorism, whose intent to inflict destruction is unconstrained by human feeling; and whose capacity to inflict it is enlarged by technology.

This is a battle that can't be fought or won only by armies. We are so much more powerful in all conventional ways than the terrorist. Yet even in all our might, we are taught humility. In the end, it is not our power alone that will defeat this evil. Our ultimate weapon is not our guns but our beliefs.

There is a myth. That though we love freedom, others don't, that our attachment to freedom is a product of our culture. That freedom, democracy, human rights, the rule of law are American values or Western values. That Afghan women were content under the lash of the Taliban. That Saddam was beloved by his people. That Milosevic was Serbia's saviour.

Ours are not Western values. They are the universal values of the human spirit and anywhere any time ordinary people are given the chance to choose, the choice is the same. Freedom, not tyranny. Democracy, not dictatorship. The rule of law, not the rule of the secret police.

The spread of freedom is the best security for the free. It is our last line of defence and our first line of attack. Just as the terrorist seeks to divide humanity in hate, so we have to unify it around an idea and that that idea is liberty. We must find the strength to fight for this idea; and the compassion to make it universal.

Abraham Lincoln said: 'Those that deny freedom to others deserve it not for themselves.'

It is a sense of justice that makes moral the love of liberty.

In some cases, where our security is under direct threat, we will have recourse to arms. In others, it will be by force of reason. But in all cases to the same end: that the liberty we seek is not for some but for all.

For that is the only true path to victory.

But first, we must explain the danger. Our new world rests on order. The danger is disorder and in today's world it now spreads like contagion. Terrorist and the states that support them don't have large armies or precision weapons. They don't need them. The weapon is chaos.

The purpose of terrorism is not the single act of wanton destruction. It is the reaction it seeks to provoke: economic collapse; the backlash; the hatred; the division; the elimination of tolerance; until societies cease to reconcile their differences but become defined by them. Kashmir, the Middle East, Chechnya, Indonesia, Africa. Barely a continent or nation is unscathed.

The risk is that terrorism and states developing WMD come together. When people say that risk is fanciful, I say: we know the Taliban supported al Qaeda; we know Iraq under Saddam gave haven to and supported terrorists; we know there are states in the Middle East now actively funding and helping people who regard it as God's will in the act of suicide to take as many innocent lives with them on their way to God's judgement. Some of these states are desperately trying to acquire nuclear weapons. We know that companies and individuals with expertise sell it to the highest bidder and we know at least one state, North Korea, that lets its people starve whilst spending billions of dollars on developing nuclear weapons and exporting the technology abroad. This isn't fantasy. It is twenty-first-century reality and it confronts us now.

Can we be sure that terrorism and WMD will join together? Let us say one thing. If we are wrong, we will have destroyed a threat that, at its least, is responsible for inhuman carnage and suffering. That is something I am confident history will forgive.

But if our critics are wrong, if we are right as I believe with every fibre of instinct and conviction I have that we are, and we do not act, then we will have hesitated in face of this menace, when we should have given leadership. That is something history will not forgive.

But precisely because the threat is new, it is not obvious. It turns upside down our concepts of how we should act and when. And it crosses the frontiers of many nations. So just as it redefines our notions of security, so it must refine our notions of diplomacy.

There is no more dangerous theory in international politics today than that we need to balance the power of America with other competitor powers, different poles around which nations gather. Such a theory made sense in nineteenth-century Europe. It was perforce the position in the Cold War. Today it is an anachronism to be discarded like traditional theories of security.

It is dangerous because it is not rivalry but partnership we need; a common will and a shared purpose in the face of a common threat.

Any alliance must start with America and Europe. Believe me, if Europe and America are together, the others will work with us. But if we split, all the rest will play around, play us off and nothing but mischief will be the result of it.

You may think after recent disagreements it can't be done. But the debate in Europe is open. Iraq showed that, when, never forget, many European nations supported our action and it shows it still, when those that didn't, agreed Resolution 1483 in the UN for Iraq's reconstruction. Today German soldiers lead in Afghanistan. French soldiers lead in the Congo where they stand between peace and a return to genocide.

We should not minimise the differences. But we should not let them confound us either. People ask me, after the past months when let us say things were a trifle strained in Europe, why do you persist in wanting Britain at the centre of Europe?

I say: maybe if the UK were a group of islands twenty miles off Manhattan I might feel differently; but we're twenty miles off Calais and joined by a tunnel. We are part of Europe – and want to be.

But we also want to be part of changing Europe. Europe has one potential for weakness. For reasons that are obvious – we spent roughly 1,000 years killing each other in large numbers – the political culture of Europe is inevitably based on compromise. Compromise is a fine thing except when based on an illusion. And I don't believe you can compromise with this new form of terrorism.

But Europe has a strength. It is a formidable political achievement. Think of its past and think of its unity today. Think of it preparing to reach out even to Turkey, a nation of vastly different culture, tradition and religion, and welcome it in.

Now it is at a point of transformation. Next year ten new countries will join. Romania and Bulgaria will follow. Why will these new European members transform Europe?

Because their scars are recent. Their memories strong. Their relationship with freedom still one of passion, not comfortable familiarity.

They believe in the transatlantic alliance. They support economic reform. They want a Europe of nations not a super-state. They are our allies. And yours. So don't give up on Europe. Work with it.

To be a serious partner, Europe must take on and defeat the crass anti-Americanism that sometimes passes for its political discourse. What America must do is to show that this is a partnership built on persuasion, not command.

Then the other great nations of our world and the small will gather around in one place, not many. And our understanding of this threat will become theirs. The United Nations can then become what it should be: an instrument of action as well as debate. The Security Council should be reformed. We need a new international regime on the non-proliferation. And we need to say clearly to UN members: if you engage in the systematic and gross abuse of human rights, in defiance of the UN charter, you can't expect the same privileges as those that conform to it.

It is not the coalition that determines the mission but the mission, the coalition. I agree. But let us start preferring a coalition and acting alone if we have to; not the other way round.

True, winning wars is not easier that way.

But winning the peace is.

And we have to win both. You have an extraordinary record of doing so. Who helped Japan renew or Germany reconstruct or Europe get back on its feet after World War II? America.

So when we invade Afghanistan or Iraq, our responsibility does not end with military victory. Finishing the fighting is not finishing the job.

If Afghanistan needs more troops from the international community to police outside Kabul, our duty is to get them. Let us help them eradicate their dependency on the poppy, the crop whose wicked residue turns up on the streets of Britain as heroin to destroy young British lives as much as their harvest warps the lives of Afghans.

We promised Iraq democratic government. We will deliver it. We promised them the chance to use their oil wealth to build prosperity for all their citizens, not a corrupt elite. We will do so. We will stay with these people, so in need of our help, until the job is done.

And then reflect on this.

How hollow would the charges of American imperialism be when these failed countries are and are seen to be transformed from states of terror to nations of prosperity; from governments of dictatorship to examples of democracy; from sources of instability to beacons of calm.

And how risible would be the claims that these were wars on Muslims, if the world could see these Muslim nations still Muslim, but Muslims with some hope for the future, not shackled by brutal regimes whose principal victims were the very Muslims they pretended to protect?

It would be the most richly observed advertisement for the values of freedom we can imagine. When we removed the Taliban and Saddam Hussein, this was not imperialism. For those oppressed people, it was their liberation. And why can the terrorists even mount an argument in the Muslim world that it isn't? Because there is one cause terrorism rides upon. A cause they have no belief in, but can manipulate.

I want to be very plain. This terrorism will not be defeated without peace in the Middle East between Israel and Palestine. Here it is that the poison is incubated. Here it is that the extremist is able to confuse in the mind of a frighteningly large number of people, the case for a Palestinian state and the destruction of Israel; and to translate this moreover into a battle between East and West; Muslim, Jew and Christian.

We must never compromise the security of the state of Israel.

The state of Israel should be recognised by the entire Arab world.

The vile propaganda used to indoctrinate children not just against Israel but against Jews must cease.

You cannot teach people hate and then ask them to practise peace. But neither can you teach people peace except by according them dignity and granting them hope.

Innocent Israelis suffer. So do innocent Palestinians.

The ending of Saddam's regime in Iraq must be the starting point of a new dispensation for the Middle East. Iraq: free and stable. Iran and Syria, who give a haven to the rejectionist men of violence, made to realise that the world will no longer countenance it; that the hand of friendship can only be offered them if they resile completely from this malice; but that if they do, that hand will be there for them and their people.

The whole of the region helped towards democracy. And to symbolise it all, the creation of an independent, viable and democratic Palestinian state side by side with the state of Israel.

What the President is doing in the Middle East is tough but right.

And I thank the President for his support and that of President Clinton before him, and members of this Congress, for our attempts to bring peace to Northern Ireland. One thing I've learnt about peace processes: they're always frustrating, often agonising and occasionally seem hopeless. But for all that, having a peace process is better than not having one.

And why has a resolution of Palestine such a powerful appeal across the world? Because it embodies an even-handed approach to justice.

Just as when this President recommended and this Congress supported a $15 billion increase in spending on the world's poorest nations to combat HIV/AIDS it was a statement of concern that echoed rightly round the world.

There can be no freedom for Africa without justice; and no justice without declaring war on Africa's poverty, disease and famine with as much vehemence as we remove the tyrant and the terrorist.

In Mexico in September the world should unite and give us a trade round that opens up our markets. I'm for free trade and I'll tell you why. Because we can't say to the poorest people in the world: we want you to be free but just don't try to sell your goods in our market. And because ever since the world started to open up, it has prospered.

That prosperity has to be sustainable too.

I remember at one of our earliest international meetings a European prime minister telling President Bush that the solution was simple: just double the tax on American gasoline. He wasn't exactly enthusiastic.

But frankly, we need to go beyond Kyoto. Science and technology is the way. Climate change, deforestation and the voracious drain on natural resources cannot be ignored. Unchecked, these forces will hinder the economic development of the most vulnerable nations first, and ultimately, all nations. We must show the world that we are willing to step up to these challenges around the world and in our own backyard.

If this seems a long way from the threat of terror and WMD it is only to say again that the world's security cannot be protected without the world's heart being won.

So: America must listen as well as lead. But don't ever apologise for your values.

Tell the world why you're proud of America. Tell them that when the Star-Spangled Banner starts, Americans get to their feet: Hispanics, Irish, Italians, Central Americans, Eastern Europeans, Jews; white, Asian, black, those who go back to the early settlers and those whose English is the same as some New York cabbies I've dealt with, but whose sons and daughters could run for this Congress.

Tell them why they stand upright and respectful.

Not because some state official told them to. But because whatever race, colour, class or creed they are, being American means being free. That's what makes them proud.

As Britain knows, all predominant power seems for a time invincible; but in fact it is transient. The question is what do you leave behind?

What you can bequeath to this anxious world is the light of liberty.

That is what this struggle against terrorist groups or states is about.

We're not fighting for domination.

We're not fighting for an American world, though we want a world in which America is at ease.

We're not fighting for Christianity but against religious fanaticism of all kinds.

This is not a war of civilisations because each civilisation has a unique capacity to enrich the stock of human heritage.

We are fighting for the inalienable right of human kind, black or white, Christian or not, left, right or merely indifferent, to be free.

Free to raise a family in love and hope.

Free to earn a living and be rewarded by your own efforts.

Free not to bend your knee to any man in fear.

Free to be you so long as being you does not impair the freedom of others.

That's what we're fighting for. And that's a battle worth fighting.

I know it's hard on America. And in some small corner of this vast country, in Nevada or Idaho, these places I've never been but always wanted to go, there's a guy getting on with his life, perfectly happily, minding his own business, saying to you the political leaders of this nation: why me? Why us? Why America?

And the only answer is: because destiny put you in this place in history, in this moment in time and the task is yours to do.

And our job, my nation that watched you grow, that you've fought alongside and now fights alongside you, that takes enormous pride in our alliance and great affection in our common bond, our job is to be there with you.

You're not going to be alone.

We'll be with you in this fight for liberty.

And if our spirit is right, and our courage firm, the world will be with us.

Labour Party conference speech

Bournemouth, 30 September 2003

Blair's speech to the Labour Party conference in Bournemouth in September 2003 opened with the joke that he looked his age. And he did. The youthful looks of the new Party leader in 1994 had been tempered by six years as Prime Minister, several political crises, and major military actions in Sierra Leone, Kosovo, Afghanistan and Iraq. This section from the speech, the peroration, shows a tougher, wiser, experienced Blair. But, he warned delegates, he had no reverse gear. 'More battered without but stronger within' might serve as a description of Tony Blair himself as he weathered the storm over Iraq and steeled himself for his third general election as leader of the Labour Party.

Forward or back?

I can only go one way. I've not got a reverse gear. The time to trust a politician most is not when they're taking the easy option. Any politician can do the popular things. I know, I used to do a few of them.

I know it's hard for people to keep faith.

Some of the people may have a different take on me. But I have the same take on them. I trust their decency. I trust their innate good sense. I know I am the same person I always was, older, tougher, more experienced, but basically the same person believing the same things. I've never led this Party by calculation. Policy you calculate. Leadership comes by instinct. I believe the British people will forgive a government mistakes; will put the media onslaught in more perspective than we think; but what they won't forgive is cowardice in the face of a challenge. The answer to any of these challenges is not easy.

During the past months on Iraq, I have received letter from parents whose sons have died as soldiers. One believing their son had died in vain and hating me for my decision.

Another, a beautiful letter, said they thought Iraq was the right thing to do and though their son was dead, whom they loved dearly, they still thought it was right. And don't believe anyone who tells you when they receive letters like that they don't suffer any doubt.

All you can do in a modern world, so confusing with its opportunities and its hazards, is to decide what is the right way and try to walk in it. It's not being out of touch.

After six years, more battered without but stronger within. It's the only leadership I can offer.

And it's the only type of leadership worth having.

The purpose: to rebuild the public realm, to discover amongst all the modern pressures, the virtues of community, of tolerance, of decency, of respect. To bring to the self-interested consumer age the value of solidarity. Not to cease to want the best for oneself but to wish it for all.

To build a country not just proud of their own achievements, but proud of what we can do together.

Proud not just of how they get and spend but what we in friendship with each other can do for each other.

This is our challenge. To stride forward where we have always previously stumbled. To renew in government. Steadfast in our values. Radical in our methods. Open in our politics.

If we faint in the day of adversity, our strength is small. And ours isn't. We have the strength, the maturity, now the experience to do it. So let it be done.

Statement on the Hutton Inquiry report

28 January 2004

The Hutton Inquiry into the death of government scientist Dr David Kelly marked the most extraordinary and turbulent period of Tony Blair's time in office. In January 2004, Lord Hutton delivered his findings on the events surrounding Dr Kelly's suicide, which exonerated the government, and severely criticised the BBC. This statement to Parliament was delivered in a week when many observers believed that Blair's career would be coming to an abrupt end. Instead, Blair came out fighting, with the demand that the BBC made an apology.

In a week which had seen such a narrow victory on tuition fees that one Conservative MP described him as a 'dead man walking', Blair seemed keen to move on quickly from the Hutton issue. Instead of using his statement as an opportunity for rousing rhetoric, he gave a relatively brief, forensic response to the report.

With your permission, Mr Speaker, I will make a statement following Lord Hutton's report into the circumstances surrounding the death of Dr David Kelly.

I am immensely grateful to Lord Hutton, his team and inquiry staff for the work they have carried out. The report itself is an extraordinarily thorough, detailed and clear document. It leaves no room for doubt or interpretation. We accept it in full.

Lord Hutton has just finished reading the summary of his findings. Before coming to those I want to echo one thing Lord Hutton said about Dr Kelly himself. Lord Hutton makes his findings about Dr Kelly's conduct in respect of the matters at issue here, but as he says, nothing should detract from Dr Kelly's fine record of public service to this country. He was respected here and abroad. I am sorry that as a result of the gravity of the allegations made it was necessary to have this inquiry and that the Kelly family have had to go through reliving this tragedy over the past months. I hope now it is over, they will be allowed to grieve in peace.

Lord Hutton has given a most comprehensive account of the facts. It is unnecessary for me to repeat them. But let me emphasise why I believed it right to establish such an inquiry. Over the past six or more months, allegations have been made that go to the heart of the integrity of government, our intelligence services and me personally as Prime Minister. There are issues, of course, as to how the case of Dr Kelly was handled in personnel terms; and I shall come to those.

But these have not sustained the media, public and parliamentary interest over all this time. What has sustained and fuelled that interest has been, to put it bluntly, a claim of lying, of deceit, of duplicity on my part personally and that of the government. That claim consists of two allegations: first that I lied over the intelligence that formed part of the government's case in respect of Iraq and WMD published on 24 September 2002; the second that I lied or was duplicitous in respect of the naming of Dr Kelly, leaking his name to the press when it should have remained confidential.

* * *

Let me now return to the two central allegations.

On 29 May 2003, following the end of the conflict in Iraq, the BBC *Today* programme broadcast a story by its defence correspondent, Andrew Gilligan. It dominated the morning bulletins and reverberates to this day. It alleged that part of the September 2002 dossier – that Saddam could use WMD within forty-five minutes of an order to do so – had been inserted into it by Downing Street, contrary to the wishes of the intelligence services and that moreover we 'probably knew it was wrong even before we decided to put it in'. There could not be a more serious charge. The source for this extraordinary allegation was said by the BBC to be 'a senior official in charge of drawing up that dossier' and an 'intelligence service source' implying a member of the JIC or assessments staff who would be in a position to know. If true, it would have meant that I had misled this House on 24 September and the country; that I had done so deliberately; and I had behaved wholly improperly in respect of the intelligence services.

From that day, 29 May onwards, that story in one form or another has been replayed many times in the UK, and all over the world.

It dominated my press conference in Poland on 30 May; and PMQs when I returned. It led that week to the Foreign Affairs Committee deciding to conduct an inquiry into the issue. In particular, on the Sunday following the story, Mr Gilligan wrote an article in the *Mail on Sunday*, not merely standing by the story but naming Alastair Campbell as the person responsible in Downing Street. The headline read: 'I asked my intelligence source why Blair misled us all over Saddam's weapons. His reply? One word … CAMPBELL'

This again, was completely untrue; and not merely stood up but further inflamed the original allegation of deceit.

The BBC has never clearly and visibly withdrawn this allegation. This has allowed others to say repeatedly I lied and misled Parliament over the 24 September dossier.

Let me make it plain: it is absolutely right that people can question whether the intelligence received was right; and why we have not yet found WMD. There is an entirely legitimate argument about the wisdom of the conflict. I happen to believe now as I did in March that removing Saddam has made the world a safer and better place. But others are entirely entitled to disagree.

However, all of this is of a completely different order from a charge of deception, of duplicity, of deceit, a charge that I or anyone else deliberately falsified intelligence.

The truth about that charge is now found. No intelligence was inserted into the dossier by Downing Street; nothing was put in it against the wishes of the intelligence services; no one, either in Downing Street or the JIC, put any intelligence into it, 'probably knowing it was wrong'; and no such claim to the BBC was made by anyone 'in charge of drawing up the dossier'. Indeed, Lord Hutton's findings go further. The claim was not even made by Dr Kelly himself.

The allegation that I or anyone else lied to this House or deliberately misled the country by falsifying intelligence on WMD is itself the real lie. And I simply ask that those that made it and those who have repeated it over all these months, now withdraw it, fully, openly and clearly.

* * *

That is how this began: with an accusation that was false then and is false now.

We can have the debate about the war; about WMD; about intelligence. But we do not need to conduct it by accusations of lies and deceit. We can respect each other's motives and integrity even when in disagreement.

Let me repeat the words of Lord Hutton: 'False accusations of fact impugning the integrity of others ... should not be made'.

Let those that made them now withdraw them.

Speech on public services

The Grove, Hertfordshire, 29 January 2004

The day after Lord Hutton delivered his report, Tony Blair made a speech on public service reform to a conference in Hertfordshire organised by the Guardian *newspaper. Just two days after a knife-edge vote on university funding which saw government's majority evaporate to just five, Blair gave an upbeat and confident speech. The chairman of the conference David Walker made the gaffe of his life by introducing Blair as 'The Prime Minister Neil Kinnock' (Kinnock had been the previous speaker). Blair, laughing, said, 'And so it should have been!' In another characteristic ad lib, Blair remarked on the patterns on the carpet, and said, 'You wouldn't want to walk down them with a hangover.' This levity, followed by his serious remarks about the public services, showed his relief at surviving his most testing week in politics. The speech itself laid out the battleground issues for the coming general election.*

In respect of university finance, I am delighted that the proposals can now proceed. They are a vital reform to put our university sector on a secure footing for the future. It is true the majority was narrow. It is true that there are lessons to be learnt. The lesson the Labour Party in government should not learn is to shy away from radical reform. A future fair for all. That is our mission. Cease to meet the challenge of the future – the reason for the reforms in education, health and crime – and we cease to have a purpose in government. My purpose in politics is governed not by doing the job, but by what the job can do. It's the only basis worth being Prime Minister. When our further reforms, to which I will turn in a moment are published in June, and taken to Party conference in October, they will not be a retreat from reform but a quickening of its pace.

Some of my colleagues have said to me after the vote this week, 'never again'.

I cannot promise it will be 'never again' in the sense of asking MPs or the Labour Party to make a tough and important choice. To do so would not just be an absence of leadership, more importantly it would be a dereliction of responsibility towards those who will benefit from the opportunity and better public services brought about by reform.

But, that said, there is a lesson that should be learnt about the way I have conducted the debate on reform. We have made a mistake in allowing the changes we are making to be portrayed as being contrary to our values. In fact the opposite is true. It would be easy to talk about values like opportunity and ignore the fact that for too many people, that's all it would be – talk. In their real lives, too often the reality is, opportunity and choice are for someone else.

Public services have a crucial role to play in our society. They extend opportunity by caring for the sick, by giving people an education, by leading the fight against crime and disorder.

I know I have been fortunate in my own life. I have had chances and opportunities that I know many others do not. I don't pretend everyone can exercise exactly the same choices in life whatever their background. But I do say this – the purpose and principle behind the changes I am fighting for is to extend to others the kinds of opportunities currently enjoyed by the few.

It is a progressive aim and one that is at the core of our beliefs as a centre left party.

Furthermore, policy first and explanation later is not the way to do things, and this was the problem with the way the debate on university finance happened. Some MPs felt the university finance measures were sprung on them with too little explanation and too sparse a tilling of the ground of debate and argument about the nature of the problem. Hence we had the bizarre situation of some MPs who voted against the government telling me that they agreed with 90 per cent of the proposals but were too far exposed in their public position to climb back.

Precisely for this reason, we started the Big Conversation – the Party discussion with the public – to elucidate and describe the future challenges Britain faces. And what is more through government, there is now a detailed process of discussion that allows full and informed debate including with backbench MPs.

Partly, it is through the process of dialogue and discussion that some of the myths about reform can be examined and demolished.

I would not be in politics, New Labour would not exist, if we accepted the idea that the modern world has somehow made futile the pursuit of our progressive values. That all we can do is cling on to fragments of the post-war settlement while we let the tide of individualistic modernity wash around us. The aim of reform is modern social justice: to ensure that the values of public service – equity, universality, public accountability – not only survive but thrive in a world of rapid change, of increasingly complex needs and of ever more demanding people.

So, lessons to be learnt, bridges to be rebuilt, but no wavering in our political purpose. A new progressive settlement; solidarity and justice for a modern world.

In recent times there have been lively debates among public service commentators between the virtues of centralism and localism, between those who see the public as consumers and those who prefer the idea of citizens. But the approach I lay out today seeks to move beyond these debates. I want to show how at the centre, in local government and at the front line we can work together with a shared point of reference; putting the public at the heart of public services. For it is only by truly transferring power to the public through choice, through personalising services, through enhanced accountability, that we can create the drivers for continuous improvement in all our services.

But first I want to explain how over the last six and half years we have got to this crucial moment on the path of reform. New Labour inherited fundamental weaknesses in Britain from the Tory years – economic instability, social inequality, international isolation – perhaps worst of all, the state of our public services. These challenges held our country back and deprived millions of our people of the opportunities they needed to do well and prosper.

Our first task was to stabilise the economy taking tough decisions to get inflation, interest rates and the costs of unemployment down. It is our commitment to meet the need for sustained investment while maintaining sound finances that mean we are the only developed world government which last year, this year and next is increasing the proportion of national wealth going to health and education and fighting crime.

So it was on the basis of sound public finances, providing the stability that is essential to the generation of wealth, that we began to expand investment in our public services. Recruiting hundreds of thousands of new workers, embarking on the biggest programme of capital investment the country has ever seen.

To ensure the money counted, we also made sure the basics were in place across each of the public services. Gathering and publishing performance information, establishing national frameworks and targets, tackling outdated practices and underperforming institutions. Getting the foundations right in each public service.

Now our aim is radical reform, redesigning public services around the individual pupil and patient, working with public service managers – like all of you – to give people the services they today expect services that are prompt, convenient, responsive, and of the highest quality.

Each of these stages on our journey is connected. Our economic management and investment, our commitment to social justice and public service provides an unprecedented opportunity, a different world from the years of social division and the rundown of the public realm. But the authors of the failed neo-conservative experiment have not given up. It is still their absolute priority to show that public provision is inherently inefficient, unresponsive and second rate. We will only win and keep winning the argument for public investment if we can show that every penny we spend is spent in the interests of the public, offering to the public a standard of service that matches and surpasses the best in the world.

And you are succeeding; services are improving. The best ever school results, waiting lists falling, crime levels down, council performance improving. The facts ought to speak for themselves. But polling evidence on public perception of the services we offer reveals a paradox. While people's own experiences are generally positive and improving, this is not reflected in their perceptions of services as a whole.

The disconnection between first-hand satisfaction and second-hand scepticism is both fuelled and exploited by those – never far away – who are hostile to the very idea of universal public services.

This gap between reality and perception also inhibits informed public debate. Effective public accountability means ministers being answerable when things are seen to go wrong but also responding when they are going right. Building on success is as important an imperative for public policy as addressing failure.

So we need to find new and better ways of communicating our shared successes in public services improvement, connecting people's experiences to our programme of investment and reform. We need to tell the stories that lie behind the statistics. Let me tell you just two:

The facts tell us there are:

- 55,000 more nurses;
- 14,000 more doctors;
- 213 more consultant cardiologists;
- 24 major new hospitals;
- waiting lists at their lowest level for a decade;
- heart disease deaths down by 23 per cent.

Behind these facts lies a transformation in the patient experience. In 1997, a person arriving in his GP surgery complaining of chest pains faced a bleak prognosis. A wait of several days to see his doctor, more for a series of diagnostic tests and an initial outpatient appointment with a hospital consultant. When we came to power, it was not uncommon for patients to wait up to two years for a heart operation.

Today, someone in the same position has a choice of ways to access rapid help and support. For instant advice, he can call a qualified nurse at NHS Direct. This service did not exist when we came to power and now gets over 6 million calls a year. He could then either get a rapid appointment with his GP – nine out of ten patients are now seen within two days compared to five in ten in 1997 – or choose to attend one of the national network of Rapid Access Chest Pain clinics we have created. He might have been prescribed cholesterol-lowering statins to reduce his risk of a heart attack – now going to 1.5 million patients. He would have benefited from the 89 new Cardiac Catheter Laboratories being installed around the country and the increase in consultant cardiologist and cardiothoracic surgeon numbers. If he needed surgery, he would be guaranteed it within six months or given the option of going anywhere in the country or abroad – NHS or private – that could provide surgery more quickly, or even travelling abroad for treatment. Now no one waits over nine months for heart surgery and we are confident that, by March 2005, if not sooner, no one will have to wait longer than three months.

The facts tell us the UK has one of the highest rates of employment and lowest rates of unemployment in the developed world, that we have virtually eradicated youth long-term unemployment; that we have helped over 225,000 lone parents move off benefit and into work through the New Deal. But behind the facts is the story of a service completely rebuilt around the needs of the user.

In 1997 a lone parent on Income Support would have made a claim for benefit in local benefits office – in some inner-city areas those offices would have had queues hours long, screens separating adviser from client, a depressing unwelcoming environment, no facilities for children, no help with finding a job or help with tackling the barriers to work. Today, a lone parent going into one of our new Job Centre Plus offices – now numbering 350 – would be faced by a transformed environment – open plan offices, screens done away with, comfortable chairs, many with facilities for children. Instead of feeling like a second-class citizen everyone is welcomed at the entrance by a dedicated floor manager and directed to the best source of help. Every client has an interview with a personal adviser whose role is both to process the benefit claim and provide a work-focused advice. The personal adviser can draw on a range of private and voluntary sector providers to develop a flexible package to meet the client's needs or direct the client to Job Point – the internet Job bank – where at the touch of a button you can find information about jobs in your local area, broken down into types of jobs, hours available, skills required. The new Adviser Discretion Fund provides the personal adviser with the freedom to pay for a new bus pass, to settle a debt, to buy a work suit – practical help to enable their client to take a job.

So, over the last six and a half years we have substantially enhanced the offer that public services make to users. But an entitlement is only meaningful if people know about it and use it. Since the creation of the modern welfare state politicians and managers have tended to see their job as damping down public expectation, minimising the scope for complaint or redress, suppressing dissatisfaction. We are starting to change this culture, to understand that service users with high expectations and the power to choose and to be heard are the best drivers of further improvement. By arming the public with greater choice and by strengthening their individual and collective voice we are making them partners in service improvement.

This might seem like common sense but we need to understand the legacy of professional domination of service provision. The 1960s and 1970s were a period of unprecedented expansion in public services. Government provided the funds for services but allowed the professionals and their managers at the local level – whether housing managers, consultants or teachers – to define not just the way services were delivered but also the standards to which they were delivered. And this too often meant services where standards were too low, an unacceptable variability in delivery which entrenched inequality and service users – parents, patients and tenants – who were disempowered and demoralised.

In recent decades governments across the developed world have sought to address underperformance. Separating the role of purchaser of public services from that of provider has been possible to break up some of the old monolithic public service bureaucracies. The use of explicit contracts has raised standards of performance. And regulation and inspection, together with the publication of an increasingly wide range of performance indicators, have increased the accountability of public service professionals. These new approaches have significantly raised standards.

But change driven from the centre has its limits. It is vital that service reform is to be driven from the bottom, as well as enabled by the centre. That is why the priority for reform – the principle tying together the different elements of change – is to put the public at the heart of public services, making 'Power to the people' the guiding principle of public sector improvement and reform.

What are the key elements if we are really to put the public at the heart of public services? First, it means a continuous drive to increase the scope and scale of choice available to public service users. Whenever the expansion of choice has been proposed in the public sector there have been the doomsayers arguing that such freedoms would be exploited by the assertive few at the expense of everyone else. Each time these predictions have been wrong. Go to any secondary school on the day prospective parents come in to look around, you will see parents of all backgrounds each wanting to know more, to engage more, to get the best for their children. The evidence on school choice has now clearly disproved the argument that it would drive social polarisation. We heard the same arguments when we began bringing choice into the NHS. But early evaluation of the London Patient Choice Pilot suggests that over two-thirds of patients offered the choice in London have taken up the offer to be treated more quickly at an alternative hospital. We are still at the early stages but the path of reform is clear. In the NHS as we move towards electronic patient records, we will give each patient greater knowledge, greater control and greater choice, not just over elective surgery but over primary care provider.

Putting the public at the heart of public services also means services that fit the individual needs and preferences of each service user. From the best practice in individual social care commissioning to the package of training and support offered a job seeker, a commitment to personalised services is beginning to reverse the decades-old assumption that the task of public service delivery was to fit the user to the service. Diversity and contestability in public service provision, both between public service providers, and bringing in the private and voluntary sector adds to the choices available and creates strong incentives for more personalised services. Again, there is much further to go. In secondary education, future reform must have as a core objective a flexible curriculum providing a distinct and personal offer to every child.

Through choice and personalisation our aim is ambitious and progressive; 'services fair for all, personal to each'. Public services that harness the drive of competition, and the power of choice to the public sector ethic of altruism and equity.

Along with choice we must also provide the public with a louder and clearer voice. This means direct user engagement whether in school governing bodies, Foundation Trust Boards, tenants' forums. In the bodies we have set up since 1997 like Sure Start and New Deal for Communities we have built in user engagement from the start. These new forms of engagement are not an attempt to supplant local government, but to enhance it. Both in central and local government we are exploring how to increase turnout in elections, but as we do this we need to recognise that voting is a blunt tool for the expression of complex opinions and detailed preferences. Now we need to explore how we can provide a stronger voice for the public in new areas. For example, David Blunkett is consulting over models of greater police accountability. As part of the Big Conversation exercise we are asking how we can decentralise decision-making in areas like public order and local liveability to community level. Indeed, many local authorities have already experimented successfully with forms of community governance.

Enhancing both choice and voice also means providing robust and trusted performance information. Some commentators assert a false dichotomy between national standards and local decentralisation. In reality, a strong framework of national standards backed up by enforceable entitlements are important levers for users and citizens to drive local improvement. For example, our national programmes for literacy and numeracy have provided parents with the information and confidence to want to know more about how their children are progressing.

There are those who believe that the very idea of choice, of diversity and competition, of giving people a greater say in the services they receive must drive inequality of provision and outcome. But this is wrong on three counts. First, it ignores the fact that the old monopolistic, paternalist model of public services failed to address inequalities, indeed in some cases worsened them. The privileged have always had choices. Second, it is a view that patronises poorer people, and says for example that they are not capable of choosing to invest in their own higher education or aspire to the best school for their children – the evidence shows that this is simply wrong. Third, it fails to see that by tackling exclusion, by supporting people through the system we can make choice and personalisation work for everyone. It is no accident that at the heart of many of our reforms – Job Centres, the Connexions service, to name two – is the development of the personal adviser role, a trained professional understanding the full needs of service users and helping them get the most of the system. We are exploring how we can apply the model of personal adviser to enhance the choices and rights we are providing to NHS patients.

So, our strategy for continuous improvement through giving power to people involves greater choice, greater voice and more personalised services. But there is one more element. As you all know, public services are a partnership. Parents are key partners in the education of their children. The cooperation of local communities is vital to tackling crime and anti-social behaviour. Employers are key to finding the right jobs for the right people. We can only make real strides in improving the nation's health if citizens themselves lead healthier lifestyles.

These are issues that can be discussed in the context of the Big Conversation and the government debates. In examining them, I want to answer one crucial question that somewhat unnerves part of the progressive left about this agenda. This is the idea that the reform programme comes with a hidden agenda of 'marketising' services; that if we create diversity, for example between universities, we create inequality; that we make some parts of the services different or better than others. I remember being told during the Foundation Hospital debate by some MPs that foundation hospitals were a bad thing because staff would want to work in them and that therefore they would gain an unfair advantage over the hospitals that weren't foundation ones.

The truth is that diversity in quality and type of public services is not a reform; it is a reality. Students don't think all universities are the same. Parents don't think all schools are. Patients know darn well some hospitals and doctors are better than others.

The question is: how do you drive up standards across the board? And the answer is partly money; partly accountability; partly the spread of best practice; partly government initiative. But it is also the knowledge that the consumer can go elsewhere. That is not to create 'a market' in the sense that whether they can go elsewhere depends on their wealth – the private sector market solution. It is choice and contestability based not on wealth but on one's equal status as a citizen. And it is wholly healthy. Because our approach to public services must never be about levelling down but levelling up.

Index

Index